Igniting Brilliance

Integral Education for the 21st Century

Willow Dea, Editor

Next Step Integral

Integral Publishers
Tucson, Arizona

First Published by
Integral Publishers, LLC
1418 N. Jefferson Ave.
Tucson, AZ 85712

Published in the United States with distribution in the United States,
Canada and the United Kingdom.

© Integral Publishers, 2011

ISBN: 978-1-4507-2224-7

Cover Design by John Philip King

Graphic for on page 192
Figure 18.1: Ken Wilber's Great Chain of Being, from *Sex, Ecology and Spirituality*
Used with permission.

Table of Contents

Appendices

Preface

Willow Dea

Conception is a mysterious process. This book was conceived in a vision that ensued quite vividly during the Integral Education Seminar in 2007. During his morning presentation, John Gruber simply asked all forty of us to close our eyes and imagine where we might be in three to five years. I saw that I was holding a book, felt the weight of a paperback about an inch thick, with a blue and yellow cover. I paged through it, and glanced to my left, where I saw that I was sitting next to a woman and another man at a table. They were signing the book, and when I looked up, I saw that there was a long line of people awaiting our signatures. Indeed we had written this book together. It was called Integral Education in Action, and those two people have indeed helped put it together!

After a brief period of silence, we were asked if we saw anything, and I raised my hand halfway, hoping to avoid being called upon. To my dismay I was asked what I saw, as apparently I was the only person who raised a hand. I hesitantly shared this little vision, fearing that it was just a crazy thought, yet I was wholeheartedly received by John's response.

The proposal for the book came through in a single writing session and for never having done this, I was amazed that this project seemed to have a life of its own. I called Stephan Martineau, the president of Next Step Integral, and asked him if he'd be interested in partnering with me to write the book. He readily agreed, and we got straight to it. The rest has been a lovely process of working with world class educators from all over the planet. I've learned a tremendous amount about writing, editing, integral theory, and the benign reality of coordinating a project such as this. Each person volunteered many, many hours to their writing, revisions, peer editing and solid scrutiny of their own and each other's work. Both visionary and granular, the process had a wholeness that was consistently palpable to me. I continue to be grateful for the opportunity to have been a part of this project.

Igniting Brilliance: Integral Education for the 21st Century is an anthology comprising chapters by educators, ranging from elementary teachers to university professors, who exemplify the integral approach. The emerging field of integral education is a holistic, multidimensional approach with a basis in Ken Wilber's all-quadrant, all-level framework. This book offers a snapshot of the field through a series of light, nonacademic memoirs. It is designed to inspire teachers to personalize the lessons and methods for adopting an integral approach.

You'll find that we've described the integral framework as it's applied to education, while exploring what it means to embody an integral approach in the classroom. We've then collected a series of eleven teachers' greatest hits; those lessons, practices or methods that have been consistently successful, each a gem. Following these, a section on conscious teaching practices guides the reader to cultivate an integral perspective by means of a series of educationally relevant inquiries, framed by the integral framework. Assessment, curriculum and program design, and the transformational power of our relationship as teacher and student are then explored from an integral perspective, offering new insight to the field. The book ends with an offering of personal and professional practices, laid out for further development of an understanding of the actual utility of an integral approach. Finally, we speak to the evolution of the field of education, the future trends of integral education, programs in development, and key areas in which integral education could enhance the quality of education at large.

With respect to research, each author drew directly from professional and personal experience, as well as the leading references needed to support their contribution. Many of the contributors have been published in academic journals, and were able to draw from their own work, or the recent works of educational and integral theorists. Tom Murray took the cake with his reference list, at over five pages. He nonchalantly added a chapter that distinguished the field of integral education from progressive education, blazing the path forward.

Words cannot adequately express the level of gratitude that I have for each person's capacity to deliver the work that occurred. While I was distinctly aware that this book was a labor of love, I was also aware that everyone who contributed had a full time teaching practice, a family and other interests. Yet their commitment to this field and their love for integral education inspired a level of interaction and writing that never failed to impress and move me. I would like to thank Miriam Mason Martineau and Stephan Martineau for founding Next Step Integral and carrying the responsibility for a particularly beautiful expression of integral education into the world. John Gruber, Nancy Davis, Lynne Feldman, Patricia Gordon and Terri O'Fallon were sister and fellow torch-carriers on the board of Next Step Integral from the very beginning, striding boldly forward to evolve this field and for that I am deeply grateful.

I'd like to thank Jonathan Reams, who served so selflessly so many times, even when the dark of the Norwegian winter lent him to subsisting on special lighting, to keep his spirits bright. He kept the spirit of this book bright with his many contributions and enduring optimism.

Jamie Wheal hatches the idea for Teacher's Greatest Hits, which quickly became the core offering of this book, and for that I am eternally grateful. I bow in gratitude to each of the educators that delivered a Greatest Hit. Lynne Feldman rings the bell for the transformative power of love and its lessons, in high form. John Gruber illuminated us with a multi sensory approach to botany. Olen Gunnlaugson, to my delight, shines light on the presence of collective intelligence. Kyle Good crafts a wonderful tale about creating community in class. Chris Nichol bakes up a warm share on homeschooling from an integral perspective. Nancy Simko dazzled us with an early education adventure making a wooden bench, and Sue Stack became a compassionate voice for the invisible children in schools everywhere. Andrew Suttar opened our eyes to the connection between bubbles and an integral model, in such fine fashion. Each of these short chapters is just pure gold.

My gratitude extends further for the level of professional acumen that the following authors added. Nancy Davis burnishes her contribution on integral assessment to a hue of clarity that has sheen of its own. Terri O'Fallon enlightenes us all with her multi-pronged approach to curriculum design and online program development for the 21st century, with panache and a smile. Shayla Wright reflects on engagement, commitment and the power of relationship with a distinctively nuanced voice. Patricia Gordon elucidates the alchemy between the personal and professional aspects of our work as educators beautifully.

A special thanks to Miriam Mason Martineau for diving in at unexpected times to unearth the precious aspects of the relationship in education, voice the importance of inner work in teaching, and for boldly spearheading the conclusion of the book with an eye to the horizon. Thank you for serving in such timely and generous ways, Miriam.

This list wouldn't be complete without acknowledging my husband David, for spurring me on, cooking dinner and listening to my chapters come spilling forth in fits and spurts. Ever the steady heart, David plays a huge and silent role in support of this book. Thanks, David.

For the most part, the book came together without a hitch. The only exception was that I got to learn to prod more clearly, nudge more firmly and lead more boldly. The greatest obstacle to our collective process was the speed at which we moved. Rather than swimming upstream and rallying for the latest deadline, I learned to accept that this book would be done at the speed of Love. I relaxed my expectations of ever finishing anything on time, and understanding that each person was navigating their life's work at a pace that was manageable. It worked!

Integral Education

1

What Can Integral Do for Education?

Jonathan Reams

Why Read This Book?

As educators, we have been motivated to some degree by the desire to enable younger generations to have better opportunities in life. This motivation, which can be or feel like a calling, takes us down the road of educating ourselves in order to learn appropriate pedagogical skills, subject matter expertise and the host of other skills that teachers require to do their job. But what kind of approach to this education will serve us best?

It is the experience of the contributors to this book that an integral approach to education has served them best, and in the following pages we will aim to describe what we mean by this. To get us started, a first pass description of an integral approach to education is one where all perspectives are acknowledged, organized and drawn upon in a manner that has integrity with the educational situation. (How this might differ from other modern or progressive approaches to education will be fleshed out later.)

In this introduction I will provide you with ideas about what we mean by an integral approach to integral education, briefly describe the journey from the various educational philosophies we may have been brought up with to an integral one that those of us here have taken, and survey the contents of the book. My intent is to provide you with a foundation from which you can get the most out of the chapters that follow. If it all comes together as intended, the answer to the question above will shine through clearly. This book offers you the possibility to have your horizons expanded, heart inspired, and hands eager to try out something new.

What is Meant by Integral?

So to begin, our aim with this book is to enable a broad audience of educators to get a taste of what those of us contributing have experienced and come to label as integral education. We do not claim to be experts in this, but more like pioneers out exploring new territory. We realize that many of you will come to the book because of a familiarity with integral ideas, and for you some of what follows will be repetition, but hopefully with some framing that can contribute new insights. For the broader audience of educators new to integral ideas, I will aim to provide a succinct overview of what can at times be an overwhelmingly complex meta-system of ideas.

Part of this complexity is evident in how our current world situation is often described. Most, if not all of us are by now familiar with the realization that our world is changing, evolving or even transforming in ways that we could not have imagined only a short while ago. There have been plenty of descriptions of this; complete with strong calls to action based on a given author's current interpretation of what it all means. The emergence of so many new perspectives on this situation adds to the complexity, and even to the confusion. An attempt to integrate these complexities, and the many perspectives, into a coherent whole is not a simple task. Yet, when done well, there is often a quality of simplicity evident in the result that resonates deep within us. It is this simplicity on the other side of the complexity that integral claims to rest in.

The idea of integral is not new, some scholars see traces as far back as pre-Socratic thinkers or early Indian or Asian philosophies, but it has manifested more recently in a form that has gathered interest and support from a number of people. Various scholars have identified authors who are seen to have initiated the use of the term integral in a manner reasonably aligned with the specific form this book will focus on. In particular, the names of Rudolf Steiner, Sri Aurobindo, Jean Gebser and Ken Wilber are most associated with the term integral. These thinkers were all comprehensive in the scope of their work and have all left legacies (Wilber's being the most recent and in progress) that include educational philosophies and/or systems (such as Waldorf schools.)

What appears common among these thinkers is that there is a mode of consciousness available to us that are qualitatively different from our common, ordinary, rational, everyday consciousness. The goal for each model is also to develop or evolve into this being normal for us. There are characteristics that set integral consciousness apart and form a difference that makes a difference. This integral consciousness allows one to perceive, conceive and make meaning in ways that go well beyond how we are trained to do these things in our society today. It allows us to cut to the heart of matters while also attending to the wholeness of things. It gives us the capacity to find the simplicity amongst the complexity.

This view that emerges is not merely cognitive. It explicitly engages head, heart and hands, or truth, goodness and beauty, to name two variations on this integrative theme. There is a theme of transcendence as well, particularly around going beyond the limitations of rational thought. There is also an integration of what were previously considered as paradoxes, a capacity to see previously disparate perspectives as interconnected. All of these point to broad generalizations of the qualities and characteristics of integral consciousness.

We see signs and symptoms of this new consciousness in various ways. Within many if not all disciplines there appears to be what might be called a set of "new paradigm" ideas. In addition, there is a growth of multi-, inter- and transdisciplinary discourses emerging. One can even talk about contemporary research that identifies new stages of consciousness and those that enact it without necessarily describing it as such.

Thus it can be useful to have a good map that enables us to distinguish the characteristics of all of the abovementioned ways of describing integral. The territory we are traversing has many riches awaiting us if we are able to have them pointed out. In this context, the chapters of this book aim to describe some of this territory as the authors have experienced it. What I will aim to do here is provide a rough and ready map to give you some bearings along the way. In order to do this, I will draw on the particular formulation of integral that is the focus of this book, that of Ken Wilber. It helps that he explicitly frames his work as a map-making project, so it is an appropriate choice for this purpose.

Integral as AQAL

Ken Wilber is a modern American philosopher whose many volumes over the last three decades have explored the range of human consciousness in many forms. Through his work, Wilber came to formulate what he described as an integral map, framework, theory or meta-theory. The particular approach he took led him to map out the territory of an integral view of human experience in five main categories: quadrants, levels, lines, types and states. Thus AQAL is shorthand for all quadrants, all levels, as well as including all lines, all types and all states. Through mapping out all of these domains of experience, Wilber gives us a framework for understanding the context of any given perspective and how it can be related to other perspectives. It is this capacity of the AQAL model that takes it a step beyond the postmodern view that, while recognizing the existence and value of different perspectives has a hard time understanding the relative merit of different perspectives, leading at times to a problematic relativism. Thus an integral or AQAL framework enables us to make sense out of the at times bewildering complexity of our current world.

Quadrants

To look a little more closely, let's go over each of the five major components of the model in a bit more detail. What is meant by quadrants? Well, in many disciplines, it is quite common to take two pairs of factors and arrange then so that you get a two by two matrix. In this case, Wilber looked at a vast range of human discourse in a comprehensive list of sciences and noticed a pattern emerge. He saw that you could arrange these as to where they fit along two axes; individual to collective on one, and interior to exterior on the other. From this you get individual interiors, collective interiors, individual exteriors and collective exteriors. There are other similar terms that can be used, but they pretty much describe the same things. If you lay these out, you get a figure like the following:

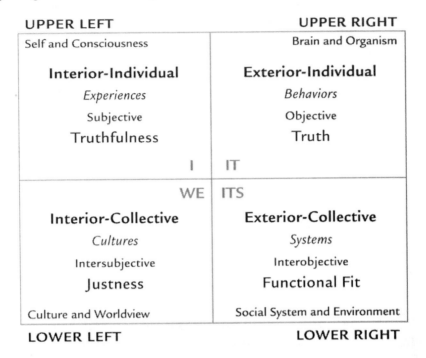

These four quadrants (leading to the commonly used term "the four quadrant model") provide a framework that enables us to map out the various domains of truth that different discourses disclose. It enables us to understand that any given discourse in itself will disclose a true but partial view of the world and our experience within it. We can more readily see the boundaries or limits of the truth claims of various disciplines. As well, we can then also use this to see that in order to more fully study or understand a given topic we should think about addressing how it looks in each of the four quadrants. (There is a further explication of this model into eight, with each quadrant being looked at through its interior and exterior, but that is beyond our needs at this moment.) Thus the four-quadrant model provides us with a handy tool to make useful distinctions, and to help us pay attention to the wholeness of any given subject.

Stages or Levels

Yet the four quadrants are only one slice of the integral map. There are also stages or levels of existence. These show up differently in each quadrant. The general pattern is one of going from simpler to more complex and more comprehensive. So for instance one can go from elementary particles to atoms to molecules to cells to organisms and so on up the chain. In parallel, one can follow the stages of inner development along say cognition, using Piaget's understanding of stages of cognitive reasoning and extending it into more recently mapped out post-formal stages. Another commonly used version is to talk about moral reasoning going through levels of ego-centric to ethno-centric to world-centric.

The principle that is used here is one of transcend and include. Each successive stage goes beyond the previous ones in identifiable ways. At the same time, each stage includes the qualities and capacities of those before it. You cannot have molecules without atoms, but atoms alone are not capable of having all the properties of molecules. A child of 4 may utilize a pre-operational mode of reasoning that can be characterized as magical and mythical. They are not yet ready for formal schooling, one example being that arithmetic reasoning is not firmly grasped yet. (This generalization does not include the recent programs to teach younger children reading and arithmetic skills. It can be argued that how they learn these tasks is still not fully at the concrete operational level.) A child of 8 can learn arithmetic, but not yet be ready to learn algebra. A 12- year old can incorporate the concrete operational logic to do arithmetic and begin to use abstract reasoning (or formal operations in Piaget's terms) to understand the principles of algebra successfully.

Where this trajectory gets really interesting is when we get to the post-formal stages of consciousness. While Piagetian formal operations are generally considered the norm for being a mature adult, recent advances in neuroscience and adult developmental psychology have shown that while our bodies may stop maturing by the time we are about 20, our minds can continue to grow. As we move into post-formal stages of consciousness, we can eventually come to what Wilber calls vision-logic. This level of consciousness enables a qualitatively different kind of reasoning that goes beyond the rational, analytical kinds of thinking we normally employ. One of the characteristics of this consciousness is its ability to integrate multiple systems, seeing to the essence of them and weaving connections where at previous stages none may be perceived to exist. This is what I referred to near the beginning of this introduction as characterizing what appears in common to thinkers describing integral consciousness.

Thus an understanding of development, or evolution is central to the integral model. This also helps us make a distinction between having, coming from or embodying an integral consciousness (referring to this specific level of consciousness) and using an integral map, framework or model as a tool from whatever level of consciousness we might be at. Of course, it makes it easier to fully use the framework if you have access to the level of consciousness. It can also be used from a wider range of levels of consciousness with great success.

Lines

The next step in understanding the AQAL model is that the development through various levels described above is not simply a generic occurrence. It is a basic observation of human nature that we are more developed in some areas and less in others. These can be seen as lines of development. The notion of multiple intelligences such as social, emotional, kinesthetic and so on allow us to recognize that there are many areas possible for us to grow in. We also recognize that we cannot really hope to be equally well developed in all categories. Thus we have lines of development.

While we can easily enough see that the diversity of lines (Wilber has identified up to 24 such lines) helps us understand the diversity of human growth, we also know that some things tend to hang together. As well, some things seem to be prerequisites for others. In this way Wilber talks about a set of lines related to the self. These include cognitive, moral, emotional and ego lines of development. Our growth in these areas will tend to roughly hang together. As well, Wilber proposes that in our society today we tend to lead with the cognitive line. The development of cognitive faculties is seen to enable other closely related lines to develop.

In a similar fashion, we can see how for instance societies grow in various lines of development such as economic, cultural, political and others. The basic principle of different aspects or lines evolving through different levels or stages is both a common enough understanding (think of Darwinian evolution) and as part of the larger whole of an integral view, essential to be understood in context. So in the AQAL framework we can make the further distinction around lines of development that occur within the various quadrants of our experience.

Types

At the same time, there is another aspect to the diversity of human experience. We have different types of religions, types of entertainment, body types and so on. There are many aspects of who we are and what we do that are not the product of levels of development. In psychology we find a number of theories and assessment instruments that can help us categorize ourselves. Things like the Myers-Briggs, Big Five, Enneagram and a host of others identify ways to make distinctions about how we show up in the world.

What is distinct about the notion of types is that they are what we might call horizontal areas of growth, in contrast to "vertical" development described as stages or levels. We can become better at being who we are without going through the vertical movement to a higher level of development. We can fill out a particular area of development at a given level. In doing this, we see that what distinguishes types from lines or levels is that we can be any given personality type (introverted or extroverted, kind, choleric etc.) at any level. Thus types enable us to see aspects of our experience that represent qualitatively different ways that are different from the kinds of distinctions made in the category of levels of development.

States

The last of the five main categories in the AQAL model aims to describe those aspects of our experience that are independent of lines, levels and types. We experience different states of consciousness on a regular basis. We can make a broad distinction between waking, dreaming, and deep sleep states. We can also distinguish a range of affective states such as happy, sad, angry, excited and so forth. We can talk about non-ordinary or altered states of consciousness. We can talk about a state of being present or grounded versus one of being scattered or flighty. There is an entire domain of such aspects of our experience that come under the category of states.

While we can experience various states of consciousness as mentioned, what the AQAL model points out is that we will interpret what those states mean according to where we are in relation to other aspects of the model. We know that it is easy enough for two people to have the same experience and yet describe it as if they were talking about something totally different. A good example that we sometimes see today is that people will have experiences of non-ordinary, altered or transcendent consciousness. They will then filter that experience through a given belief system. Further, within that belief system they will further filter it according to their level of cognitive development. To go on, they may act on it in various ways depending on their level of emotional or social maturity. In an extreme case, someone might claim that God spoke to them and told them to convince all their friends and neighbors that they need to radically change their lives in some manner to fit with how this person interprets their experience.

At the same time, we have a freedom to experience any given state at pretty much any time. This separates states of consciousness from levels or stages of consciousness. What can happen is that a transitory experience of a higher state of consciousness can open up a window of possibility for us, and motivate us to make it a more stable and accessible place to come from. This can lead to developmental growth along one or more lines, eventually allowing us to have as everyday what was once a peak experience.

Thus these five categories aim to cover the full range of our experience and to enable us to recognize the different aspects of them and how they might relate to each other. This brief overview only provides a small sample of what is possible applying the model in full, but it should give you an idea of the basic contours and how it aims to integrate in a systematic and comprehensive way the full range of human experience. Now, on to the focus at hand: how does this apply to education?

Integral and Education

There has always been a tension in education between conserving forces, philosophies and pedagogies that aim to keep doing what works and progressive pedagogies that aim to reform education, progress it into new areas. From within one perspective, the other side appears as wrong, uninformed and so on, leading to reactive battles over educational policy decisions, pedagogical practices and how teacher education is structured. Large amounts of time, energy and seemingly endless seesawing back and forth go on as one side or the other gains the upper hand in these arenas.

While the current model of integral being described and drawn on in this book is a more recent take on how to address this tension, it is not the first. Early use of the term integral education can be found in the approaches of a few French and Russian socialists as far back as the early 19th century. Also during the 19th century, there developed strands of Catholic education that described an explicitly integral approach. In the early 20th century the work of Sri Aurobindo led to an explicitly integral form of education to go along with his integral yoga. Similarly, the work of Jean Gebser produced a brand of integral education in the mid 20th century. As mentioned above, Rudolf Steiner's work inspired the Waldorf school movement. These educational experiments and movements all described their approach in ways that would not be out of place in the context of this current book. While some are still alive others were too far ahead of their time, or too dependent upon a founding figure to carry forward the work in a sustained manner.

At the same time, there have also been voices of integration within American education. These aimed to recognize the positive contributions of each perspective and limit their weaknesses. John Dewey's approach can be seen as an example of taking a less embedded perspective and working towards an integration that takes the whole conversation to a higher level. In our current educational context, it is not always clear how to sort out the strengths and weaknesses of not only the traditional polarity of conservative and progressive strands of education, but also of the many variations and subtle gradations that also have emerged. It is in this context that the integral map can address this complexity.

The above brief overview of the AQAL framework can give an indication of how the multi-faceted complexities of educational systems can be contextualized. In this process the unique contribution of each educational theory, process and philosophy can be situated and linked to the educational environment to see what will really best serve the interests of the students. It is possible to find multiple right answers or pathways to this end, opening up ways to allow for the diversity of preferences and capacities that we bring as educators.

It is not only in this mapping capacity that integral makes its contribution. It can also serve as a methodology for all phases of the process. The training of teachers could be designed to take into account the five different domains mentioned above. This could happen in both the way the training of teachers itself is undertaken and in the methods that teachers are given to use in the classroom. Thus as a methodology, integral can shape the way we approach education in substantial ways.

In order to do this, a community of practice is necessary in order to test out the steps along the way. It is certain that taking an integral approach to education is not going to result from a weekend seminar. Within a community of practice we can have the space to learn from others' efforts, get feedback on our own applications and steps as well as keep current with the evolving nature of understanding how these ideas can actually work in practice. A community can also lend credibility to the work, keeping us from being a lonely voice in the wilderness.

As well, one of the desired results of all this work is to enable teachers (as well as students) to enter into this stage or level of human consciousness. While there are huge benefits that can be derived from using the map to help understand and navigate the territory, applying the model and participating in a community of practice around this, there is yet a fuller stage of realization that can be gained when the course of our personal growth enables us to internalize all of this and come from an integral consciousness. The opportunities that emerge when one begins to operate from this level of consciousness are enormous. Being able to take a meta-perspective on complex systems, being able to reframe and recontextualize concepts, experiences and interpretive frameworks so that others can glimpse something in a new way is a powerful capacity for teaching on many levels.

While the vision of taking all this in may seem far off in the distance, the reality is that we are all taking steps along the path all the time. In the chapters that follow, you will hear from many educators who are at various places in their own journey of applying integral to education. You can think of integral as having its own line of development. One might begin as an enthusiastic novice, eager to apply ideas that while resonating deeply also are still primarily being held as an intellectual map with plenty of emotional enthusiasm. This can end up making one a kind of proselytizer for integral (and annoying everyone you come in contact with as well.) One can move on to a more measured and rational relationship to integral where some more settled discernment arises. This can enable one to work in a more sustained way with the ideas, applying them over a longer period and in a more systematic manner. Eventually, one can move on to reaping the deeper benefits of sustained work with the integral model and even move more into the integral consciousness.

Chapter Overviews

Each of the authors contributing to this book is at various places along this journey. We have approached integral and education from a wide variety of starting places. Our lives have led us through a similarly wide variety of attempts to make sense of and improve our ability to educate. Finally, we are also at various stages with respect to different aspects of the journey. Together, it is our hope that you can find voices that resonate with you and provide insight, inspiration and ideas for application. In this section of the introduction, I will give you a brief survey of the territory that follows. The next two chapters give in-depth explanations, overviews and insights into two core issues: what makes integral education actually integral, and what does it take to get there? The fourth chapter speaks directly to some of the elements of embodying ones' teaching practice with awareness. While the next section of the book is a collection of shorter chapters where the authors focus on specific applications of integral education in their own teaching, a "Teachers' Greatest Hits." The third section, Conscious Teaching Practices, offers more detailed descriptions of specific areas such as assessment, curriculum and program development, engagement and transformation and integral practices. The book closes with a look to the future.

Tom Murray brought forth the second chapter From Progressive Pedagogy to Integral Pedagogy, which describes the similarities between progressive and integral education as well as delineating the differences between them. To show what integral can offer beyond the range of progressive educational approaches, Tom describes several facets of integral methodology and the skills that result from the use of these methods. This includes using several hallmark areas of the integral framework to shed light on the importance of their consideration, such as: systems thinking, cultural evolution, and individual development. The chapter takes some of the distinctions made in this introduction and expands on them in sufficient detail to give a clear picture of how integral can offer something genuinely new to education.

In On the Value and Importance of Personal Development, Miriam Mason Martineau and myself dialogue about the value, role, and importance that personal development plays in integral education. We discuss the growing awareness of the interior and exterior dimensions of teaching, with consideration for students' capacities along various lines of development. Personal qualities such as humility, openness to learning, and the willingness to fully engage in co-facilitating students' development is discussed. We draw on personal experiences that have shaped our journey to illustrate how we have evolved towards this integral approach.

Willow Dea, the editor and torchbearer for this book, offers An Overview of Embodying Awareness. This chapter is about a few of the subtle elements that involve embodying your highest level of awareness while teaching. She describes several ways to understand embodiment, and invites you to try a few of these methods on.

The section on Teachers' Greatest Hits, replete with 11 hits, opens with a brief introduction, before diving into the juicy stories that comprise the core of the book.

In Mrs. Feldman and Her Students Learn About Love, Lynne Feldman demonstrates the power and intensity of deeply applying an integral framework and awareness in service of building student's capacity to understand love. Lynn does a masterful job of showing how something as simple as a Hollywood movie can be used as a pedagogical instrument to reveal the depths of human experience and love.

Next we have Botany in All Dimensions: The Flowering of Integral Science by John W. Gruber. In this chapter John describes how he put together a botany curriculum based on eight elements of integral practice. This leads to a case study description and John telling what this work has enabled him to do as a teacher.

Presencing the Optimal We: Evoking Collective Intelligence in the Classroom is Olen Gunnlaugson's contribution. Here Olen draws on his research and teaching to describe how we can better cultivate the collective "we" or intersubjective space. In addition to some theoretical aspects, he presents techniques for facilitating the opening of this kind of space.

Kyle Good has contributed Integral Education: Community Building where he opens with two stories exemplifying the benefits of creating a solid sense of community in the classroom. From these stories, he then points to the goals of this work and some expectations for students to support it. He lists a number of helpful tools and techniques teachers can use in building the community of their own classrooms.

Chris Nichol explores Homeschooling from an Integral Point of View. In this chapter, Chris aptly described the joys and challenges of living the dictum that we teach who we are. In her experience of homeschooling she covered a deep array of issues in how to consciously raise her children and educate them in ways that supported their best growth, even when that meant letting them attend regular school.

In The Cradle of Education, Miriam Mason Martineau focuses on the impact of relationships on education. Before anything can be learned, we need to establish a relationship with our students. By also drawing on her experience as a parent, Miriam enables us to see the often overlooked and yet profoundly impactful ways in which we are always creating relationships. She also provides practices to sharpen our awareness of how we co-crate these relationships.

My own contribution to this section is Classroom Conversation: How to Move Beyond Debate and Discussion and Create Dialogue. In this short piece I outline the distinctions I see between debate, discussion and dialogue, grounding them in some theory and describe a structured process I have used in the classroom for enabling students to experience a taste of the kind of dialogue that can open new conversational horizons.

Nancy Simko of the Blue School contributed The Peace Bench, an early elementary story about a collaborative learning process. She illuminates the highlights of a simple solution that her students created for resolving conflict in the classroom.

The Invisible Children: A parable in which the invisible become visible, and the visible invisible is by Sue Stack. Sue tells the story of how a group of teens took on a project that led to a number of "teachable moments." The challenges of being present to student needs, one's own needs and those of student teaching assistants are all described with a depth and dexterity that provide insights for everyone.

With A Frothy Edge, Andrew Suttar takes us on a journey to see the world through the eyes of bubbles. His life's passion of using bubble making as an educational practice shows us how integral ideas can be perceived and used in pretty much any modality.

High Upon a Mountaintop: Teaching, Doing, and Being is by Jamie Wheal and describes an experience he had of balancing the tension between Rightness and Effectiveness. His context is teaching while on a backpacking adventure in the Colorado Rockies, engaging the students in the wonder of nature in real time while simultaneously helping them reflect on the personal and collective illusions about such engagement with their worlds.

As the book enters the third section on Conscious Teaching Practices, we open with Cultivating an Integral Perspective in the Classroom by Willow Dea. This chapter's goal is to help the reader actively apply the integral model to current issues, questions, or themes in the educational setting. By this we mean an integral analysis for working out the answer to particular questions. A series of inquiries designed to support the reader to ask missing questions is provided. The aim is to support the reader to cultivate an integral perspective while teaching.

Learning from Assessment by Nancy Davis follows. This is an area of specialty of Nancy's and her experience in applying an integral framework to the topic lends great strength to the chapter. By acknowledging and valuing the multiple purposes of assessment while also understanding that students bring varying perspectives of assessment to the learning environment, we, as educators, can develop skilful means that can help us align our intentions with our practices as we consider how the learners are interpreting what we do. We can act with compassion as we use the wisdom we gain from looking at our own practices and our students' conceptions of those practices through integral lenses. This chapter tells the story of Nancy's ongoing journey of understanding of assessment as a tool, a skilful means to be used to enhance development.

Terri O'Fallon brings a lifetime of experience at almost all levels of education to Integral Curriculum and Program Development in a Technical World. Her chapter foregrounds the often hidden benefits of the online classroom and explains how to design curricula that take advantage of these benefits. Infusing integral programs with an online focus can add benefits to learning that face-to-face experiences alone cannot deliver. It is critical to engage the world of technology because this is the primary platform for learning for young people today.

Shayla Wright is a long time teacher of yoga and personal development. Her chapter on Mutuality, Engagement, and Transformation asks questions essential to the support of learning the lessons of value in life: what is the source of long-term commitment and engagement in our students, and how do we draw forth this capacity? How do we evoke their innate courage and intelligence, and support them in nourishing these fundamental aspects of their being? Shayla uses a case study to describe her way of engaging these questions and the impact of coaching from a non-dual perspective.

Integral Practices: The Personal in the Professional brings us a taste of Patricia Gordon's sustained inquiry into how to use one's self as an instrument of teaching. She has also provided two appendixes to give even more detail to these issues. Her chapter is an invitation to a series of personal and professional practices aimed to help us inhabit an integral worldspace in our teaching. Personal and professional practices are entwined, creating a seamless way of embodying integral in our lives and of lighting up the many facets of Being. Patricia invites the reader to explore these practices as part of an evolutionary process.

We close with Future Horizons where Miriam Mason Martineau explores the future trends of integral education, programs in development, notable research, technology, and key areas in which integral education could enhance the quality of education at large. How the community of practice emerging around integral education can evolve to support these trends is also examined.

It is our sincere hope that this book opens up new horizons, inspires and engages you in the journey of being a teacher. All of us contributing have taken journeys similar to yours, in that we have wanted to teach as a way of making a difference in the world, enabling the students of today to grow in the best ways possible into the citizens of tomorrow. The path we have taken has brought us together in a loose community of practice around learning our way to being integral educators. We hope that some of you will want to join us and contribute your own journey and learning to the ongoing collective journey.

2

From Progressive Pedagogy to Integral Pedagogy

Tom Murray

Education is everything. We don't need little changes we need gigantic revolutionary changes. Schools should be palaces. Competition for the best teachers should be fierce. They should be getting six-figure salaries. Schools should be incredibly expensive for government and absolutely free of charge for its citizens, just like national defense. That is my position. I just haven't figured out how to do it yet.

—Aaron Sorokin

Education is a private matter between the person and the world of knowledge and experience, and has little to do with school or college.

—Lillian Smith

Integral means many things to many people, and the same is true for integral education. For educational practitioners, any particular school of educational thought may feel constraining and bound to a particular model or founder. The integral approach, on the other hand, embraces most of the values and deep principles embodied in progressive thought. It not only is compatible with these principles, but offers us a generous and welcoming meta-container.

The integral model places progressive educational ideas within a larger transdisciplinary web of ideas about culture, psychology, philosophy, science, etcetera, and also cleans up some shortcomings. A theory can fit comfortably within the integral camp and have the elbowroom to grow—and to play (not take itself too seriously.) Likewise, the community of people drawn to integral theory seems to be on board with the key assumptions of progressive pedagogies, and more importantly, seems to be more likely than not to embody these theories.

For about 20 years I have participated in instructional technology R&D that applies new learning and cognitive theories to advanced computer learning environments. I have taught graduate classes and facilitated teacher training workshops that explicitly use constructivist, inquiry-based, and other progressive pedagogies. My entry into the integral theory community about five years ago was motivated by interests in philosophy and systems approaches to the social sciences, not by education per se. I eventually connected with educators drawn to integral theory, and found that for some of them, integral theory had been their primary doorway into the wider world of progressive pedagogies. In fact, what excited them most about this new integral approach often turned out to be well-established (nothing novel) principles within progressive educational communities.

Many who have been inspired by a variety of particular progressive pedagogies find their way to the comforting and energizing umbrella of integral, which supports what they have in common and provides space and perspective on where they differ. Clearly, integral education is more than the sum of these various theories (or the overlap among them.) However, it is not always clear exactly what integral has to add over and above these other theories. If you ask someone interested in the integral approach to education to describe it, the response may not be differentiated from other progressive approaches, or it might be a description of other theories peppered with an integralized vocabulary, or repackaged in an AQAL model. When the integral approach to education is described in this old-wine-in-new-bottles fashion, as I have heard it described, especially by those enthusiastic and new to it, its legitimacy in the eyes of experienced educational practitioners, administrators, and theorists is jeopardized. Therefore, I think it is important for those of us who write about or teach integrally informed pedagogy to clearly differentiate it from existing progressive models and to articulate the value added.

Though it is a new and emerging field, much has been written already about integral approaches to education. Integrative Learning and Action: A Call to Wholeness (edited by Awbrey, Dana, Miller, Robinson, Ryan, & Scott, 2006) focuses on how aspects of spirituality and new ways of knowing can be integrated into education. Integral Education: New Directions for Higher Learning (edited by Esbjörn-Hargens, Reams, & Gunnlaugson, in press) focuses on higher education and also offers various perspectives on the field as a whole. These books contain material originally published as articles in journals, conference proceedings, and other venues; thus, several dozen papers have been published in this field (Moltz, in press, gives an overview of related research studies, to date). The topics in these books include the theoretical and pragmatic roots of integral approaches to education (Esbjörn-Hargens et al., in press), case study reports of using integral approaches (both books), and a diversity of theoretical perspectives on integral education (Esbjörn-Hargens et al., 2010).

Integral can be seen as pointing to four things: a (meta-) model or framework (a system of concepts for interpreting the world,) a methodology (a set of injunctions or principles for inquiring about the world,) a community (the embodied group or groups of people using integral models and methods), and/or a set of skills or capacities (a developmental stage that points past modern and postmodern cultural perspectives, and past formal operational modes of thinking.) In this chapter I address each of these perspectives on what being integral means, in the context of education.

In this chapter, I speak primarily to practicing educators and those who work with educators (e.g., administrators, curriculum designers, educational tool designers, and those who teach teachers) who are using or interested in integral approaches. The chapter may also be useful for integrally aware readers in training, coaching, leadership, and other fields involved in intentional learning. My overall goal is to help us clarify, to ourselves and to others unfamiliar with integral theory, who we are, where we come from, and where we seem to be going as integral educators. I start with a birds-eye overview of key principles of progressive pedagogies, then describe what the integral approach adds to these in terms of a model, a methodology, a consciousness, and a community. I discuss integral community in the context of responding to the challenges of realizing the visions of integral education. Along the way, I try to illustrate some elements of the integral approach by applying it in situ in my analysis. I assume you have at least a passing familiarity with Ken Wilber's integral theory and the AQAL and spiral dynamics models (see Wilber, 2006, 2000; Beck & Cowan, 1996).

Progressive Pedagogies

The mind is not a vessel to be filled, but a fire to be kindled.

—Plutarch

Education is an admirable thing, but it is well to remember from time to time that nothing that is worth knowing can be taught.

—Oscar Wilde

Education, therefore, is a process of living and not a preparation for future living.

—John Dewey

Progressive (or reform or alternative) pedagogies and educational approaches include the works of thinkers such as John Dewy, Jean Piaget, Lev Vygotsky, Rudolf Steiner, Paulo Freire, John Holt, Ivan Illich, Parker Palmer, Maria Montessori, Jerome Bruner, Jack Mezirow, and Howard Gardner, who developed alternative pedagogical theories in response to the perceived deficiencies of traditional institutional education, theories of learning, and social knowledge creation modalities. The theories and models of these educational leaders include constructivism, Montessori schools, Reggio-Emilio schools, Waldorf education, transformative learning, un/de-schooling, and situated learning. It is not my goal here to compare or contrast each of these, but to point to what they share in a general sense, and how we can approach their totality and their differences as a system.

An Overview of Progressive Pedagogies

I use the terms progressive (or integral) method, approach, theory, principles, world view, and pedagogy interchangeably. They all point to more or less the same thing, but highlight different aspects. (I use the term framework only for Wilber's theory.) I assume you are familiar with a handful of progressive educational models, assumptions, and value-orientations. Even though they seem like separate principles, each has a significant overlap with many others because there are many ways to cut the pie that constitutes the common appreciation of progressive pedagogy. In real world application, the lines between these principles blur significantly.

Holism: An acknowledgement and appreciation of the whole person or whole child—mind, body, heart, spirit, and community are all interconnected and important. Artistic expression, bodily movement and health, spontaneity and fun, interaction with the natural world, and service are as important to creating good citizens and realizing students' full potential, as is the learning of content. The physical arrangement of the classroom, what a student had for breakfast, and whether caring parents saw him or her out the door all affect a student's learning and engagement.

Multiple intelligences: All forms of intelligence should be acknowledged and nurtured; each student may have his or her own path to learning due to some of these lines of development or styles of learning being stronger than others (Gardner, 1983).

Creativity: Success in the world, especially the complex modern world, requires creativity (lateral thinking, right-brained thinking). This includes considering multiple hypotheses, or alternative solutions, or perspectives, and not committing rigidly to any one too quickly. Nurturing creativity requires bracketing the logical mind and opening to other forms of intelligence (deBono, 1970; Polya, 1973; Robinson, 2001).

Individuality and human potential: Each person has a unique set of capabilities and potentials, and something unique to offer the classroom and the world. Learners should be treated and respected as unique individuals.

Constructivism: Each person constructs his or her knowledge in a unique way, depending on prior knowledge, preconceptions, and experiences. Meaning making is idiosyncratic and personal. Instruction must move beyond the pipeline theory of learning that assumes that if curriculum could only be organized and presented skillfully enough, one learning path will fit all students (von Glasersfeld, 1995; Collins et al., 1989).

Developmentalism: Learning happens through natural processes, such as integration and differentiation, or assimilation and accommodation, or horizontal and hierarchical learning (depending on the theory). This puts limits on the speed of learning (it cannot be pushed too fast) and the order of learning (some concepts and skills necessarily come before others) (Piaget, 1972; Fischer & Farrar, 1987; Commons & Richards, 1984).

Zone of proximal development (ZPD): Instruction should aim for the zone of proximal development that has the right balance of support and challenge to avoid the extremes of boredom and being overwhelmed (Vygotsky, 1987; Murray & Arroyo, 2002).

Meta-learning: In today's dynamic world, one needs to learn how to learn. One also needs to think about thinking (metacognition) and understand the nature and limits of knowing (i.e., have epistemic knowledge). Education should strengthen the learner's ability to monitor, reflect upon, and adjust problem solving processes and outcomes on the fly (Schoenfeld, 1985; Winne, 2001; Kegan, 1994).

Adaptivity/individualization/differentiation: The content, style, and speed of curriculum should allow for, adapt to, and/or differ for the various types of individual differences noted above. This can be done by dynamically steering the instructional path to respond to individual student needs and/or by immersing learners in open-ended environments that support many paths (Tomlinson, 1995).

Learning by doing, case-based learning, situated learning, discovery learning, and inquiry learning: Progressive theories say learning activities need to be authentic, rich, or realistic enough to engage student motivation and to allow for transfer to real-life problems. Taking guesses and making mistakes are seen as normal, inevitable, and positive. Learning that comes from real engagement and curiosity is far superior in depth and longevity to rote memorization or cramming for a test. We learn by designing and building things, playing, and getting our hands dirty, and trial and error.

Situated learning: Most authentic learning happens in social contexts, often through apprenticeship or mentoring relationships. The social fabric and dynamics of the learning context are critical success factors. Collaborative learning is beneficial, as are peer learning and peer tutoring. We learn by showing, explaining to, questioning, arguing with, negotiating with, teaching, and helping others. Social and emotional intelligence are as important to learning as is intellect (Brown et al., 1989; Lave & Wenger, 1991; Vygotsky, 1978).

Empowerment and liberation: Education happens largely through institutions that perpetuate habits of disempowerment, oppression, conformity, orthodoxy, and life alienating thought forms (Freire, 1970; Illich, 1975; Rosenberg, 1999; Ewert on Habermas, 1991; Dewey, 1926; hooks, 1994). Education should be designed to support the ideals of freedom, equality, self-determination, justice, and open mindedness that enable democratic society. Students can be given more choice and power over what and how they learn; they can be supported in acquiring the skills of dialog and conflict resolution. Teachers can relinquish some control and reveal their areas of ignorance and uncertainty; they can be "guides on the side" rather than "sages on the stage."

The ethical classroom: If the classroom is a learning laboratory for life, then it should support such qualities as compassion, caring, respect, empathy, and dialog, and model quality relationships and community building (Palmer, 1998; Elbow, 2008).

Transformative education: Some focus on education as a vehicle for spiritual growth, the flowering of human potential, and/or the evolution of human meaning-making capacity (or action-logics, see Torbert, 2004). They suggest that the classroom can support contemplative, transpersonal, and transformative experiences (Mezirow, 1991; Steiner, 1965).

Community/service-based learning: Community-base and service-based learning are strongly situated and have ethical implications. Connecting schooling tightly with family, community, and society has clear benefits for students and allows learning through doing to directly benefit the larger whole. This engages multiple intelligences and modalities, and gives students a sense of empowerment and purpose.

Lifelong learning and emergence: We never stop learning, or at least need not stop. This is true because of the constantly changing social and technological landscape, and also is true from the perspective of human potential and emergence. Expertise, wisdom, leadership, and innovation are continually deepening skills developed over years of adult life.

Teacher presence and embodiment: Of critical importance is how teachers and other leaders embody and model the qualities they intend to teach and support. This highlights the critical and too often neglected fact that educational reform requires significant investment in teacher training. In addition, the deep qualities of compassion, presence, metacognitive reflection, and mind/body/emotion/spirit integration cannot be taught in a teacher training classroom. Teachers and leaders are called to engage in personal transformative practices of emotional healing and self-realization, and also to risk a deeper authenticity and transparency in the classroom.

Participatory/action-based curriculum development and research: At the graduate level, teachers in training begin to become engaged in tasks such as curriculum development and research. Here (and in other contexts), progressive pedagogies are combined with progressive methodologies, such as action research (Argyris, 1985; Feldman & Minstrell, 2000); user-participatory design (Barnathy, 1992); and qualitative, interdisciplinary, and mixed-method research (Bogdan & Biklen, 1982; Patton, 1980).

Progressive Pedagogies Compared

The descriptions of progressive approaches comprise theories of learning (claims about scientific truths), prescriptive practices, and educational values (claims about how people should act and be treated). Most progressive pedagogical models emphasize a handful of the basic principles and values and are compatible with most of the others. Each of these principles points to an entire literature of inter-referencing papers and an entire community of practitioners and scholars, complete with journals and conference meetings. Furthermore, each theory has become the central construct for a world of real practice. Because implementing theories into real educational contexts tends to require fleshing out a wide range of universally encountered concerns, in practice, the full articulation of each has much overlap with the others.

These progressive approaches cover a wide range of issues echoed in integral theories:

- Addressing the many aspects of being human: body/mind/emotion/spirit,
- Including multiple systemic layers: the individual, aspects/parts of the individual, the classroom, the wider community and society,
- Allowing for multiple ways of knowing: in terms of quadrants (i.e., subjective, objective, intersubjective; and types); multiple intelligences; and so-called masculine and feminine modalities,
- Giving full attention to both internal realities (values, visions, feeling, motivations, relationships) and external realities (measurement, action, physical health, educational infrastructure),
- Seeing knowledge in terms of the coordination of perspectives (e.g.,critical approaches to knowledge and power, epistemic or meta-knowledge, and dialogic approaches).

Although significant overlap and compatibility exists between the integral and progressive approaches, the integral approach adds several elements (e.g., except for a few exceptions, progressive approaches do not incorporate principles from modern theories of dynamic systems, adult development, or cultural evolution). The progressive educational principles, models, and value orientations were developed in a social and cultural context critical of mainstream institutional forms of education. In the mirror image of each of the principles is a pointer to some elements of traditional education seen as detrimental (e.g., knowledge presented as fragmented bits or in disciplinary silos, inadequately connected to real life practice and concerns; cognitively impoverished metaphors for learning, such as the pipe line model; rout memorization, teaching to the test, and standardized curricula; hierarchical and oppressive forms of personal and institutional relationships; capitalistic, materialistic, and bureaucratic educational systems) (Feldman, 2008).

If you are a progressive-thinking individual, you may find the list of progressive approaches quite appealing and bemoan the fact that public education is so far from these ideals. If you are a teacher, you may be thinking, "How the heck can any one person learn all of those principles, much less practice them?"

Any teacher skilled in progressive pedagogical methods will be implementing a bit of this and a bit of that, and probably is familiar with a few but not all of these principles. The massive interconnectedness of the principles means you might be working in alignment with many of them implicitly, as a matter of intuition more than explicit theory application. It also means a teacher in training can assimilate the gist of many of the principles simultaneously through mentoring with a skilled practitioner. Of course, a full understanding also can come from a traditional academic-style study of the theories and from reading texts, taking advanced study classes, and attending conferences. Also, as I note later, understanding and using progressive versus traditional modalities (as well as integral modalities) assumes a certain set of developmental competencies.

Where's the Integral?

Education forms the common mind. Just as the twig is bent, the tree's inclined.
—Alexander Pope

I think people are starved for a truly holistic and genuinely integral approach to the world—in psychology, in spirituality, in politics, in education... [Alternative] education in this country is at a crucial turning point. For several decades the counter-cultural and "new paradigm" thinkers imagined, with good reason, that they were fighting a lonely battle against conventional education. But in the last five years or so, everything has profoundly changed. Mainstream institutions... are now quite open to integral studies...
—Ken Wilber

A main theme of this chapter is that nothing in the progressive pedagogies points to the uniquely integral part of integral education (or what integral theory brings to education). Having said that integral can be understood as a (meta) model or framework, a methodology, a community, and/or a stage or phase of human development, now let's explore what each of these perspectives means for integral education.

It is worth noting that while Ken Wilber's Integral Theory (capitalized here) with its AQAL model is by far the most well-known and influential integral model, many who identify their work with integral (not capitalized) do not primarily base their work on Wilber's work. Therefore, when I say integral theory, model, or approach, I usually mean the body of work being developed in the greater community of integral theory and practice.

AQAL: A Framework That Transcends and Includes Progressive Pedagogical Principles

For many readers, integral is, if not synonymous with Ken Wilber's work, strongly identified with it. Though his work consistently and brilliantly points to postformal, dialectical, metasystematic, and even (I hesitate to use a term so overused in the integral community that its meaning is ambiguous) non-dual ways of perceiving the world, Wilber has chosen to frame or package his ideas in terms of a formal-looking model with seemingly precise categories. His AQAL model, which includes the Four Quadrants (or 8 Zones), 8 Developmental Stages or Levels, 3 primary States, and a variety of Types of human capacities, should be familiar to most readers (see Wilber, 2006, for a description). I assume Wilber and his associates choose to foreground such a model because its benefits in terms of allowing integral theory to appeal to a wider audience and appear applicable to a larger range of domains outweigh the problems of using formal structures to promote post-formal ways of knowing.

AQAL is a meta-model that can hold within it the full set of progressive education principles, allow them to be compared, and set them in a larger meta-theoretical context. It can be the kitchen sink into which all of these ideas are thrown. More than being merely a conceptual container, it organizes them and clarifies core elements. Some of the principles focus on the understanding and development of internal mental, emotional, or spiritual capacities (upper left quadrant.) Others prioritize collaborative, community, or ethical elements (lower left.) Yet others emphasize in-the-world action, the creation of artifacts, or physical embodiment (upper right quadrant,) while others highlight the systemic factors in classrooms, the institutions of education, or social and political realities (lower right quadrant.)

We could describe the major insights of the integral approach in terms of two elements. The first is a deeper appreciation for and understanding of the interior dimensions of reality, which have been neglected in many aspects of modernity. The second is in bringing the rigor of systems theory to holistic and transdisciplinary approaches. Systems theory brings insights about structural complexity. This complexity is seen, for example, in the understanding of systems as nested holons and with co-arising interior, exterior, individual, and collective components. Systems theory also adds insights about dynamic complexity, which includes the evolutionary and developmental perspectives so central to the integral approach.

Integral theory explains the massive overlap among the principles. In real systems (e.g., including people, groups, and societies), all four quadrants interact. In fact, they are four sides of the same coin (if a coin could have 4 sides.) The I, We, It, and Its of a system arise and develop simultaneously (they tetra-emerge.) The four-quadrant model (and Wilber's eight zones, or primordial perspectives) can be used as a diagnostic tool for assessing missing components in an educational situation.

AQAL's exploration of states versus stages helps us as teachers think about how to design experiences that induce states of mind that support learning. AQAL's elaboration of distinct lines and levels of development, types of intelligence, and states of mind (or consciousness) together incorporate the intuitions articulated in theories of multiple intelligences and the holistic approaches to mind, body, emotion, and spirit. This helps us avoid overemphasizing any particular learning modality or pedagogical theory. In a later section, I examine the merits of evolutionary, developmental, and systems-theory approaches, which are central to AQAL and all integral approaches.

Upper Left (1) **Educational Experiences** **Contemplative** **Critical** **Somatic**	Upper Right (2) **Educational Behavior** **Skilled** **Practical** **Active**
Lower Left (3) **Educational Culture** **Connected** **Perspectival** **Ethical**	Lower Right (4) **Educational Systemic** **Ecological** **Social** **Global**

Figure 2.1. Esbjorn-Hargens' Twelve Commitments of Integral Education

As an example of how the AQAL map can illuminate and organize educational themes, consider Sean Esbjörn-Hargens's (2007) table of Twelve Commitments of Integral Education. It illustrates what he calls the essential dimensions of an integral approach to education by situating a mind, body, and spirit element in each of AQAL's four quadrants. The table describes twelve "forms of engagement…modes of interaction [and/or] ways of knowing the world" (12).

Integral Methodology: Perspectives, Knowledge Building, and Dialog

The AQAL model is as limited as it is powerful. In fact, some of its limitations are because it is so powerful. It can trick us into thinking that it represents an accurate picture of reality, when in fact, like all models, it is one interpretation of reality, presenting one way to categorize the elements of our experience and understanding. When we try to use it in complex real-life situations, we see that surrounding its clear and insight-producing distinctions are grey areas, like square pegs forced into round holes, and a diversity of opinions about the exact meaning and implication of the model's categories. These difficulties come unavoidably with any conceptual system. Wilber entreats us not to "confuse the map for the territory," yet assuming that reality reflects our constructs instead of the other way around is an ingrained human tendency difficult to avoid.

The integral approach (as articulated by Wilber and many others) provides something deeper than a categorical framework within which to neatly organize our untidy reality. It suggests a certain attitude with which we can approach knowing, conceptualizing, and theorizing. It suggests not so much what is true about the world but how we can work together to discover what is most true, just, and useful in a particular context. In other words, it includes an epistemology as well as an ontology. This method or way of thinking is not as well defined as is the AQAL model, so the description of it is something we circle around and weave through, rather than a crisp diagram of a model.

Educators have increasingly acknowledged that, in the modern context, education should involve not only the learning of content, (i.e., information and specific skills), but also the learning of more general (higher order) skills and knowledge. Among these are learning how to learn (i.e., self-directed learning that reflects upon what we should be learning and how the learning process is going), and epistemic (or meta-) knowledge (i.e., some understanding of how knowledge is arrived at and the limitations of knowledge) (Schoenfeld, 1985; Mayer, 1998). The integral approach requires this type of meta-level perspective on knowledge, method, learning, and doing.

The relevant modern (or postmodern) insights about knowledge include:

- **Complexity:** Many aspects of the world are highly complex. We need concepts from systems theory (e.g., co-evolution, chaos, non-linearity, and self-organization) to understand (a) the world in general and (b) educational and learning processes in particular (Reigeluth, 2008).

- **Meta-perspectives:** For citizens to address the complex problems of modern society, educators must help learners develop higher level skills (e.g., meta-cognition, or thinking about thinking); meta-knowledge (knowledge about the nature and limitations of knowledge); meta-learning (learning how to learn); and meta-dialog (dialog about how we engage in dialog) (See more in Murray, 2008).

• **Knowledge is personal:** Knowledge, understanding, and truths are, at least in most instances, constrained by the world view, experiences, biases, perspective, developmental level, etcetera of the speaker and listener (Polanyi, 1962).

• **Multi-methodology:** Different methods of observing (or inquiry or experimentation) lead to different conclusions or claims. Different disciplines tend to use different methodologies, leading to different conclusions about a phenomenon. Each of these conclusions can be seen as valid perspectives on a complex reality, rather than as opposing camps battling for the truth (Norgaard, 1989).

• **Indeterminism:** Terms, concepts, rules, models, and theories all have a certain degree of indeterminacy (i.e., fuzziness, uncertainty, or ambiguity in their meaning) (Murray, 2006). It is often important to pay attention to the grey areas at the boundaries of seemingly precise categories or rules (Lakoff & Johnson, 1999; Mervis & Rosch, 1981).

• **Negotiation, ethics, and power:** Knowledge is constructed, or negotiated, via communicative processes situated in authentic contexts. Truth finding is an evolutionary process requiring dialog (Lave & Wenger, 1991; Habermas, 1998). Knowledge also has important moral/ethical aspects (Habermas, 1999; Kögler, 1992). The quality of knowledge building outcomes can depend on how carefully the knowledge building process pays attention to elements such as freedom, equality, empathy, sincerity, inclusivity, reciprocity, integrity, and mutual regard.

How does a learner, knowledge worker, or educator deal with the added levels of complexity and indeterminacy that come when he or she begins to acknowledge these insights? An additional set of methods is needed.

All of the insights just described fall into what we could call a postmodern or progressive understanding and world view. What I listed under progressive blends with what I am calling an integral level (e.g., the indeterminacy involved in creating categories.) What constitutes the difference? For me, a progressive perspective involves identifying and describing the problems with traditional modes, leading to a critical attitude that is suspect of all claims and perspectives. It involves a discerning analysis about the nature of the problem(s). However, with respect to dealing productively with the problem, it gives only vague advice or ends with acceptance or despair that things are so complex, unknowable, subjective, and so on. An integral perspective, while not pretending to any easy or complete fix, does more to help us understand the nature of complexity itself, the nature of indeterminacy itself, and the nature of subjectivity itself. We can use this higher level of understanding to improve upon a situation.

If every perspective is like a lens or filter that distorts perception and inference, then we can correct for these distortions to the extent that we understand something about the lens or filter itself (turning subject into object, as Kegan frames it.) At the integral level, we are not only learning and using a set of pedagogies, but we are adopting a critical (and appreciative) meta-perspective on those pedagogies. We also are noticing how our self (including our values and assumptions) fits into the system of teacher-applying-pedagogy-within-an-educational-system.

Three Ways to Use Integral Methods

We can apply integral (or progressive) methods and models at three levels. First, we can teach them explicitly. That is, the students know they are learning and using, for example, "the AQAL model" or "systems theory" or "the Believing Game." Second, teachers can learn these methods and models and use them implicitly. They can bring their knowledge of integral (or progressive) methods and models to bear in designing and running educational activities without explicitly mentioning these models or methods to students. In this case, teacher educators facilitate teachers in learning about these methods and models. Third, administrators, curriculum designers, or teacher educators can use integral (or progressive) methods and models to design the materials or environment within which teachers work. In which case, teachers (and secondarily students) benefit from these methods and models without necessarily learning about them. In addition, we can differentiate between methods and models designed through integral consciousness and those that require integral consciousness to understand and adopt. The level of development required to conceive and design a professional development program for, for example, constructivist pedagogy is higher than the level required to understand and implement constructivism in a classroom.

All three levels are possible when teaching young learners or adults, and also when teaching teachers. The point is that integral (or progressive) methods and models can have a strong impact even if the student, or teacher, is not aware the method or models are being used. Integral is as much a type of consciousness or awareness as a set of models or methods. An integral learning environment might have an indefinable but recognizable look and feel, or texture of breadth and depth. It has been argued that people who work or learn under the implicit umbrella of a worldview, milieu, approach, or type of consciousness will implicitly assimilate some of that world view or consciousness. I propose that when students or teachers are immersed in curricular, social, or administrative environments that are integrally informed, the seeds of integral consciousness are planted and nurtured.

In the Fourth Grade

My descriptions thus far may sound rather sophisticated, esoteric, and philosophical. Indeed, fully working at an integral level requires a grasp of developmental skills. Even though these skills mature later in life, they begin to develop early in life, and we can do much to nurture this developmental process at all ages and stages.

Let's briefly consider how these philosophically rich issues and methods can be simplified and brought into a fourth grade classroom. Imagine the students are working collaboratively to research what to do on a school trip to Washington DC. They gather information from diverse sources and have facilitated classroom discussions to decide (a) what the case is (e.g., how much gas will cost) and (b) what should be done (e.g., whether to stay at a campground or hotel.)

If the activity is facilitated well, students can learn that knowledge is complex and perspectival and that it has subjective (what I think,) objective (what Wikipedia says,) and intersubjective (what we all agree upon) facets. They can learn that words and rules may not have one single meaning and can be interpreted differently in different contexts. Moreover, they can learn that biases and assumptions are hidden in beliefs and preferences, and that it takes a triangulation of different perspectives and inquiry methods to arrive at an adequate understanding or solution. It is not hard to imagine a teacher fashioning simplistic forms of integral methodological pluralism, polarity mapping, contemplative practices, the Believing Game, and even indeterminacy analysis that apply to this age group.

Progressive Pedagogies as a Dynamic System of Principles

I believe that school makes complete fools of our young men, because they see and hear nothing of ordinary life there.
—Petronius, Satyricon

[Public education is] the single most important element in the maintenance of a democratic system...The better the citizenry as a whole are educated, the wider and more sensible public participation, debate and social mobility will be... The most difficult and the most valuable is a well-educated populace. (John Ralston Saul, Doubter's Companion: A Dictionary of Aggressive Common Sense) The difficulty is the perception that [one is] dealing with a problem that can be solved by choosing either one or the other... fear of getting stuck in the opposite pole gets you stuck in your own pole... paradoxically, opposition becomes a resource.
—Barry Johnson

Thus far I have stressed how the principles of progressive pedagogies tend to mutually support each other and form a complex system or dense meshwork of co-defining ideas. Let's continue by shifting focus from the commonalities to the differences. Each principle emphasizes a particular theoretical perspective or value. Principles are ideals. Overemphasizing any one principle or value may cause another to be minimized. Practical applications require tradeoffs and balancing acts.

Polarity mapping (Johnson, 1996) can be used to illustrate and explore this issue. Here are some of the polarities or dialectical tensions within our set of progressive pedagogies:

- **Self-determination versus helpful hierarchy.** A polarity exists between student empowerment or discovery and the need for teachers to skillfully employ guidance, limitations, expertise, and leadership. Traditional schools often underestimate the learners' abilities to self-steer their learning experiences. How far into the background should a teacher step?

- **Individual freedom versus group needs.** A polarity exists between methods that focus on individual students (meeting their needs, giving them a voice, supporting their autonomy, respecting their complex personal histories) and methods that emphasize the group, the community, and caring about the needs of others. Sometimes a student's needs must go unmet for the greater good of the class. So at what level does that approach become oppressive?

- **Equality versus special treatment.** A polarity exists between the desire to treat all students equally and the fact that students have a range of capacities and motivations. Should the most capable and motivated students be given extra resources? Should underprivileged students be given extra resources? If yes to both, where does this leave the middle group?

- **Support versus challenge.** A polarity exists between acknowledging the wonderfulness of every impulse and creative product a student produces and supporting self-esteem and learning enjoyment, and the benefits of challenging students by providing cognitive or emotional disequilibrium. When and how does a teacher tell students they are wrong, need to improve, or are not stepping up to their potential?

- **Creativity versus rigor.** A polarity exists between supporting creativity, play, and intuition, and teaching logic, critical thinking, rigor, and discernment. Both can be taught; however, in any given activity or course, one may be highlighted at the expense of the other.
- **Process versus product.** Progressive pedagogy stresses learning to learn, higher order thinking skills, and the importance of good problem-solving reasoning over getting the right answer. However, usable knowledge must include some amount of facts and memorized procedures; real world performance often needs a correct or best solution. How should education balance these poles?

- **Change versus stability.** Progressive pedagogy values adaptation, dynamic flow, and customization. Yet, to some degree, people flourish when given clear and stable constraints, rules, and/or boundaries. How predictable should the classroom experience, including teacher expectations, be for students?

- **Cognitive (mind) versus social and affective (heart).** Developing wisdom includes developing the capacities of both the heart and mind, as well as their skillful interpenetration. However, when designing curriculum or activities, priorities often must be made to focus primarily on content and cognitive skills rather than on social or emotional skills. In addition, the educator must decide how these priorities influence methods of evaluation, grading, and feedback (e.g., what type of evaluation and feedback is appropriate for a student who tries hard and is a good team player, yet fails to grasp key subject matter concepts.)

In many situations, these dichotomies are imaginary in the sense that the human needs that seem to be in conflict are in fact not, and an elegant solution exists that can satisfy both sides. However, these polarities also are real, in that real life decisions will often unavoidably benefit one side of the equation at the cost of the other. The perennial advice regarding such polarities is true: practical application involves balance and compromise, and a forswearing of ideology and dogmas, even progressive dogmas. Integral, or dialectical, consciousness can take us a bit further still. Note that the above polarities are within the set of progressive pedagogies. Additional polarities can be mapped/managed/balanced when we include a full spectrum of traditional, modern, progressive, and integral pedagogies.

As described in polarity mapping theory, opposing poles of some situations are interdependent and mutually defining, rather than either/or choices or opposite ends of a spectrum (Johnson, 1996). Effective learning environments need change as well as stability, creativity as well as rigor, support as well as challenge, and so on. Moreover, real systems are dynamic, so a solution that works at one point in time may not apply later. For instance, a teacher correctly evaluates a situation and decides to move in the direction of supporting more creativity (versus rigor.) After the teacher begins to do this, he or she will not know how far to go in that direction until the class has gone a bit too far, and the downsides of creativity and the importance of rigor start to come alive. Even if the teacher finds a perfect balance, when the class moves on to the next topic in the curriculum, or an additional student comes to town, or the warm winds of spring start to blow through the winterized classroom windows, the appropriate balance point will shift. In addition, just introducing a pedagogical change can affect the classroom system in unpredictable ways. A teacher takes a measurement of the class, compares it with an existing goal, sets a bearing in some direction, and implements the change. As soon as the change is implemented, the landscape changes and both the measurement and the bearing are uncertain (in a type of social Heisenberg uncertainty principle; see Reigeluth, 2008.)

The solution is the development of a dialectical intelligence capable of constant (or frequent) assessment and awareness of the situation and flexible adaptation (Basseches, 1984). This includes an understanding of the dynamic tensions between the polarities and a perception of the whole as a dynamic system. This skill is one element of what we are calling integral consciousness or second-tier capacity.

Integral Consciousness

To teach is to touch the heart and impel it to action.
—Louis Sullivan

We teach who we are... Good teaching comes from good people.
—Parker Palmer

Like progressive pedagogies, the integral approach has roots in the human potential movement (and in humanism more broadly; see Hampson, in press). Both approaches (a) value multiple lines of human capacities and needs, (b) acknowledge that each person has a unique set of capacities and needs, and (c) speak to the possibility of more fully realizing these capacities and needs. Yet unlike most of the progressive pedagogies, the integral approach draws heavily from both developmental theories and transpersonal psychology. From developmental theories we gain an appreciation not only of the abilities and limitations of students according to their developmental profiles, but we also gain an appreciation of the developmental requirements that the integral approach places upon teachers (in general, and upon oneself). From transpersonal psychology and its humanist and spiritualist threads (e.g., transformational learning,) we gain a valuing of the psychological and spiritual wholeness and adeptness of the individual teacher (which is itself developmental.)

Integral points to a capacity (a level of skill development also called second tier by Wilber, and closely related to Kegan's fifth order of consciousness) as well as a model and a methodology. In fact, the most complete or appropriate application of the integral models and methods actually requires a certain developmental capacity.

Progressive teacher educators tend to realize that learning new methods requires personalized mentoring, patience, and the trial and error of extended practice. Still, they are often befuddled by the difficulty some have in learning progressive methods. They may attribute it to a stylistic bent, or a learning (or communication) personality type, or cognitive type, or a deficit in the so-called system. However, though they have some appreciation of how constructivist and developmental principles apply to children, they usually lack appreciation for the importance of (and limitations imposed by) adult development (along cognitive, epistemological, dialectical, social, and self lines.) Thus, in strongly emphasizing adult developmental and transformational themes, the integral approach has much to add to progressive approaches. In this section I describe some characteristics of integral or second tier consciousness as this developmental level applies to education. In a later section I discuss more about the challenges in supporting practicing educators to develop this type of awareness.

Aspects of Integral Consciousness

So what is integral consciousness, or second-tier capacity, and how does it relate to education? Though these terms have not been concisely defined, the literature points to several aspects of this broadly defined stage of development.

First consider some caveats about the constructs of developmental lines and levels (or stages)—concepts that appear prominently within the integral community. Although these constructs have powerful explanatory power; their accuracy is regarded as controversial by some in the field. Also, they represent properties of human development as if such properties could be easily categorized, labeled, and differentiated, when in fact these phenomena have fuzzy boundaries and overlap. Thus, great care should be taken when assigning individuals to a particular category. For example, it is useful to speak about traditional versus progressive worldviews, but each individual is more complex than can be captured by such labels.

Learning involves not only the accumulation and coordination of knowledge and skills, but a progression of qualitatively different capacities for learning and meaning making. A plethora of developmental models are available for mapping various interrelated sets of developmental capacities (Wilber, 2000; Harris, 2002). I draw from Robert Kegan's (1994) model, focusing on fifth-order consciousness, which has significant overlap with the concept of second-tier thinking, and was derived from empirical studies.

Kegan (1994) describes five orders of consciousness. The progressive, alternative, reform, and holistic pedagogies mentioned in this chapter are associated with his fourth order (and reach into his fifth order.) Integral approaches are more centrally fifth order. Applied to the domain of education, learners at Kegan's fourth order are self-directed (or self-authoring, co-creative) learners who can examine themselves and their culture, develop critical thinking and individual initiative, and take responsibility for their learning and productivity (303). At full fourth-order consciousness, individuals have mastered skills such as these, and in the process of doing so, likely became advocates of such skills and identified with them, believing this level of skill superior to others. Typically, they have practiced and identified with one or a small number of progressive schools of thought (from the many listed above.)

At Kegan's fifth-order individuals begin to reflect upon whole belief systems, even their own fourth-order beliefs, as limited and indeterminate systems. They begin to dis-identify with any particular belief system, and experience themselves as embodying a variety of evolving belief systems, surfacing in different contexts. Questions of "who am I," "what do I believe," "what is true," and "what is right" cease to have one best or optimal answer ("it depends!") Rather than responding to situations by looking for optimal or win-win solutions (a fourth-order approach,) fifth-order individuals see themselves as co-evolving constituents of each situation, and expect a problem situation or dilemma to transform them; they may continue to search for an adequate solution or approach to a problem—each developmental level transcends and includes prior ones, as Wilber notes. Wilber (2000) and Beck and Cowan (1996) describe this second tier of development as one in which individuals develop a working understanding of the developmental process itself and see the value of all developmental levels (all world-view systems) as coexisting within themselves (and others).

Kegan's model maps the interweaving development among cognitive (it), interpersonal (we) and intrapersonal (I) capacities. Cook-Greuter's (2000) developmental framework describes second-tier capacities called construct awareness and ego awareness, which are closely related to Kegan's cognitive and intrapersonal lines. In addition, Wilber's AQAL theory posits a systemic "its" perspective (or quadrant) in addition to the objective (it), intersubjective (we), and subjective (I) perspectives. Thus, I propose the following model for integral (or second-tier) consciousness:

- Construct aware (cognitive; "it" dimension),
- Systems aware ("its" dimension; also a cognitive capacity, but reflecting systems and networks of relationships as opposed to mental constructs),
- Ego aware (self/ego/will and being/spirit/essence; "I" dimension),
- Relationally aware (emotional/social/ethical/interpersonal intelligence; "we" dimension).

Both construct-aware and systems-aware capacities are cognitively oriented and are lumped together in much of what follows. One way to describe the cognitive skill spectrum is to say it comprises a movement away from linear, black-and-white thinking and toward more sophisticated and nuanced modes of reasoning. This includes a deeper understanding or wider perspective on the function of language and thought itself.

The developmental literature mentions three overlapping skills that can help understand second-tier cognitive development. Construct awareness (Cook-Greuter, 2005) is a flexible approach to the uncertainties; ambiguities; and paradoxes of concepts, language, and knowledge. It is closely related to what has been called dialectical intelligence (Basseches, 1984) and epistemic wisdom (Murray, 2008). It is needed for integral-level methodologies (e.g., polarity mapping). Cook-Greuter describes it as "…becoming aware of the profound splits and paradoxes inherent in rational thought [in which] good and evil, life and death, beauty and ugliness may now appear as two sides of the same coin" (28). Meta-systematic reasoning refers to an ability to flexibly coordinate multiple whole systems of ideas (Commons & Richards, 1984; Ross, 2005). It is "meta"-systematic because it goes beyond the capacity to conceptualize and work systematically with ideas and within a system of ideas, to being able to move among and perceive reality through (or by coordinating) multiple systems of ideas. Vision logic refers to the ability to use forms of reasoning that are beyond formal logic and systematic thought (Gebser, as described by Feuerstein, 1987). This includes reasoning about logic and its limitations, and also flexibly and intentionally tapping into intuitive, unconscious, or gestalt ways of thinking.

Ego awareness is easier to explain using nontechnical language than is cognitive awareness (Kegan's model highlights ego development and Cook-Greuter's model focuses on ego development). Cook-Greuter (2005) describes it thus: "This is the first time in development that the ego becomes transparent to itself. Final knowledge about the self or anything else is seen as illusive and unattainable through effort and reason because all conscious thought, all cognition is recognized as constructed and, therefore, split off from the underlying, cohesive, non-dual truth" (28). Social/emotional intelligence is a significant aspect of integral consciousness, and in this model is implied as part of both ego awareness and relational awareness, which is discussed in the next section. Kegan and Lahey (2009) and Goleman (2006) discuss the critical importance of social/emotional intelligence in real life situations, and how cognitive and social/emotional intelligences interpenetrate and inter-depend.

Being an Integral Teacher

Embodying integral consciousness may not be as mysterious, sophisticated, or esoteric as it sounds. This inner capacity can be touched when teachers finds themselves in a bit of a pickle in the classroom. For example, when two students are unable to work well together, instead of responding in his or her usual way, the teacher may pause, become quiet inside, and ask, "Okay, what is really called for here? What is the best for this class and for me right now? " In this moment, the teacher receives a quiet but certain insight into this social and interpersonal system. The insight comes with an "aha! " sense of relief and confidence about what to do. This level of development also involves a way of being with the flow of life, so the teacher can be consistently committed to concepts, values, and relationships, but also be able to gently and cleanly let go, listen deeply, and adapt when reality does not meet his or her expectations or desires.

High levels of personal development point not only to sophisticated, or higher, capacities, but to increased depth of being (related to ego awareness.) This involves being in touch with deep sources of self-knowing, intuition, empathy, compassion, and presence that are associated with wisdom and transpersonal modes of awareness. Scharmer (2007) suggests that when we release our cognitive preconceptions and emotional attachments and settle into a state of open awareness and presence, we can unleash a powerful potential for creativity and growth.

The development toward these forms of wisdom involves an increasing ability to step outside ourselves and our emotions, biases, and attachments. Such development along the self, or ego, line is implicated in all ethical/moral systems (including religions). It is not difficult to appreciate the importance of being able to put our ego aside and have some sort of objective perspective on it when operating in a classroom, parent-teacher conference, or teachers' lounge.

This picture of integral consciousness is as much about a teacher's state while in the classroom as it is about his or her stage of development. However, finding consistent access to such states and understanding how to make the most of them implies a certain developmental stage. These states/stages of higher wisdom imply an ease, generosity, and humility that are usually developed in the course of life's challenges.

Regular Old Consciousness

An obvious question is: "How does an educator interested in self-development move toward these capacities we are calling integral consciousness?" So-called integral consciousness and related advanced levels of skill and states of awareness might be great to have, but all of us have much to gain by noting what keeps us from being normally aware, alive, and intelligent in the classroom. Think about the days when you are relaxed and confident; enjoying your work; feeling connected to students and peers; knowing your thinking is not clouded by emotional reactions, exhaustion, distractions, or worries. That sounds good, doesn't it?

First, we can say that achieving a more sustained and sustainable degree of this normal-for-a good-day (NFAGD) consciousness is more important and more achievable in the classroom context than is working toward anything that sounds highly developed, super-sophisticated, or spiritually advanced. Second, sustaining NFAGD consciousness is both a prerequisite for developing higher level capacities and also implicates many of the same methods of practice. So working on sustained NFAGD consciousness is in many ways being on the exact same path as is developing integral, or second-tier, capacities. Human development is a natural process, as well as a very gradual one. It requires adequate support, which includes just minimizing the stuff that gets in the way of NFAGD, and sufficient challenge, which practicing educators don't have to worry about having—what could be more challenging than teaching?

Although the integral community tends to highlight vertical development (through successive stages,) horizontal development also is of great value. Development cannot be rushed. Developmental theorists advise teachers and learners that at each developmental step individuals need plenty of time and practice to assimilate new skills and expand their scope to of application. Working on NFAGD consciousness is in part about horizontal development, leaning more deeply and consistently into existing skills, and in part about the work of healing, remediating, or tuning prior developmental levels.

Cultural Evolution and Individual Development

I have argued that blame, scolding, and punishment in public schools… can be successfully defended. Students have a duty to learn, and can be held responsible for violating whatever rules, policies, or instructions are enforced to ensure that they do so.

—Charles Howell, Education

No use to shout at them to pay attention. If the situations, the materials, the problems before the child do not interest him, his attention will slip off to what does interest him, and no amount of exhortation of threats will bring it back.

—John Holt

A bad teacher punishes, a poor teacher complains, an average teacher explains, a good teacher teaches, a great teacher inspires.

—H. Narasimhaiah

Integral theories point not only to a particular developmental level but also address developmental processes across an individual's life. They strongly refer to the evolution of human capacities, values, and world views (or cultural memes) throughout history. This focus on individual development and cultural evolution is strong in integral approaches but is seen only rarely in progressive approaches. Integral theorists draw upon dozens of theories of human development and cultural evolution. I assume you have some familiarity with one or more of these theories, so my goal is not to describe any in detail, but rather to summarize some of the main principles they share, noting what integral theory has to add over progressive educational approaches.

Except for theories of childhood development (and the general understanding that learners construct their knowledge,) the application of evolutionary and developmental theories to the pedagogical principles generally accepted by progressive educators has been scant (in the Appendix.) The notion that evolutionary or developmental history adds significantly to an understanding of the human condition seems obvious to integralists, but these concept have only taken root in the past century or two and still are a long way from being fully appreciated (Pinker, 1997). Some psychologists, scientists, and philosophers are still developing elaborate theories about how and why phenomena such as learning, motivation, and socio-political forces in educational systems operate, without acknowledging that these phenomena owe much to evolutionary and developmental forces.

Development as a Path through Disequilibrium and Humility

In the cognitive domain, we develop the capacity to understand increasingly complex situations and to perceive more subtle patterns, more diverse alternatives, and more abstract concepts. At some point, however, understanding becomes limited to how well we understand the instrument of understanding, the mind itself, including the fallible nature of concepts and generalities and the many ways reason is unavoidably biased (Lakoff & Johnson, 1999; Murray, 2006; Wittgenstein, 1953). At first this leads to a profound dissonance as the foundations of certainty in knowing are shaken. Eventually we come to an acceptance and appreciation of the limitations of our knowing, and in so doing develop the skills of uncertainty, ambiguity, and paradox.

In the relational domain, development progresses in several ways: an increasing awareness of our emotional state and how it affects our thinking, a deeper skill in empathy (and the imaginative capacity to put ourselves in another's shoes,) and a widening understanding of the vulnerability-imbued interdependencies of social interactions. As this happens, the sphere of whom we identify with and have compassion for extends ever further out, allowing for, for example, compassion for our "enemies" or those living lifestyles very distant from and different than our own. This leads to a second form of profound dissonance. As we open to the pain and suffering of wider circles of relationship, we can become over-sensitized and immobilized in situations that require difficult choices and compromises. Eventually we develop the emotional resilience and wisdom to make choices for the good of the whole (or the highest good, as we estimate it,) even though a decision may cause pain or discomfort. We also develop the wisdom to (partially) discern how our assumptions or projections onto a situation cloud how we perceive the experience of others (i.e., our own unresolved psychological issues can lead us to draw faulty conclusions that others are suffering or not suffering.) This type of development focuses and purifies social and ethical actions.

In the domain of ego, development progresses from impulsivity through compliance with social conventions, and then into self-authoring. In this last stage, we increasingly become the master of our beliefs, values, goals, body, and relationships. Again, at some point a dissonance is reached. We can only exercise so much control over our life, our body, and even our thought processes and beliefs. We become awake to the profound levels of chaos and vulnerability in life—seeing the aspect of ourselves that is like a small boat tossed by the waves or currents of forces large and unfathomable. We may imagine those forces to be random, impersonal, or divine, but they are nevertheless beyond knowing and control. On the other side of this dissonance is a will that comes from a deeper place of "knowing without knowing." It is a place that is more like listening than thinking or planning (though thinking and planning also happens,) from which we can tap into or feel a deep intuitive source.

These three general lines of development (cognitive, ego, and relational) have similar paths, though an individual can develop along each of them at a different rate. They all pass through egocentric/pre-conventional and ethnocentric/conventional/traditional phases to a more mature phase, but then if development continues, must pass through an uncomfortable disequilibrium before emerging on the other side with an integral, or second-tier, type of flexibility. In fact, although it is not our topic here, sub-stages of disequilibrium mark the transitions from any level to the next. For all three lines, the transition out of the dissonance phase has an aspect of humility—a way of perceiving and coming to peace with our limitations (and with life's inscrutabilities, paradoxes, and mysteries.)

Having this perspective on development can allow teachers and teacher educators to shepherd learners through the difficult transitions on the way to second-tier skillfulness.

Development of Skills Versus Values

The parallels between how individuals develop and how cultures or societies seem to develop are so striking that a number of theorists (e.g., Wilber, Kegan, Torbert, Beck and Cowan, and Gebser) see individual development as recapitulating cultural evolution. There seem to be definite, but hard to capture precisely or empirically, relationships between the capacities and skills we have along cognitive, relational, ego, and other lines, and the values and world views we adopt. That is, the depth and complexity with which we can understand self, others, things, and systems (and thus their flexibility and adequacy in responding to life situations) have some influence upon what we are aware of and value. So, in the integral literature, we see terms such as traditional, modern, postmodern, and integral along side pre-conventional, conventional, and post-conventional; and ego-centric, ethnocentric, and world-centric.

These constructs can be applied (or misapplied) to students, parents, peers, administrators, local communities, and institutions. The menagerie of evolutionary/developmental terms not only describes different—but, again, overlapping—skills and capacities, but also describes an evolution of values and worldviews. Each system mixes skills and values to a different degree. Although conflating skills and value development is somewhat problematic (see Stein, 2008), it has explanatory power.

Caveats on Inferring Individual Development from Cultural Values

Wilber's AQAL model and the spiral dynamics model include the familiar color-coded developmental levels (e.g., red, blue, orange, green, and yellow value-memes) representing ego-centric, traditionalist/ethno-centric, modern techno-achievement-oriented, postmodern/progressive, and early integral. These culturally scaled systems are able to emerge historically only when enough individuals in a given society reach a certain level of individual development (along cognitive, relational, and/or self lines.) Once these cultural modes are established, individuals at any level of development can find themselves attracted to them, often for differing reasons.

For example, if we encounter a student, colleague, or parent whose value system is predominantly progressive, we cannot use that fact to make a reliable estimate of the person's developmental level. Some egocentrics are drawn to the progressive culture because of its promiscuity, and some ethno-centric progressives hold onto progressive beliefs with the fervor of a religion. Therefore, I suggest not using the spiral dynamics model (or similar ones) to judge developmental level or capacity, or at least be extremely cautious in doing so.

It is best to think of individuals as having some degree of capacity in a range of developmental levels (Beck & Cowan, 1996, 63). Although some levels (Kegan calls them meaning-making structures) predominate in a person, individuals tend to function at different levels, depending on the context. It is more difficult to access higher levels of development in situations that are novel, complex, or emotionally challenging than it is to do so in simpler situations. The same individual can display a wide variety of developmental levels in stressful and in unstressful situations, and in groups that embody awareness and support as well as in groups that reinforce developmentally inferior mindsets. In a sufficiently nonthreatening, familiar, and supportive context, even a 12-year old can show the precursors to many second-tier skills (e.g., realizing he or she has a bias about a subject, and trying to step outside his or her ego and worldview to enter into another worldview [ego awareness] or engaging in a polarity mapping analysis of the situation [construct awareness].)

All of this is not to ignore the real challenges and imperatives of human development, but to suggest that the seeds of integral consciousness can be planted and nurtured much earlier than might be thought. As I have implied, applying and deepening these skills often is limited more by emotional and social factors than by cognitive ones.

Transcending and Including the Traditional and Progressive

As noted by Wilber and others, many who advocate progressive (or postmodern) principles seem to be at war with the mindsets called traditional/conventional and modern. We say that green has a problem with blue and orange (e.g., that new age thinkers resist traditionalist and capitalist ways.) The integral, or second-tier, perspective allows us to understand the deep value of all levels and world-views. The thrust of the integral movement is to help more people, especially teachers and others in leadership roles, transition from a progressive (green meme, or Kegan's fourth order) stage into an integral (or fifth order) one. The overall thrust is to support all humans at all levels to thrive at their current level, and when that level is not meeting their needs, to transition to a higher one; however, the programs and rhetoric of most integralists indicate the main audience is at levels just below and above the second-tier threshold.

Some progressive modalities were developed in reaction to the excesses of traditional value orientations, but all too often in progressive classrooms (or policies) the pendulum swings too far. As our discussion about mapping the polarities of progressive educational principles implied, traditional/conservative (and modern) values are as important as progressive and integral ones. It is a matter of maintaining the right dynamic balance.

As practicing teachers know all too well, traditional values (e.g., basic skills, memorization, respect, self-control, loyalty, conformity, responsibility, and accountability) are essential on the playing field of the real classroom. Equally important are modernist values (e.g., efficiency, achievement, measurable standards, and resource accumulation) and pre-conventional/egocentric values (e.g., self-protection and enjoyment.) The integral approach can help teachers integrate what progressive models prescribe with the realities of the classroom. It also helps teachers understand that particular students, classrooms, and even communities have developmental differences that require very different pedagogical approaches. Plus it can help teachers empathize and communicate more effectively with students, principals, parents, and others who have value systems different than their own.

From Being There to Getting There: Pathways and Communities for Integral Educators

I am of the opinion that my life belongs to the community, and as long as I live it is my privilege to do for it whatever I can.

—George Bernard Shaw

There can be no vulnerability without risk; there can be no community without vulnerability; there can be no peace, and ultimately no life, without community.

—M. Scott Peck

Education would be much more effective if its purpose were to ensure that by the time they leave school every student should know how much they don't know, and be imbued with a lifelong desire to know it.

—William Haley

To recap, integral models and methods can help practitioners coordinate a panoply of progressive pedagogical principles and can help them reevaluate the importance of good old traditional and modernist pedagogical principles and values. The integral approach also adds meta-perspectives that can be used to more adequately and systematically address the values and goals behind progressive pedagogies. Adopting integral pedagogies involves not just the application of methods, but new ways of thinking (and meaning making and being) that we are calling integral consciousness. I have described how embodying integral, or second-tier, capacity is part of a developmental journey. Now we ask: How does an educator step onto and develop along this path and/or help others to do so? What difficulties are we likely to encounter, and what support strategies are available?

A full answer to these questions is beyond the scope of this chapter, and because integral education is a new domain of inquiry, these questions are still in early stages of being explored by practitioners and scholars. Briefly, I start by addressing the challenges we face. Do you want the good news or the bad news first? Okay, I'll start with the bad news.

Second-tier consciousness is rare, and learning integral level pedagogical methods and teaching with integral consciousness are difficult. In fact, just moving from traditional to progressive pedagogical approaches is challenging. For most practitioners, this transition requires teaching in ways not experienced during their years of formal education. Kegan (1994), in discussing how to support the fourth-order self-authoring/co-creative worldview, notes that the literature "reflects a goodly amount of frustration, disappointment, surprise, and even, at times, disdain toward the large numbers of adult students who have difficulty achieving or who do not achieve these [skills] " (274). Humility-inducing disequilibrium awaits those on developmental paths. Harris (2002) notes that "learning to reflect on and alter one's perspectives and behaviors can arouse feeling of fear, loss, guilt, anxiety, and anger. These emotions, if sufficiently strong, can elicit counterproductive defenses that block further learning. [Educators] lack strategies to help people manage the emotional distress when the old order is shaken..." (19). She follows by saying that developmental theory offers a perspective that can help address this gap.

Supporting an integral (or progressive) approach is not just a matter of introducing new methods (Fosnot, 1996). Practitioners with stable progressive (or conventional) worldviews can find it extremely difficult to grok, or appreciate, many integral (or progressive) educational principles, much less learn and adopt them (see Steckler & Torbert, in press; Gunnlaugson, in press). Empirical evidence indicates that very few people are at an integral or second-tier developmental level; the percentage is only between 0.5% and 5%, depending on how the second tier is defined (Wilber, 2006).

In addition, the classroom and institutional logistics of new, liberating instructional approaches can be complex and can meet with resistance from peers, parents, and administrators. Kegan (1994) notes that "the distinguishing feature of contemporary culture is that for the first time in human history, three mentalities [i.e., orders of consciousness] exist side by side in the adult population" (303). During frustrating days in the educational trenches, we can appreciate the deceptive allure of the traditional hierarchical one-size-fits-all factory model of learning.

Now for the good news, or at least some glimmers of hope. Actually, I have been offering these glimmers of hope throughout the chapter:

1. I noted how the integral approach can be used at the systemic level (administration or curriculum design), implicitly at the classroom level (using but not teaching about integral concepts,) and explicitly (teaching integral ideas.) Thus, many can benefit while not explicitly learning about in integral approach.

2. Though it is rare to find individuals with a developmental center of gravity at the second tier, the skills and capacities of the second tier begin to show up much sooner, and can be modeled and nurtured. I suggested how integral pedagogical principles can be brought into a fourth-grade activity of planning for a school trip.

3. I described how an individual can exhibit a wide range of developmental mindsets, depending on the level of stress, support, and developmental scaffolding of the context and group in which they are. It may be difficult to advance a person's developmental level per-se, but it is relatively easy to create contexts that allow learners' existing integral skills to flourish and expand.

4. I have described the integral approach as including models, methods, and capacities (skills or consciousness.) Models must be explicitly learned. Methods are more powerful when explicitly learned, but can be learned somewhat through informal modeling and practice, wherein an approach or worldview is passed on through apprenticeship or even osmosis (unconscious learning.) Integral consciousness is even more susceptible to being passed on informally through witnessing of and participation in contexts that embody it.

5. I described how educational practitioners can cultivate states and personal practices that support NFAGD consciousness, which, when it becomes connected with deep inner listening and cognitive empathy in the classroom, creates horizontal development and directly supports some aspects of the vertical development into integral consciousness.

The integral approach to education has many facets. It can involve using models such as AQAL and methods such as integral methodological pluralism to support a metasystematic understanding of many methods or of the multiple systems in which we are embedded as teachers. These facets are for the cognitively oriented among us—those who like theories and abstractions and big-picture models (I must count myself among them.) The integral approach also involves a consciousness with softer facets, such as ego awareness, construct awareness, relational awareness, and vision logic, which are really just ways of describing a type of wisdom—a wisdom just as likely to be observed in people who speak simply, do not display scholarly linguistic skills, and have no taste for abstract models.

At the level of classroom activity, curriculum, and school system design and administration, the developmental and systems-level insights of the integral approach address how belief and value systems become stabilized and resistant to change through communicative processes and social structures. These insights can support sustainable transformation in classroom, school, family, and community systems—whereas an oversimplified grasp of these human systems, which can occur when progressive methods do not include integral level insights, can lead to solutions that cause more harm than good.

A Readiness to Learn

I will share a story as a further illustration of item 2 in the previous list. Recently I was spending time with a 7-year-old girl and her 5-year-old brother, who are close friends of my family. We were on an outing and watching two older children about 20 feet from us doing tricks on bicycles. The girl was observing with the keen eyes of an ethnographer. The boy wondered aloud about how they did those tricks, and where they got their bicycles. Since the older children seemed quite safe, I suggested that he could go over and ask them, and that I could help. Unsurprisingly, he felt too shy to do so and said, "You do it." I asked, "Are you feeling too shy to ask them?" And he nodded, and again said, "You ask them." I said I did not really want to do so by myself and that perhaps I was feeling shy also.

Upon a moment's reflection I added, "I could help you find out, but actually I'm not very curious about it. It's like there is a part of me that gets curious and a part of me that gets shy. And when the curious part feels stronger than the shy part, I might go over and ask someone something, but right now the curious part isn't very strong and the shy part is medium strong." I was trying to teach something in that moment, and was actually saying it for the benefit of the girl, who is a bit precocious. Appropriate to his age, the boy was not particularly interested in this observation, but I could see the girl was taking it in, absorbing it like a sponge.

I don't have a follow-up story illustrating how she assimilated it, but I would not be surprised if she began to work with this concept of having different parts of ourselves that are in a constant state of negotiation and balancing. Even though the ego-awareness skill of disembedding from our thinking enough to reflect on multiple inner voices is a second-tier skill many adults do not seem to have, especially in the contexts we think they need it most, the story illustrates that people can begin to learn such skills quite early in life.

So, even though few adults are centered at the integral developmental levels, the percentage of people who have a readiness to begin to develop some of the second-tier skills is much larger (perhaps 25% of the population, probably at least 50% of teachers.) There is much the average teacher can gain from working with integral principles, including a more systemic and flexible understanding of classroom and institutional dynamics; a deeper and more flexible understanding of thinking, learning, communication, and knowledge in general; and as I indicated, a greater ability to coordinate and utilize a range of progressive pedagogies. They also can be supported in gaining a more flexible perspective on themselves and their teaching.

Communities of and for Integral Educators

Having described the challenges and reasons for hope about the general question of helping educators (and their students) acquire and/or use what the integral approach has to offer, I now address the question of what an educator (or teacher trainer) can do personally.

First let's state the obvious advice, the unsurprising basics that bear repeating: apply the attention and effort required to take good care of yourself—body, mind, and spirit. Balance high expectations that energize, with sufficient doses of compassion and acceptance for what is—with your students and yourself. Keep learning to deepen and broaden your understanding of yourself and your professional work.

Easy, yes? You may be thinking: Do you have any idea how busy a teacher's life is? Eating well, exercising, getting enough social/emotional contact and R&R to stay sane—not to mention any sort of contemplative practice—seem hardly the norm for the average teacher. Verily, our social structures—from the expectations and compensation levels set up by educational institutions, to the cultural materialism and work ethic that keep citizens on their daily tread mills—do not support this type of self-care and growth, especially for educational professionals. Of course, you would not be reading an essay like this if you weren't interested in stretching outside the status quo. So, one additional crucial item on the list of suggestions is to build community and peer support into your efforts.

As mentioned, communities of learning/practice are associated with most of the progressive pedagogies. One added value of integrally informed communities of learning/practice is that they explicitly value whole-self (mind/body/emotions/ spirit; interior-I, exterior-it, relational-we, and systems-its) approaches to personal and professional development, and have developed methods and workshops toward this end (e.g., see material on integral life practice, Wilber et al., 2008). Many localities have integral salons or MeetUp groups.

The integral approach, unlike approaches used in most other learning communities, contains an explicit inquiry into psychological growth and healing and into contemplative practices (e.g., the 3-2-1 Shadow Process and Big Mind voice dialog, Wilber et al., 2008). These tools can help clear away the psychological detritus that stands between us and the clear and easy states of mind implied by NFAGD consciousness, and the deeper states and stages implied in integral consciousness.

Although the integral movement has deepened and widened significantly in recent years, communities and programs supporting integral education are far from plentiful. A number of organizations exist that help professionals understand and use specific integral models, particularly AQAL, but far fewer systematized opportunities are available to develop integral methodological skills or integral consciousness. For more information, check the websites for the Integral Institute, JFKU's Integral Studies degree program, Fielding Graduate University's Integral Studies certificate program, the California Institute of Integral Studies, Next Step Integral, and Pacific Integral (and see O'Fallon, in press; Esbjörn-Hargens, in press).

Conclusions

Don't worry that children never listen to you. Worry that they are always watching you.
—Robert Fulghum

Live as if you were to die tomorrow. Learn as if you were to live forever.
—Mohandas Gandhi

This chapter has explored what the integral approach has to offer above and beyond what is offered by progressive (or alternative, or reform) educational theories, principles, and values. We began with a kitchen-sink overview of progressive pedagogical principles and values. Educators who associate themselves with a subset of these principles and values and are wondering how to understand them as a whole, struggling with how to deal with the dialectical tensions among them and between them and traditional pedagogies, or intuiting that there may be a higher perspective, are likely to find something of value in an integral approach and integral community.

The value added by the integral approach was described in terms of integral as a model, a method, a developmental stage, and a community. AQAL is the most popular integral model being used, and I gave an example of its skilled application. I suggested that, though AQAL is useful and powerful, employing integral methods and consciousness is more important than is the use of any particular model. I elaborated on the primary principles that integral emphasizes and that progressive approaches do not: the development of human capacities and evolution of human meaning making (or worldview) systems. The teacher with an integral perspective on human development will serve as a stronger facilitator of progressive (and integral and traditional) pedagogies. Successfully applying integral models and methods requires a type of consciousness or meaning-making capacity, and I described integral consciousness in terms of higher levels of construct awareness, ego awareness, relational awareness, and systems awareness.

The integral approach is not a simple picture. Realizing a vision of integral education involves, as is only appropriate for an integral vision, a complex but dynamically flexibly process of engaging self, others, artifacts, bodies, and socio-cultural systems. In this chapter, we explored some of the challenges in learning and teaching the integral approach. Although these challenges are substantial, and the integral approach is complex, the seeds of integral consciousness and methodology can be planted and nurtured in many ways.

In addition to what is gained, something also can be lost by taking the integral approach. While it coordinates many different progressive principles, it does not (at least in my reading) specialize or deeply describe any. It may be best to adopt an integral approach only after being mentored and immersed deeply in one (or several) specific progressive methods.

I mentioned several integral level pedagogical approaches in the section about integral methodology, but you might still ask: What does integral pedagogy, or an integrally informed classroom, actually look like? What uniquely integral methods would we see being used there? I could point to specific methods or models used to anchor an integrally informed classroom. For example, students may be systematically investigating the world from each of Wilber's eight perspectival zones. However, that would overly constrain our vision. An integral curriculum is so much more than that and probably includes most of the 20 or so principles listed as progressive pedagogies. In fact, a teacher who has a sophisticated grasp of progressive pedagogy, but who has never heard of integral theory, would probably be observed to intuitively be employing most or all of the eight zones. Of course, an integral approach can help this teacher better understand what he or she is doing and to transfer this wisdom to others.

What I would like to propose at this historical moment in integral pedagogy's evolution is that the integral approach points not so much toward a new set of methods, but toward a way (or ways) of coordinating, integrating, practicing, and embodying already existing specific methods. These methods come mostly from progressive approaches, but also include traditional (and modernist) approaches, as appropriate. Integral methods look and feel like progressive methods applied with wisdom and adequatio, and with an ego-aware and construct-aware consciousness.

For me, integral is an emerging wave of human capacity, difficult or impossible to define, but still tangible and recognizable. It is a form of human understanding and skillfulness that takes the insights about the human condition, the critiques of existing systems and mores, and the experiential openings in human capacity that we associate with the progressive and New Age movements, and adds new levels of rigor, reflective self-and-system understanding, and hope for the possibilities of improving the human condition.

In the domain of education, the integral approach is not just a new set of beliefs about teaching and learning, but also indicates new ways of being in the classroom and making meaning of the educational process. In this sense, it is not a theory to be taught but a pointer to a naturally occurring next wave of human capacities. These capacities are desperately needed to meet the complex and urgent problems of the times. For many educators, then, what is of ultimate concern is helping learners—both as global citizens and future citizens—move vibrantly toward developing these capacities.

3

On the Value and Importance of Personal Development

Miriam Mason Martineau and Jonathan Reams

What does it take to be an integral educator? This question lies behind the dialogue that follows between Miriam Mason Martineau in Winlaw (near Nelson,) British Columbia, and Jonathan Reams, in Trondheim Norway (formerly of Nelson.) While we have worked for a while now from the notion of being "integral" educators, we also experience this very much as a living question and quest. Thus in the dialogue that follows we will convey what we feel distinguishes integral from other approaches to education, what inspires us about this, what has challenged us in embodying our inspirations, and some stories of our journeys through the process of becoming increasingly integral in our work as educators.

Previously we have spent many hours face to face in conversation over issues related to this topic, as friends and as colleagues. Working together on developing curriculums for a proposed integral school, planning for integral education seminars, and sharing stories of our lives as educators have all contributed to our understanding of the joys and challenges of this journey. This dialogue then represents a distillation and updating of these conversations, mediated now by the technology involved in communicating over the Atlantic. We began by drafting a set of questions we felt were important, and then seeing how our responses to these questions and each other directed the conversation.

We began by asking ourselves, "What do we think it means to be an 'integral' educator?"

Jonathan: As I think about the question what makes an educator "integral," what comes up mostly for me is an awareness of interiors as well as exteriors. When I think about how consciousness develops, one aspect of it is how awareness expands gradually, from simple external features, through more complex external features, to rudimentary awareness of internal aspects such as affective states, leading to the awareness of complex emotions, and even how language shapes consciousness. The awareness of interiors arises at later stages of development, and of course there are many levels of this. So, when I think about an integral educator, I have an image or expectation of someone who has sufficient awareness of the subtleties and complexities of these interior states to be able to attend to them consciously when working with students.

This quality of attention can then be applied to how curriculum is designed, what pedagogical strategies will be employed, and where students' attention is directed. It also means for me that there is a sensitivity to and acceptance of where students are in their own development. I think that this is especially important as a mark of an integral educator. At an earlier stage, prior to moving into an integral awareness of education, I know I had a strong and unconscious tendency to expect all my students to have the same implicit or tacit knowledge, capacity and worldview that I had, and if they appeared not to, my job was to help them see it my way!

So I think that one central mark of an integral educator is this awareness of deep structure differences in the tacit knowledge students bring to the learning situation, and then being able to meet them where they are, rather than where one wants them to be. This is no small task! Of course one place that I think this is actually already being done to a degree is in elementary schools. The cognitive differences between teacher and student are obvious, and there has been a significant effort to make use of child cognitive developmental theory in designing pedagogy and curriculum for students.

This does not mean that all elementary school teachers are "integral," but it does mean that there is a larger culture that creates a structure that socializes and trains teachers into taking development seriously. Thus teachers may not have personally developed into a realization of the importance of attending to development in students, but their own education as teachers and the larger system they work in creates an environment that allows them to accept and make use of these ideas. What thoughts arise for you in relation to this, Miriam?

Miriam: I have often noticed this—how in the case of younger students and children, the reality of developmental stages is much more present and integrated in an educator's awareness and thus in the educational process. However, I have also noticed that whilst this is true, there is generally a much greater emphasis placed on certain developmental lines, such as a child's physical, cognitive, and emotional experience and growth, and on what we as educators and parents can do to nurture and strengthen these lines of development. One aspect that distinguishes an integral educator/parent in my view and experience is the willingness and the increasing capacity to grow into the fullness of who we actually are—body, mind, soul and spirit—and to see and nurture that same fullness in our students and children. What does that mean? For one, to pay as much attention to their soul and spirit as to their bodies and minds. You can see right away that, besides conventional religious frameworks and the New Age treatment of childhood spirituality that tends to insufficiently consider the stages of development each human being passes through (thereby confusing a young child's prepersonal consciousness with transpersonal consciousness,) there is very little information available regarding an integral nurturing of a child's soul and spirit. When touching on these dimensions of self we step into realms that are much less measurable. Accurate cross-referencing of direct experiences is harder to come by. Including these dimensions of the human being is part of the work of an integral educator/parent, and it involves lifting the context within which education happens, seeing education, as educator Jamie Wheal says, as a process that takes place from "Cradle to Kosmos." So, another distinguishing mark of an integral educator would be the increasing awareness and placement of oneself as an educator or parent within the Great Arc of Life.

This means that instead of seeing the purpose and aim of a human being's journey, and in this case, specifically of education, to mainly help a person grow up into a well-adapted, well-functioning ego, we include this earlier leg of the journey, while also understanding that following this outer arc, there is the potential of traveling along the inner arc, of gradually dis-identifying from the constructed frontal self. This means that we include all the valuable skills and knowledge that have been gained, and we transcend our attachment to all of it. In doing so we begin to educate for eternity, we seek to grow up for our students (as well as for all of existence), and we allow the full potential of the human journey—an awakened, embodied and evolving human being—to inform how we educate. So, rather than viewing education as a passing down of knowledge, we include that perspective, as well as set forth within ourselves and with our students to co-create emerging culture, to live at the edge of what is known, to continue to learn, grow and discover.

Another aspect of placing education in an evolutionary context is understanding that as we aspire and stretch toward bringing evermore consciousness to our work as educators, we will at times undoubtedly fail and "land flat on our faces." Thus, it is also important to offer kindness toward ourselves and to our students; otherwise we run the risk of falling into one of two traps: We may give up because we'll "never get it." Or we may keep trying, but waste a lot of precious energy feeling guilty because "we never fully get it." Instead, as we realize that we are somewhere along the evolutionary trajectory, that each of us has come to a certain point in our development and each of us still has great distance ahead to travel, we can extend forgiveness and compassion, as well as challenge and aspiration toward our efforts, wherever we may stand at present. We do not seek a "perfect" way of educating, but rather a "perfecting" way. We are curious to find out how much more present and expanded our awareness and embodiment as teachers can be, we are willing to try out, and to take ourselves lightly amidst profound and serious commitment.

Finally, I would say that becoming an integral educator has a lot to do with Presence. How present can I be, how aware and conscious can I become to Life itself, to who is before me, to who I am, and to what is unfolding between myself as an educator and my students?

What has your experience been around the theme of spiritual awareness and growth in regards to integral education?

Jonathan: Bringing attention to the spiritual domain of our work as educators is tricky. There is the context of explicit attention to this in places such as religious, or as you mention New Age education. I view this element as being how it shows up in the everyday and mundane aspects of our lives. Yes, we need to pay attention to this, but how? It is easier to say and use these words than to enable our attention to encompass not only the demands of the physical, emotional and mental lives of self and student, which is challenging enough in itself, but to also perceive self and student as soul. In this manner, I think what is being put forward as "integral" education really makes significant demands on us. To be able to pay attention to this spiritual essence in a dynamic and evolving relationship with the other aspects of our being in this world requires that we have sufficient personal awareness of this in ourselves first and foremost.

This then means that we as educators must first travel this inward arc if we wish to have the capacity to guide others in a manner that is sensitive to it. For me, this is how we develop presence. I view presence as the capacity to be consciously aware of these deeper aspects of self and maintain this awareness in the face of an array of worldly circumstances. What this brings is the ability to be conscious of the reactive tendencies embedded in mind, emotion and physiology and to suspend or restrain them to allow the deeper self or soul to be the source of response. Reflecting on this, it seems clear that to both of us what may distinguish integral is the attention to and inclusion of this spiritual dimension, not simply in an intellectual acknowledgement, but as the "self-as-subject," as Kegan would say.

This has taken us deep into the territory of what we perceive and experience as key elements of being an integral educator. Another element that I see in relation to this is similar to what I described above. That is, having developed sufficient personal awareness or consciousness of interior complexity, that we are able to recognize that there is a stage progression through different levels of this kind of awareness. Then, being able to make use of that awareness to craft learning strategies appropriate to the consciousness of the student(s), teachers can apply their insights appropriately.

Along with the development of this perspective-taking capacity, it seems to me that there is a need for a high level of qualities like compassion and patience. This becomes evident by its lack when you have teachers who are harsh to students simply because they are not able to grasp the higher consciousness the teacher is implicitly demanding of them. This compassion can be said to arise naturally in higher stages of consciousness, but I think that it is also necessary to go through a certain depth of personal work, psychological healing as it were, to enable a genuine depth of compassion to be present. This brings out the need to work on developing states as well as stages for becoming an integral teacher.

How do you see this aspect of perspective-taking ability? How do you experience this need for compassion?

Miriam: I agree with you. A basic requirement of an integral educator is that we, as educators and parents, approach education/parenting as an integral practice, which includes psychodynamic and shadow work. Since who we are is ultimately what we bring to our teaching and parenting, our own evolution is intimately connected with how we teach and parent. As we develop our capacity to witness ourselves in action, we can make conscious choices. We can stop resorting to all forms of projection (negative and positive), free ourselves from being held hostage to our own unseen shadows and from acting upon the myriad knee-jerk reactions and whims of conditioning. In this way we can actually see our children and students more fully and can respond to them more adequately, more integrally.

Also, as teachers and parents we have a potent and daily "in-our-face" reason and motivation to grow in self-awareness. Our students and children are entrusted to us for the time they spend in our presence. We provide orientation, information and modeling. The combination of the huge potential inherent in education as a way of affecting positive change in the world and the fact that our students are entrusted to us (the younger the student, the more vulnerable and dependent) calls for utmost integrity in our intentions, communications and actions. As you mentioned earlier, another key requirement of an integral educator is the capacity to hold multiple perspectives, which in turn facilitates our ability to hold and work with paradoxes. Then, we are not attached to one particular way of seeing life. We can inquire, feel into and see through a variety of perspectives. We can validate and make use of the insights of each. We can engage with sincere curiosity. This helps us to be more fully present with and to each student, to "get behind their eyes," which I feel is a central expression of authentic care and interest in their wellbeing and learning. It also enables us to offer our students and children support and challenge; each of us generally tends toward one or the other—a more lenient, embracing or a more strict, firm style and posture. As we ourselves evolve, we can increasingly stretch into ways of being and acting that consider more fully what our students and children actually need, instead of mainly being guided and driven by our natural tendencies and strengths. And yes, I agree with you that compassion and patience are an essential piece of what integral educators brings to their work — often brought about through the humbling effect of life experience. I think that is one of the aspects I appreciate most about living into a more integral perspective—it is that dynamic right in the midst of my being between stretching upward/forward and simultaneously feeling kindness/gentleness toward myself, and extending this to others. I expect from and challenge my students and my child, and I simultaneously seek to embrace them where they presently are. We all are "evolving wholes"—"human becomings" with much room for growth and improvement, who also deserve respect and integrity, and are whole just as we are right now. In some mysterious way, the two co-exist, moment to moment.

Jonathan: Yes, Life, with all its ups and downs, and humbling moments is also our best teacher! It is also our best teacher in those moments. The modeling aspect of teaching is something that I think is key and yet most often neglected. It is something that I had to learn the hard way, as when I began teaching college freshmen, the content of my teaching was all about consciousness and spiritual development, but the way I taught, how I presented myself through my way of engaging and creating a space for the students was not in line with this. This then brought me the opportunity to see my own shadow(s) projected very loud and clear into the teaching situation. It was certainly "in my face!" So first, I had to see myself clearly and go through my own process of healing and then integrating the aspects of my ego structures that were driving this behavior. The gift of this was that it enabled me to understand the challenges of this journey in a very grounded way. For example, when some students disagreed with the perspectives being presented in class, I was so identified with those perspectives that my reaction was to defend them. I thus pushed harder at the students to "see the light" of my way, and of course they learned quickly from my modeled behavior to defend their views right back! Reflecting on these experiences later, I could see how strongly the self as subject can be tied to perspectives, and that a bit of detachment can go a long ways towards creating a different quality of educational space. As you say, from these kind of experiences we begin to develop some compassion, first for ourselves, and this then gives us the capacity to have compassion for others.

If I were to reflect on and try to summarize our conversation thus far, I would have to say that central to becoming an integral teacher is simply developing oneself as a person. Some aspects of this personal development are pointed to above, but in another way it will be unique for each person. The circumstances of one's life will shape development and growth, as well as the pace that is just right for that person, but the central trajectory will be similar. That trajectory could be called one of self-transcendence. Whatever form one's education and growth takes, this growth always leads one to go beyond oneself, to expand one's horizons.

Miriam: Yes, it's so true…what we offer as educators has so much to do with who we are. Daunting in a way; but also invigorating, that simplicity beneath all the theory and methodology. As Parker Palmer says, we teach who we are: "As I teach, I project the condition of my soul onto my students, my subject, and our way of being together" (1998, 2). This requires that we as educators and parents discover and become evermore present to who we are, and where we are coming from—which ties into what you mentioned earlier, how integral education has a lot to do with a growing awareness of both exteriors and interiors. Basically I feel that however integral a lesson plan or an entire curriculum is, Integral Education ultimately hinges upon us as teachers being, thinking, feeling, and acting integrally. Since educating our students is intimately connected with our own development, where we stand in our own life trajectory becomes a central consideration. I like to think about this: If everything we do, say, are, gesture, react to… is imitable, and quite likely, especially with younger children, will be imitated (or reacted to,) and at the very least create some imprint upon our student/child and his/her understanding of and orientation to the world, to relationships, to how things are and how s/he is supposed to be in this world, then what does that leave us with? A big responsibility and a big opportunity!

I think another reason why developing as a person is so central to integral education has to do with what I said earlier about growing evermore into the fullness of who we are, of not limiting what this life existence is all about, but seeking to co-facilitate a foundation during the earlier years of life that is most conducive toward a child/student growing into an integrated adult who is poised at the cutting edge of consciousness evolution, ready and willing to take next steps on the trajectory of the human adventure. In order to be as attentive to our students' deeper nature—their soul and spirit—as we are to their developing egos, we need to awaken the deeper layers of our self, and grow in our discernment of who we are and where we are coming from in each moment. Thus, inner work on behalf of the educator becomes as important, if not more central than the teaching methods. Our doing flows from our being.

Jonathan: I agree that our doing does indeed flow from our being. And I recognize that my being and doing have been influenced by the being and doing of many others along the way. Their modeling provided the guidance and inspiration at times for my own growth. Reflecting back on my own life experiences with educators, I will begin with my grade 5/6 teacher, Mr. Babchuck. He stands out for me as someone who had a knack for knowing how to engage and motivate students. While he used a number of, at that time, creative and new-to-us learning strategies, he always made sure that we had a good foundation of basic skills and knowledge to build on. As well, I remember how he had us working on improving the school grounds. Being a small rural school we had overgrown forest around the edges of the playing fields. He had us clearing undergrowth, taking down small trees (by learning how to use leverage to hang from them to bring them over and uproot them!) and using our creativity to improve our environment. While I would not necessarily say he was "integral," there was something about my educational experience with him that stayed with me.

Next came my grades eight and nine social studies teacher, Mr. Nasser. He opened me up to the world at large. At the beginning of every class, we would listen to five minutes of the world news report from a major news agency, live on radio if it was first period, and on tape if later in the day. As a young adolescent, my world tended to be pretty narrow, centered on self and close friends. His persistent practice of exposing us to what was happening in the world at large exposed me to the beginnings of a world-centric perspective.

The third and final example is Mike Carey. He taught me during my masters program in organizational leadership. His classes and teaching exposed me to concepts of development and transformation, and gave me my first real experience of dialogical pedagogy. I recall meeting outside of class with a small group of students in his transformational leadership course. Half way through the semester we went to him, saying that we were certain that he knew a whole lot more than he was telling us. We asked him to give us more information so that we could understand what he was trying to teach us. He deftly gave us a small something to keep us happy for the moment, but continued to teach without dumping knowledge onto us. At the end of the semester, our small study group noticed that we had come to a place where we did not have to think about the subject in an intellectual or analytical manner—we simply saw the world differently. The dialogical pedagogy had helped us to go beyond our more familiar analytical knowledge, and had actually transformed our capacity to perceive the world.

Miriam: I appreciate your looking back and noticing what and who influenced your being and doing along the way. Reflecting on what might be identified as "beginning seeds" of becoming an aspiring integral parent and educator... how far back do I go? I remember my most fervent prayer as a teenager being to "grow" and to keep growing in a spiritual, inner sense. Side by side with this intense desire to "grow," I was also deeply touched by what I felt was a call to "live life to its fullest," not able to articulate exactly what that meant, but having a clear sense that we are invited to "more," that we often live our lives within 8-foot high rooms instead of filling out and living into the universe. That search continues. I love the invitation to lift the bar. I am often amazed by how sometimes I also simultaneously stubbornly resist doing so. I am intrigued by the notion and exploration of how we can bring evermore consciousness to our work as parents and educators, that there is no end in sight. Rather than feeling overly daunted by that, I generally feel a thrill. I do indeed fall flat on my face on a regular basis—my daughter and husband can attest to that! I am sure my parents' generous and consistent embrace of who I was and am has made it easier for me to offer myself kindness and forgiveness over and over again, perhaps sometimes too easily.

I am a gradual, persistant and steady climber. So far along my journey, I haven't often been a sudden "quick through-the-roof evolver." Meeting my husband and growing through our relationship has had a huge effect on my ability to see further, to challenge myself to grow even when my egoic self resists, which of course it does—that's its job, right?! I really think, in looking back, that a balance or interweaving of eros and agape (reaching for the "goal" and embracing the "journey") has a lot to do with my growth toward becoming a more integral person. The glimpses of what is possible—either through spiritual state experiences, insights offered by friends, books, teachers, community, song and dance—combined with an intuition and a determination not to save those "peak moments" for "Sundays," but to attempt to bring them into daily life, step by step (Ah, God must be patient...) keep me at it.

And since I have become a mother, I have experienced a new depth of commitment. I have before me this incredible human being, who I am largely responsible for. She matters so much. When I lack presence, and allow the consequences of that lack to make their way past ego defenses to where a deeper part of me can "see" and "hear" and let sink in, I am finally brought to tears and I, with a cracked open heart, renew my commitment to try my best, and to let "my best" continue evolving. It is sometimes so tempting to let myself be comforted by what is "normal." The lifting of the bar, the stretching required in me…all that is heard by deeper layers in myself, but cleverly resisted to by the ego. It is as if my soul says a great big "yes" to that—and then when it comes to embodying the sacred presence in the midst of everyday life, that's really when the rubber hits the road, that's when it depends on how accessible I let that soul dimension within myself be. There is not much in society that supports this movement. Though, it is so worth it! The fruit of this labor, such as the greater depth, insight and growth that can emerge in a counseling session, or the vitality that bursts and shines through a child's eyes and entire being when met with full presence, or the learning that can take place in a student when he is held in the fullness of his being, make that very clear. Those are the parenting, counseling and teaching moments that truly stand out and shine.

Jonathan: It is interesting how we focused on different aspects of our lives in reflecting on what has helped us grow. If I look back and see the inner thread of my life, I can also recall stretching limits constantly. By the time I was about eight I learned to quit asking my father questions. I would ask something, he would answer, and it would not get at the core of what I was seeking, so I would ask another question about his answer. I can see I was a hard case to deal with, because no answers ever satisfied me! So, there was clearly a dynamic energy for growth and learning active in me from an early age.

At the same time I was always looking for people who had answers to the questions that remained for me. Thus my recollections of these three teachers, and many more who each in their own way had a piece of a puzzle that gifted me with what I needed to carry on this growth.

Miriam: As we reflect on what key experiences led us to be intrigued, touched and eager to grow into a more integral perspective and way of being, I am struck by the interweaving of inner impulse and outer experience, the two work together; we are formed both by what we meet and experience, and we seek out who we meet and what we experience, guided to some degree by our inner being. When I was studying psychology at the University of Zurich, it was very clear to me that I would and could only engage in a career in this field if I combined spirituality with psychology. I would have long conversations with a handful of fellow student about how the two required each other, were incomplete without the other. This was definitely not the stance of the university where psychology was seen as a science, with no place for spirituality. Still, a few of us felt this deeply, and this has hugely formed who we have become as counselors, and how we now work. I find it fascinating to look back and to notice that who we have become actually has a lot to do with what was going on way back then…almost like there is a pull to become integral, perhaps a call, a yearning, an enthusiasm or a recognition that is already there and simply takes time to emerge more fully and develop.

One of my favorite attributes about anything integral is that it can always become more integral; once you consciously step onto the evolutionary trajectory, it keeps on going, inviting us to a fine meeting place between a growing humility and confidence.

Jonathan: In addition, all aspects of our lives are interwoven. We build capacity in one domain and find that we then are applying it in another. For example, I often use literature from education when talking about leadership. As well, being a parent was certainly a journey full of learning. One thing that stood out is how much early parenting experiences revealed to me how deeply entrained and habituated I was to repeating the patterns of behavior from my own parents. As much as I swore I would not be like my parents, when the stresses of the world met with the challenges of raising children, it was scary to see how those deeper patterns asserted themselves. For me, this experience brought awareness to these patterns, and allowed me to do some very conscious work on them. This kind of personal work then became one thread in this theme of personal growth as being the central necessity for integral education.

Being in relationship has had the deepest impact on my personal growth. When you are in a situation where all your good qualities bring you into relationship with someone, and then gradually the shadows emerge and are present to be dealt with, the opportunities for growth are immense. Of course at the same time the opportunities for divorce are also great, as evidenced by the statistics for this! As with anything in life, it depends on what you make of it. So this points to a quality that I think is central in the capacity for growth into an integral consciousness: a willingness to be open to learning from the curriculum that life presents you with. My view is that life has an innate intelligence to it that is far beyond our human consciousness' capacity to understand, and that if we can see, be open to, and learn from the opportunities presented to us, then we can make our way bit by bit to this place of learning deeply from the curriculum of life.

In a relationship, the intensity and intimacy of the situation allows for a tremendous depth of learning. However, these situations, while allowing for this intensity and depth, do not always provide the diversity of learning that we need. In this way, being engaged in community can allow for the diversity of learning experiences that can help round out our education.

Then there is also the relationship we can have with ideas. We can be inspired by them, educated, informed, or become embedded in them, zealots in service of them. It is in this context that I view coming across the concepts of integral theory. Actually, there is really no such thing as integral theory in a way—it is really a meta-theory, a way of relating to and situating theories. It was this feature and capacity of the framework that inspired me upon coming across it in the late nineties. It allowed a number of ideas and theories I had been exposed to, to be put in perspective. Of course it is this ability to take perspective on something that is central to the growth of consciousness.

Miriam: "Curriculum of life"—what a wonderful term! It reminds me of this paradoxical dance we engage in…that whilst we work and aspire I have often thought about this paradox—that whilst we aspire to become more integral as educators and as persons, life itself is actually already integral. The whole territory is already there— the inner, the outer, the individual, the collective, the development, the states, the types… As you say, Integral Theory offers us this incredible perspective and tool with which to notice areas we are not naturally paying as much attention to. Life does the same thing, don't you think? When we don't hit the mark, when we are "less than integral," which most of us are most of the time, life will tell us so. If, for example, I ignore my need for rest because I am trying to fit in all the pieces of my "integral practice"—have you ever noticed how much time this can take?!—I may get sick. My body steps in and says, "Hey, that's not integral, better sleep some more." Pretty simple, and like you say, our intimate relationships and any relationship for that matter, do the same thing—should we fool ourselves into thinking we are rather evolved, just bring on the interpersonal realm and we are met fair and square with all the areas of our being, subtle and not so subtle, that we have not yet faced and integrated.

On the theme of Integral Theory and the journey of an integral educator… I don't think an educator needs to know the theory, but it can provide very useful and helpful orientation and organization. As Wilber says, it is a map, not the territory. I have found the theory most useful when I use it in conjunction with life—to make sense of life experiences, to highlight areas I fail to notice in my teaching and parenting, to round out my natural tendencies as an educator, and to be able to better articulate next steps, professionally and personally. At first, my delight and deep appreciation of Integral Theory led me to overly "paste" it onto life. Now, I feel it has percolated through my system more; it is there, has become more a part of me rather than something I carry around like a new bag. It continues to inform me, and I continue exploring how the practice and the theory can interweave and serve one another.

In my work as a teacher, parent and counselor, as I seek to bring an integral perspective into action, I have been struck many-a-time by how "practical" the theory is when it is applied, "practical" in the sense of what a very real difference it can make. For example, when I take the time to study in-depth the developmental stages of early childhood, I am much more capable of not expecting too much nor too little from a child. The knowledge facilitates greater presence and also confidence in how best I can serve their development and accompany them with sufficient stimulation and challenge, but also enough understanding and acceptance. Holding the aspect of developmental lines in my awareness, I can more consciously work with those lines in a child that are already strong and use them to "spill over" into areas that need strengthening. For example, if I am working with a highly active 4-year old who has a hard time sitting down for longer periods of time, I can get him on the trampoline and begin introducing math while counting jumps. Holding awareness that he tends to spend a large part of each day in a very physical way, I would also encourage him to discover other ways of being, pairing him up, for instance, with a child who loves and is very adept at role plays and can help him get immersed in imagination and social interactions. A further aspect of the integral framework that I have found extremely useful when working with young children, and students of any age for that matter, is that it points to "types" as a key element to consider. There are so many books available on certain approaches to parenting and teaching, but what many don't consider is that depending on a personality type, one approach may well work for a particular child, but not for another. This, too, is an awareness that asks me to pay more attention to each unique individual I interact with.

Since teaching and parenting are about more than one person, we are immediately brought into the realm of the collective. The emphasis author Joseph Chilton Pearce, developmental psychologist Gordon Neufeld, and other attachment theorists place on healthy relationship as a basic foundation for healthy learning resonates deeply, and have provided great inspiration and challenge for me. I am easily led from the "inside out." I am generally quite in touch with myself, have a pretty clear idea of how I think things should or could go, and can get rolling in an impassioned monologue. Most of my work, however, involves at least another human being! To seek to get behind their eyes, to speak to them from a "listening" stance rather than a "speaking at" posture has become a key practice. Given my tendencies, I see how important it is to balance these and to learn to be present with another from the "outside in," allowing them to inform me. Perhaps for another teacher/parent whose awareness is already very much out "there," informed and influenced by everyone more than by themselves, a shift in the other direction, toward more listening within, is called for. What role has the Integral framework played in your development as a teacher?

Jonathan: At first it was simply to have my students (college freshmen) read bits of Wilber and then we would discuss it. This is pretty typical, and in many ways naïve. Some got something out of it, but the framing of it and engagement was not necessarily skillful. Gradually I began to dig deeper into the sources and implications for education. This has led to being more sensitive to where students are at in multiple areas; developmentally, learning style, personality type, and so on. I have especially found the value of providing framing and structure that aims to liberate students to inquire and create knowledge for themselves, rather than prescribe learning.

Of course the elements of these approaches are found in many places. I was influenced by Paulo Frière's notion of helping students create their own knowledge, which began to move me away from a "sage on the stage" image and practice of education. Parker Palmer's work deepened this and led me to work for a number of years on helping students create a relationship with the subject as a way of facilitating this creation of knowledge. His work also informed my approach to and awareness of the importance of one's presence as being the deeper curriculum that goes on beneath the spoken words. Later on, Bill Torbert's notions of action inquiry and ways of framing and directing attention helped me gain skills in using language as a more conscious and explicit tool.

Miriam: It is fascinating to hear of the various impulses and insights that contribute to your present understanding and practice as an educator. What do you see as some of the steps along this ongoing journey for yourself?

Jonathan: I found that over the years I had many opportunities to test and hone ideas about education, beginning with volunteering in my children's elementary school, through the alternative junior high I worked with and finally into teaching at a university. It was in the latter venue that I really saw how deeply the more traditional model of "teaching" was embedded in me. While I consciously espoused all these new ideas about how to teach, the responses of my students quickly made it apparent that I had simply taken new ideas and delivered them in a traditional skin. The shadows that were illuminated were primarily around an insecurity and need to validate my beliefs by getting others to confirm their value. This drove my stance in relation to the curriculum, which when the students reacted by pushing back, led to a reactive digging in and arguing with them over technical merits of the ideas or other means to convince them of the "truth."

This led to a lot of reflection and work to understand what was implied in the works that had inspired me. What emerged for me was a much clearer sense of what was going on in the classroom that enabled or disabled learning. What clearly disabled it was when I created a space that was infused with this deeper agenda of validating my beliefs. This energy acted like an electric fence, bounding the direction of the inquiry and giving students little shocks when they tried to stray from these boundaries. It made the learning environment risky, and pushed the students to create coping mechanisms to deal with the shocks.

Gradually I learned how to let go of my attachments and trust that if there was some truth in my views, and if the students engaged in an open and genuine inquiry into the subject that could roam without the shocks of my fencing, then they would come to a place where they might also see what I did. They might describe it differently, or interpret its meaning another way, but they would generally come to a similar place. This letting go and trusting then paradoxically actually led to the outcome I had been driven by in the earlier reactive stage, that my views were generally validated by the perception of others.

Miriam: Sometimes I liken education and parenting to an "accompanying" of someone, perhaps for similar reasons as you mention. We are not here to enforce our agenda, nor are we here to let the whole learning be driven by the student. Instead, we are to be present to what is possible, and to direct and guide the learning in a way that includes where a student is at, while inviting or at times challenging him or her to take a next step and stretch beyond the known. It is a dance, a continually shifting balance and interweaving between what we as educators perceive needs to be taught and how we do so, and what our students and children are actually interested in learning about and how they like to learn. Additionally, this balance changes, depending on the age and developmental level of any student. In my present immersion with homeschooling at the kindergarten age, I face this very same dance…of having a clear idea of the direction the learning can and should take, being open to surprising ways in which this can take place…basically holding the larger picture and direction, and being present to the actual best way we can step in that direction through considering the individual child's type, her developmental level and the lines she is flourishing or weaker in, and which state(s) she is most receptive to learning in. It is a challenging and enlivening dynamic for me to hold—the active engagement, and the allowing and letting go. I am sometimes tempted to fall into one or the other extreme—holding the two together requires much more presence than emphasizing one over the other. What are you working on now and what does the future look like?

Jonathan: Now, as I have a regular teaching position, I find myself moving into a space where I can learn to work more consciously with a number of the elements I have worked on previously. This has led to experimenting with having the students create their own ideas about a topic rather than be guided by a text. A good example of this is in the main course I teach, which is about organizational counseling, coaching and leadership. The students have a project that involves them having a coaching session with a "live" student leader. Thus coaching is a significant focal point of the course. There was, however, no text on coaching for them to look to. Instead, their anxiety about what they were supposed to do, entering into this unknown realm of actually coaching someone, led them to ask, "What is coaching all about?" What are we supposed to do? I asked them to think about their previous experiences of counseling (they are students in a masters in counseling program) and what ideas came up in them as they reflected on it. Working with these, we together built up an idea of what coaching might be and what it was not.

This led to their creation of a one-page brochure that made them get specific about saying what they were inviting these student leaders to participate in. Given that they wrote it together in Norwegian, a still somewhat foreign language to me, I could not really guide them at a certain stage. They took the first step in creating their own knowledge of coaching in this way.

The next step was in preparing for the actual coaching experience. We discussed various issues involved, drawing again on their existing knowledge and guided by questions to get them to inquire deeply into these issues. They developed various tools to put in a toolbox that they could take into the coaching session and draw on. They discussed how to use the broader ideas about leadership development from a stage development perspective in their coaching. All of this got them to customize a plan for themselves and take into their project.

The third step was having the actual experience of coaching someone. This allowed them to apply their created knowledge and test it against reality. This testing came from the reflection they did on this, by video recording their sessions and going back over them. The fourth step came in presenting their session and their reflections on how they did in front of the class and getting questions and feedback from their peers and me. Often they found that they were harsher on themselves and overlooked things they had done well, and so this collective reflection generally built confidence. Together, this experience allowed them to create some theoretical and applied knowledge, integrating these in a way that hopefully will be transferable and carry forward in their lives. What is most present for you these days in your work as a parent and educator?

Miriam: Four things come to mind. First, the work of bringing integral visions and aspirations into action. Most of us first get "integral" theoretically, as it makes sense in heart and mind. Putting an emerging integral perspective into action is a whole other step in the journey to becoming an integral educator. I am humbled. I have thought about these things for over a decade; I have read, written and taught about them. What is really alive for me is: to what extent am I truly living all these wonderful insights, day in day out? That is really the challenge. It is a good and at times a hard one.

Second, which is connected with my first point, is the limitless degree of presence possible—the sense that there is no end or ceiling to how present we can be in relation to ourselves, our students and children, to Life itself…plus the inquiry into what that may actually look like in action. What could arise and take place in educational settings when we become evermore present and aware? I am curious about this and find it motivates me to stay present with being present!

Third, that dance I just spoke about earlier, between guiding/directing and allowing, which with young children involves being in charge but not in control, and with older students involves a continual, gradual handing over of responsibility. Often I don't know if the balance I am offering between those two is the right one; in such moments I find it helpful to focus on where I am coming from within, and encourage my deeper self to come to the fore, so that even if I am unsure, I am less likely to be reactive and working from a conditioned place.

And fourth, how helpful it is to be amongst a community of integral practitioners. It is sometimes a lonely path, as we seek to break new ground, within and without, and often with less structural societal support than if we were teaching and parenting within already existing and stabilized perspectives and systems. Do you have any final thoughts?

Jonathan: There is one more issue I would like to discuss, that of integral as integrity. The two words appear quite similar to each other, and there is a simple way in which being integral should mean having integrity. After all, if we have managed to integrate all of these various aspects of our lives that we are now more aware of through this powerful map of the complex territory of human experience, we should be able to enact a kind of alignment of values and actions. Or in other words, what are integral ethics?

This is no simple question. There are of course vast volumes of literature dedicated to questions of ethics, and one question could simply be: What could an integral perspective add to what has already been said? While this is also an area open for future exploration, I do have one thought about the demands that knowledge of an integral view of the world can make on us. It comes from viewing integral as transcending and including the rational analytical mode of consciousness predominant today. In the transcending, a different kind of view of truth can emerge. This has to do with a notion of truth not as a noun, a thing to be found, pinned down and defined as in a rational view, but as a verb, a living engagement with life.

I have found this concept discussed in a manner that resonates for me by Parker Palmer in his book To Know as We are Known: Education as a Spiritual Journey. Palmer talks of the ethics of knowledge by saying that it "begins not in a neutrality but in a place of passion within the human soul. Depending on the nature of that passion, our knowledge will follow certain courses and head toward certain ends" (7). Palmer sees truth as troth, a living pledge. "We find truth by pledging our troth, and knowing becomes a reunion of separated beings whose primary bond is not of logic but of love" (32). He illustrates this concept with a story of an early Christian desert father whose students came asking him to speak.

Some brothers went to see Abba Felix and they begged him to say a word to them. But the old man kept silence. After they had asked for a long time he said to them, "You wish to hear a word?" They said "Yes, Abba." The old man said to them, "There are no more words nowadays. When the brothers used to consult the old men and when they did what was said to them, God showed them how to speak. But now, since they ask without doing that which they hear, God has withdrawn the grace of the word from the old men and they do not find anything to say, since there are no longer any who carry their words out." Hearing this, the brothers groaned, saying "Pray for us, Abba." (41)

This story illustrates the integrity between knowing and truth, between thinking or believing and our actions in the world. It allows us to conceive of knowledge as more than a static thing to be defined, but as something integral to how our essence manifests in the world. It challenges us to embody our knowing in our doing. This is quite challenging as we have noted, and for the future, I think that one thing that will be very important is to create a community of practice for educators on similar journeys through this territory.

Miriam: Yes, I really appreciate your bringing in the theme of integrity—alignment between word and deed, awareness of responsibility and effect, and to bring us back to where we began, an inclusion of the sacred, of Spirit, in the midst of daily life, and in this context, especially in the educational realm and relationship.

4

An Overview of Embodying with Awareness

Willow Dea

Now that you've been introduced to the integral theory and have learned about what it takes to be an integral educator you're likely asking, what does this look like in action? How do I embody this?

Before we begin, I want to acknowledge your instincts, vision, and moxie. As a teacher, you already embody an undeniable commitment to service. You undoubtedly hold a positive vision for the world, which guides your daily practice with a certain quality of integrity. You are probably already navigating the territory of your role as an educator quite well. My hope is to break down the elements of what we mean by embodying awareness, as you may have gathered that this is a central practice in integral education.

As well, I'd like to encourage you to take a fresh look at your practice as a teacher, and to bring an increasingly integral perspective to your experience each day. The reason this is so important is that we need to empower and equip young people who are encountering the ever-increasing complexities of the 21st century with an integral perspective and skill set which engenders the capacity to solve complex issues with sophisticated approaches to these nonlinear, interdependent problems. Recalibrating our presence to befit the capacities required to witness these complexities is of central importance. The focal point of this chapter is the space between the map and the territory, which lies in your heart and mind. You know the way. These words are just a pointer to your way of knowing.

While considering several aspects of embodying awareness as they relate to your inner state, I'd like to acknowledge that the practices that I'm suggesting are but one way of embodying with awareness. Of course, the deeper invitation is to find your own way!

Here's a quick overview of the aspects that we will explore:

- Slowing Down
- The Importance of State Training

- Holding Space
- What are the Benefits?
- What Wants to Happen?
- Intention & Expectation : the Impact on the Class
- Divine Regard
- Flow: Unlocking Creative Potential
- Embodying with Awareness

Slowing Down

We can choose to quiet down to be with the territory and to observe it as it's arising in and around us, or we can superimpose our thoughts, our defense mechanisms, habits and addictions to resist, try to change, or argue with "what is." When we come out of resistance to what is arising in the classroom or learning environment, we are able to perceive the next obvious move more clearly.

An easy way to slow down is to take a few minutes at the beginning of a day to prepare your being. Sit down and simply pay attention to the sensations in the body, become aware of feeling your body. Bring your full attention to the sensation of your breath for a few minutes.. When we slow down, our perceptual field opens up, and as that occurs, there's an opening for us to be in more intimate contact with the nuanced aspects of what's occurring in our surroundings. For example, when we go to the woods and stay in one spot for as long as ten minutes, the smaller motion of the birds may resume. The squirrels' activity may be more apparent; we might even hear the bugs. Our capacity to be present to the smaller happenings in our field of awareness is heightened. The same practice holds true in the classroom. Slowing down allows us to make a more creative response to any given moment. The quality that fresh eyes can bring to a moment can shift the outcome in unexpected and wonderful ways.

In fact, greater precision and clarity of awareness allow us to respond to the elements of our experience that are ultimately more nourishing or effective. For example, those things we might ignore or miss when we're moving quickly are more obvious when seen with a soft, open gaze. The wider our perspective, the more easily we can see opportunities to connect, clean up that mess, initiate an activity, or handle a loose end.

Reality presents us with a constant invitation to be with what is. To bear witness to the territory from a place, which is simply seeing: not reacting, not moving away in fear, or overriding it with an agenda. You might be wondering why this would be important, and I would offer that when we slow down and become more grounded; we align with our greater purpose. There is a felt sense of connection with a deeper volition for coming to school that day. From there, greater potency and service is available in our teaching practice. A quality of fullness, rightness and clear direction often come along with deep alignment to our purpose. Allowing ourselves the pleasure of preparing in this way can help us to access and bring greater presence to our students... thus having a greater impact on their well being and learning.

The Importance of State Training

One of the fundamental practices for expanding one's capacity to bring ourselves fully to the tasks of teaching lies in the commitment to marshal one's attention for a predetermined amount of time on a single point of focus. Be it the breath, the sensations of the body, a mantra or an inquiry, meditation is an essential part of building the capacity to embody the awareness that one naturally encounters in the interiority of a daily practice.

Remember states are temporary aspects of phenomena that arise in our direct experience in all four quadrants. Three general categories of states include narrow, phenomenal states of body or mind. Waking, dreaming, and deep sleep are examples of broad, natural states of consciousness. Non-ordinary and altered states are found during meditation, while consuming drugs or alcohol are altered types of states.

As there are an array of meditative practices from which to choose, many people find one to which they gravitate. Some find that tai chi, qigong, aikido, various forms of martial arts, and/or physical yoga facilitate a state change that assists one to access higher or deeper states of consciousness—while still others may find that they prefer to ski, run, cycle, train in a gym or surf. The speed of movement is less important than the experience of a definitive state shift.

Alternately, the great wisdom traditions offer yet another plethora of practice opportunities for state training, by means of meditation, in a seated, standing or lying down posture. One might feel more drawn to contemplative Christian practices or Zen, Advaita Vedanta, or Vipassana, Tibetan Buddhist or Hindu. Essentially these practices are done in stillness, with specific techniques for the focal point of attention. As you may have gathered, the point is: pick one. Commit to it. Allow yourself to be transformed by it. Receive the daily nourishment from your practice. Bring that fullness with you, wherever you are. Be that silent aware presence.

What are the Benefits?

Though research has yet to establish a causal link between the ability to stabilize access to higher mystical states of consciousness and a faster rate of growth into higher stages of awareness, there are many benefits to practicing daily.

The intentional practice of cultivating deep meditative states, on a regular basis, has been found to increase our capacity to demonstrate resilience, to tolerate the stresses that life presents. Resilience is particularly increased when we marshal our attention to that which is arising in our bodily experience—directly. Employing our attention to bear witness to our direct experience facilitates deep shift in the body, mind and spirit. As Wilber put it, "…there is a big difference between naturally occurring states and trained states. As we said, natural states are always available to us, and do not follow any strictly sequential nature. While trained states almost always do, leading the practitioner over many years from the 'densest' states (gross states) to less dense states (subtle states) to formless states (causal states) to effortless Witnessing states (Turiya) to the seamless nondual integration of Witness and Witnessed (Turiyatita)." (Wilber, 2006)

Contemplative practices can help you improve your relationships with yourself and other people. More specifically, the benefits of practice include:

Transforming your relationship with yourself:

- Generating an overall sense of calm and well-being
- Managing your stress and its impact on your body
- Deepening your self-understanding
- Sharpening your focus, concentration, and insight
- Upholding your core values in your personal and professional life

Improving your relationships with others:

- Enabling you to treat people with compassion and wisdom
- Helping you to see conflicts from different angles, opening up creative possibilities for problem-solving and resolving disagreement
- Improving your listening skills

Enriching your relationship with the world around you:

- Increasing your global awareness and appreciation for the interconnection of all life
- Developing the ability to question, explore, adapt to rapid change, and deal with complexity

The practice of mindfulness (living in the present moment) offers an opportunity to reduce stress, increase concentration, enhance relationships, and find more peace and joy in one's personal and professional life. As an educator, you have one of the most important and challenging jobs! The relevance of state training is as simple as enabling you to better teach who you are, on an essential level.

Holding Space

One of the functional practicalities of cultivating integral awareness is the ability to hold space as a teacher. Holding space is a delicate balance between sensing, feeling and action. One maintains an awareness of one's own sensations in the body, the sense of the emotional tone in the classroom, and the choices that are most beneficial and effective for the whole class. In other words, the practice is to hold the curriculum lightly and allow for what is, to guide the next movement...whether it's to contribute more information to your students, facilitate discussion, assign an activity or take a brief break for integration. Holding space is also a balance of attention. By balancing attention, I mean the subtle navigation between the cognitive elements of your curriculum objectives, and your bodily felt sense. In this way, we are holding the paradox of being slowed down, with a quality of open attention, even as there is work to be done. There is authentic engagement in the physical world, and an awareness of the territory and map, directly and simultaneously.

What Wants to Happen?

Another way of making a decision is not to. Listening for what wants to happen is to follow the intelligence of the intersubjective space, the Field. One of my strategies for navigating how to bring a certain lesson into the territory of learning is to feel what wants to happen in a group. For me, this is another bridge between theory and practice. If it's true that what-wants-to-happen is that the class wants to gobble that lesson up, then that's what we do. If it is alternately true that instead there's some resistance, some drag, a sense that the room is bogged down, or something just simply isn't clear, then that would be where the attention goes. That's where the intelligence of that moment would lead me to attend. From a place where there is no resistance, it is easy—there is a sense of ease and obviousness about what wants to happen. This approach is about holding intention clearly and lightly, staying very attentive to the subtle, emotional and energetic signals in a group field, such that a highly customized response can be offered to facilitate flow for the whole group. See what happens when you allow your instincts and intuitive self to take the lead for a while. Is it really true that we need to "drive" the process? Can we also ride the process?

Intention and Expectation: The Impact on the Class

An intention is open ended, while expectation can have a very different effect on the culture (LL) of the class. Why? Intention allows for a unique process to unfold organically, while an expectation can foil that unfolding. An expectation can act as an inertial fulcrum in the Field, shutting out possibilities for emergent learning, rather than to encouraging spontaneity and creativity.

By definition, an intention is attention that's consciously applied to an area of focus. One might set an intention for the next hour, day, week or year. By contrast, an expectation means to await, to consider reasonable, due or necessary a specific outcome; while the connotation is that something is probable or certain. Expectations carry a certain weight and sense of attachment, as if one might experience loss if the outcome is different than expected, versus an open curiosity to the present moment, and the unfolding of that particular moment.

There is a distinct, yet subtle difference between setting an intention for a class, and having an expectation for the outcome of a class. When we expect something, we set ourselves up for an argument with reality. When we intend something, and are open to the actual (and possibly different) outcome, there's an opportunity to learn, stay curious and be with a new, perhaps better outcome.

We cannot fully know the impact of our thoughts, words and actions. Ultimately, we need to trust that teaching from authentic clarity and integrity will serve those learning from us.

"Don't play the saxophone. Let it play you." (Charlie Parker)

Divine Regard

Divine regard is the ability to hold our everyday affairs as sacred. It is the embodied understanding that all of the mundane, habitual, domestic, gritty or tedious tasks of any ordinary day are indeed sacred, exactly as they are. Divine regard refers also to the living practice that every person we come across is also sacred, just as they are. Even with all the parts of their behavior that we find unacceptable, we are invited to relate to them as part of ourselves. Seeing everyone as sacred does not mean overseeing what is unacceptable or needs improvement, it is not one or the other, rather a both/and—divine regard and realistic observation. Divine regard is a disposition of the heart, a way of staying aligned to what matters to us most deeply, even in the midst of great challenge.

Divine regard is also a practice of staying with a situation, a task or a relationship, even during periods of intense duress or strain. We do this with the understanding that therein lies an opportunity to see through our projections, to access clear seeing in an undefended, vulnerable way, and to find ways to maintain active compassion by means of communication. The opportunity is to do the inner work of decoupling the truth from the projection, whilst staying open to finding the words to speak in (at least) a neutral tone of voice, and ideally in a constructive, positive one.

Divine regard includes the ability to hold multiple perspectives (yours and theirs) and to stop making ourselves separate from another. By "making separate" I mean to suspend the mechanism in us that makes another person wrong or bad in any way—rather to see their wholeness as well as the patterns that we may have trouble accepting. Maintaining an authentically empathetic connection in the face of a difficult, or unconscious event or dynamic provides an opportunity to practice this new disposition. It's all too easy to judge others, and push them away, based on some perception of them, while staying connected and exploring how to be with the ambiguity of those feelings is truly facing our own shadow simultaneously, while witnessing the other person as a mirror, and an individual.

It seems that forgiveness or acceptance lies in the perspective taken from the eyes of Love. Love and respect for our self and for the other person. Divine regard applies to us too! We can ask ourselves: How does Love perceive me right now? What would Love say? What would Love do? How might I act more wisely in a moment like this?

Flow: Unlocking Creative Potential

When we bring our students into contact with the unique spark of life that they are, by means of helping to create states of flow with them, we optimize the potential that the Light will turn on for them. Whether they light up around math, international policy, spelling, psychology or literature is for their essence to understand. It is our job as teachers to assist our students to access that spark, such that it can light up and burn as passionately as possible, eventuating a Life purpose.

Flow is a source of mental energy in that it focuses attention and motivates action. Flow is a state—a fleeting experience of various qualities. Flow theory, developed by Mihaly Csikzentmihalyi after studying thousands of subjects has been characterized as having these qualities:

- Effortless concentration and enjoyment
- Complete immersion
- There is no room in your awareness for conflicts or contradictions.
- Flashes of intense living against the dull background of everyday life.
- Effortless action that some people feel stand out as the best in their lives.
- Athletes refer to it as "being in the zone," religious mystics as being in ecstasy, artists and musicians as aesthetic rapture.

Csikzentmihalyi asserted that "The happiness that follows flow is of its own making, and it leads to increasing complexity and growth in consciousness," which is the whole point. Higher stages of human development have been found to resemble this list of attributes, according to Hartman and Zimberoff,

"Descriptions of people functioning at an optimal level include increasing flexibility, conceptual complexity, and tolerance for ambiguity; recognition and acceptance of internal contradictions; a broader and more complex understanding of the self, others and the self in relation to others; internalized self-control and emotional self-regulation; transcendence of ego boundaries; transparency; and "postambivalence" i.e. total whole-hearted and unconflicted love, acceptance, and self-expression."

This is our aim. To evermore embody increasingly higher levels of complexity, with greater ease and fullness… and to model this for our students, colleagues and the administrative leaders with whom we work.

"Flow happens when a person's skills are fully involved in overcoming a challenge that is just about manageable, according to Hartman.and Zimberoff. We create flow by offering an opportunity in which a student/learner must stretch to acquire a new skill, whilst using all of her previously attained skills, and this with a refined level of support for facing the challenge. According to Flow theory, Flow activities allow a person to focus on goals that are clear and compatible, and provide immediate feedback. The clarity of the goal has been found to create a "self-contained universe," where everything is black and white. Flow tends to occur when a person is engaged in their favorite subject. Surprisingly, flow states occur more often at work than at leisure. Flow dissipates when the level of challenge is too low, or too high. A person's skills must be fully involved to create flow.

A note on embodying flow: When one allows oneself to relax into the mystery that we are, there is an effacement…an opening…an allowance to being touched by a silent, dynamic force which has an intelligence that, again when I <u>allow</u> it, soften into it, has an unerring potency and inherent knowing. Flow itself seems to have the "answers," the way, the depth and breadth to move us into new, deeper contact with life. There is a sense of intimacy, immediacy, wholeness and "rightness."

Embodying with Awareness

Embodied awareness is ultimately very simple. It's about listening closely to what your body and being need and want to be nourished, balanced, and flourishing. Cultivate a practice of inquiring underneath the habitual cravings for sugar, distraction, caffeine, alcohol, or busyness to discover the next level of desire—perhaps for a nap, some time alone, a good book, or intimacy. This is a wonderful way to understand the emotional needs you may be feeding or covering up with other behavior. When we feel truly fed, or emotionally met by ourselves, and we trust ourselves to provide those things, a quality of relaxation and calm can accompany us through the day. There is a deep sense of emotional safety, thus the permission to really listen and creatively choose the form of deep nourishment that would serve in the moment.

What does your body actually want? Is it really another cup of coffee, or would a nap be more supportive? It's also about being willing to let go of habits that no longer serve your wellbeing. Do you have the courage to let go of something that's hurting you? A happy, healthy body finds relaxation more easily in a delicious state of meditation. It's just that simple.

The good news is that as we progress with a meditation or movement practice, we tend to become more sensitized to the sensations in the body. This enables a greater awareness of the impact of our food choices and habits, and tends to inform us pretty quickly as the to real benefit of yet another cookie…versus a good long stretch in the sun.

Ask yourself: What would make your being sing with joy? A motorcycle ride? A walk in the garden? A game of soccer? A hug from a friend?

Greatest Hits

The next section of the book is a collection of teachers' Greatest Hits, which are first-person narratives that elucidate the pedagogical practice or lesson that an integrally informed educator found effective over the years. These chapters exemplify integral education at its best. Some of the explanations about the lessons are implicit, while others are more explicit. The material in these Greatest Hits ranges from the transformative power of love, to an integral perspective on homeschooling, to the nature of an integral science class using only bubbles!

5

Mrs. Feldman and Her Students
Learn about Love

Lynne Feldman

As my 12th grade classroom slipped into darkness and the huge screen over my whiteboard reflected the DVD of "Pleasantville," my seniors settled back to enjoy two of their generation's favorite stars, Reese Witherspoon and Toby Maguire, depict fraternal twins living in 1990s American suburbia but who represent contrasting value systems. My purpose has been to expose these sociology students to the contrasts between the culture and social norms of the 1950s and modern culture and norms.

"This Friday on TV Time...Take the phone off the hook and the plastic off the couch. That's right, it's the Pleasantville marathon! Hours chocked full of pure family values."

The plot of "Pleasantville" fit beautifully into my pedagogical intentions:

"Two modern American teenagers are sucked into their television set and end up living in a black-and-white fifties sitcom. Bewildered by their new world's naïveté and innocence, they slowly start to add color and spice to the town's life. Eventually, however, they begin to question their influence, wondering if their advanced 90's attitudes are really that much better than those of the innocent past. Sterling effects and stand-out performances make this commentary on modern life a poignant, entertaining effort."

The initial part of the lesson proceeded as I had planned and hoped. Comparisons of the two eras' economic, political, intellectual and social institutions were quickly made. I then put this shift into an evolutionary context, from where we began our human journey with a pre-modern worldview that encompassed survival bands, magic, blood rituals, and deadly competition over scarce resources.

The class has studied History for three years in high school, exploring the evolution from this pre-modern era through to the modern era as they learned about the

Renaissance and the Industrial Revolution. However, no contextualization had been offered to tie all of this into an understanding that these successes (and their accompanying negative and restrictive aspects) were manifestations of ever-widening worldviews, or changes in consciousness that enabled the population to see beyond the traditional horizons to new territories and technologies.

My students received this contextualization with me, and could understand that these shifts were not merely shifts in values and technology; these shifts involved different levels of cognition and consciousness, as discrete from one another as the teens are from their primary school-aged siblings. I had given them examples throughout history of this change of consciousness, and they understood why they would not be able to convince a Roman soldier, a Puritan fearful of witches, or a slave owner to change their belief systems by merely sharing a post-modern perspective. Each film I showed throughout the year made this central Integral point.

I keyed the "Pleasantville" assignment to Chapter 3 in their Sociology text, a chapter that describes traditional American values. The chapter discusses Robin M. Williams' study of core American values, and students are asked to learn them. There is one column on changing values, but once again, no developmental framework is presented, and no historical context is offered to help anchor the lesson for the students. The text fails, for example, to note that Williams' groundbreaking study was published in 1951 and the referenced source on changing values was published in 1971. The text, published in 2003, makes no mention of the past thirty years of phenomenal changes within American society.

To assist my students in being able to distinguish modern from post-modern values, I had them first design a t-chart where they compared and contrasted the sociocultural manifestations of American life in the 1950s and the 1990s.

The next assignment instructed them to choose from a list of twenty topics dealt within the film, such as sexual harassment, censorship and teen sexuality. They were to research the issues with an eye toward the changes reflected in the shift from modern to post-modern worldviews. For example, the issue of teen sexual activity would incorporate what they had already learned about psychosexual development. They would use what they knew about sexual mores in the 1950s in the pre-pill, conformist, in loco parentis culture. I shared with them my own background growing up in the South, when my pregnant 10th grade high school teacher had to go on maternity leave the moment she began wearing maternity clothes, lest we ask why she was "getting fat."

The students then researched the influence of technology on current sexual norms. Finally, they were to write an opinion paper on their reaction to those changes. It was fascinating to read how skeptical many of my seniors were about the absence of bright-line standards about when and how to engage in sex.

Armed with my belief that I had a clear lesson plan ahead, I was ready to assist my students in understanding the fairly obvious comparisons in the film: the twin who pined for the simpler life of the 1950's (Toby) came to see the narrowness and flatness of that worldview, whereas the post-modern lascivious twin (Reese) came to see that responsibility and conforming to social norms can lead to a more fulfilling life.

The metacognitive issues did not draw my students' attention away from their personal reactions to social issues presented in the film. As the twins are children of divorce, in one scene they overhear their mother arguing with their father on the phone. She begs him to switch their custodial schedule and supervise the teens while she takes a holiday with her new and younger boyfriend. The father refuses, and thus the twins are left alone for the weekend.

The issue of custody and the rancor that often ensues is a hot button topic among many of my students, and I permit them to discuss it during breaks in the film. Many of them have had soul-wrenching issues around this topic and want a safe place to share their stories and hear from others. It becomes yet another poignant time for them to wrestle with the progress and the downside of our current era, and I stop the DVD to permit discussion over this issue.

The entire matter of unsupervised teen parties led to tragic consequences locally, and the painful episode is revisited. One of their classmates apparently lacked all structure and parental supervision, and suffered an overdose that resulted in severe brain damage. They wonder if this tragedy could have been avoided by more structure and parental supervision.

This segues into a discussion of what makes the students binge drink each weekend. These topics are seldom openly aired. When the topic does come up, it is couched as: "Is it healthy for teens to binge drink on the weekend, yes or no?" so that the students are alerted to the fact that there is a "right" answer. Pitting the "theory in use" which actually motivates their actions versus the "espoused theory" that they have been taught is the proper answer causes great cynicism amongst my students. They do not believe that adults value the root causes of these issues, and they are much too "sophisticated" to buy into the "correct" answer. They are also cynical about the expensive and dramatic anti-substance abuse programs that most schools host periodically. Once again, I am aware that the teens need to bring these hot-button issues up for discussion in a safe environment, where the teacher provides a neutral framework that assists them in making decisions.

Shortly after we learn that the contemporary twins will be unsupervised for a weekend, a clever plot device sucks them from their living room into the black and white 1950's situation comedy that Toby, the twin who wanted to return to simpler and kinder times, had been watching. They suddenly find themselves replacing the characters of "Bud" and "Mary Sue".

The movie continues on in delightful 1950's retro fashion in black and white, with the typical modern era values paraded on-screen: the huge and unhealthy meals, the complete conformity laced with innocence, the acceptance of a truncated worldview with non-questioning compliance. Reese has now taken on the black and white persona of Mary Sue, seated in the 1950's classroom with a map of Pleasantville that has only two streets, Main and Elm.

Teacher: Now, can anyone tell me the difference between Elm Street and Main Street? Tommy.

Tommy: It's not as long?

Teacher: That's right, Tommy. It's not as long. Also, it only has houses...so the geography of Main Street is different than the geography of Elm Street.

Mary Sue/Reese: What's outside of Pleasantville?

Teacher: I don't understand.

As I watch the affect of my students, I see a wave of smiles. Not only do they get the joke, but they can relate to the common generational problems when adults fail to appropriately mirror their interior worlds, which happen most commonly in their classrooms.

Toby, as 1950's black and white "Bud," and Reese, as "Mary Sue," fails to act exactly according to the sitcom script that has been in reruns for decades, and very soon Pleasantville's routine turns into frightening chaos.

To illustrate to my students how the small ripples in the socio-cultural arena can lead to serious destabilizations, I assigned them an exercise to vary one of the following in a very small way, and to report the results in an essay: they are to change their use of body language, hand gestures, facial expressions, and social distancing. The results are mostly amusing, but in some cases it proved frightening.

Sitting too close to their friend at lunch got some of the boys punched. Not making eye contact with her Chinese parents at dinner got one student sent to her room and emotionally accused that she must be pregnant! Laughing at nothing funny in class got one boy sent to the office. Looking over the heads of her friends instead of at their eyes brought anger from them. I have taught them that 80% of our communication is done non-verbally, and after the exercise above, it was obvious to them why slight deviations from the norm can cause serious social disruptions.

"Mary Sue" continued behaving as the lusty and sexually active Reese, and she invited her new beau to Lover's Lane. While there, Reese introduced Skip to sexual activity that he had never, in his 1950's sitcom reality, been exposed to, and with that introduction of sexual knowledge into Eden, one lone black and white rose burst into luscious red.

Soon Lover's Lane is full of couples engaging in various sexual positions inside their cars, and parts of them and the landscape are beginning to burst into color.

My students are well aware of the bursts caused by Eros, whether directly experienced by now or via the culture. At first they presume that it is the introduction of carnal knowledge that enlivens the dreary conformity of the 1950's world, and they have studied about the sexual revolution of the 1960's.

However, my class of hormone-raging teens surprised me by interpreting the core message of the film more concretely: that engaging in sex is all that is necessary for personal transformation! This misinterpretation led me to present them with a more sophisticated and nuanced lesson on the levels of love from Eros to Agape. This is definitely NOT the underlying lesson that I wanted them to comprehend. I realized that I had failed to address their level of psychosocial development appropriately, and that it was necessary for me to redesign my lesson on individual and social transformation. I set out to uncover the "disorienting dilemma" that would put forward paradoxes and polarities that would stretch their minds beyond their current psychological stages. Mezirow explains its effects as follows:

"...We transform frames of reference—our own and those of others—by becoming critically reflective them of their assumptions and aware of their context... Assumptions on which habits of mind and related points of view are predicated may be epistemological, logical, ethical, psychological, ideological, social, cultural, economic, political, ecological, scientific, or spiritual, or may pertain to other aspects of experience."

"Transformative learning refers to transforming a problematic frame of reference to make it more dependable... by generating opinions and interactions that are more justified. We become critically reflective of those beliefs that become problematic."

So is it merely the physical act of sex that led to the transformation, I ask them? It certainly appears that way, especially when Bud's "mother" discovers that she can pleasure herself and achieve orgasm... and a tree outside the house bursts into flame!

Sociologists and psychologists have traced how the social and religious institutions in both Eastern and Western cultures responded to sex. Freud characterized Eros as the life instinct and Thanatos as the death instinct, and held them as polarities that are inextricably entwined. Sexual frustration, he and others held, leads to anger and aggression, while sexual repression can led to emotional numbing that leaves a person feeling dead inside.

As the characters in the movie begin to experience Eros, the establishment elders begin to recoil from the changes they observe around them in Pleasantville, much as an earlier generation split with youth over the sexual revolution in the 1960's. Rules were created by the Pleasantville elders to stop the teens from learning, acting, and questioning.

My students demand to know why going to the library and learning something new in Pleasantville actually provoked more reactivity by the elders than the sexual activity at the lake. Why is the acquisition of certain knowledge also having a transformative effect on some of the townspeople, and how is this linked to sex?

Yes, the archetypal Pleasantville had been an Eden of sorts, and yes, Adam and Eve ate from the Tree of Knowledge and were punished. Toby/Bud's girlfriend actually does pluck an apple from a tree in one scene, eats it, and we wait breathlessly to see what happens... but nothing does. Then what is so frightening about knowledge so that it causes more anger than sexual activity?

My students are restless at this point, clearly agitated over this conundrum. I ask them to recall the pre-modern mindset, and to try to put themselves into other unfamiliar perspectives. We've dealt at some length with indigenous cultures, and some quickly connect that the indigenous peoples are not at all ashamed of their bodies until the missionaries taught them Western culturally acceptable norms of shame.

One academic further explains this comparison as follows: "We must pause to imagine Adam in his state of innocence... uncomprehending of what is being told to him, and certainly uncomprehending of the possible consequences of his actions.... At this point Adam is a babe, innocent and completely dependent... Imagine what such a story might mean to our pre-reflective selves, our coming to understanding and Sex and the consciousness of sex must be part of this story, in the sense that confusion and uncertainty precede understanding and insight. Children have difficulty anticipating and appreciating the consequences their actions may bring at a later time…"

Nakedness and embarrassment were the first consequences of the decision to eat the fruit of the tree of knowledge of good and evil. Adam and Eve become aware of themselves in a way that was novel to them...

The students understand that Adam and Eve can be seen as symbolic of the developmental path of every boy and girl, and they have been exposed to Piaget, Erikson, Kohlberg and Gilligan. Tracing developmental trajectories of humans and cultures helps resolve the issue of taboos at various stages of cultural and psychological development.

But this does not solve the issue of why neither Reese nor Toby have transformed. Up until now it had appeared that everyone who experienced sex changed into "normal" and robust color, and Reese asks her brother about their lack of change into normal color.

I direct the students back to the disorienting dilemmas. For Reese's character, sex is nothing new, no dilemma for her at all. As it turns out, her transformation occurs when she settles into a glasses-wearing, serious student who wishes to continue her education in college within the enlarged geography of the Pleasantville world now born anew in color, breadth, depth, and complexity.

Fine. We all get it. But then there is Toby. For all of his insight and patience, he has not transformed. Not until he speaks up as he is put on trial for his crimes against the norms. It is then that he achieves his full palette of glorious colors. Why has this been a disorienting dilemma for Toby, our hero, my students ask?

I am left to ponder that myself overnight. I had been concentrating on the polarities of Eros and Thanatos, concepts that I considered important as social motivators. Yet to limit Eros to a sex drive was a reductionist approach, I realized, and not approached from an Integral perspective. The following day I began my class by saying, "You know, sex is about more than just the physical act of intercourse. And there is more to love than just sex."

The class hushed so quickly and completely that I turned around to see if an alien had appeared behind me while I was talking. No one so much as breathed.

I've had this experience with my seniors before. They hunger for truth being told, for things to make sense in an integrated manner. They might have read chivalric poetry and discussed its contents, but no one has brought that forward for them so that they can flesh out, no pun intended, what relationships, both emotional and physical, are in their fullness. The first week of class I explain that my classroom is a safe space, with no harassment permitted, and that we can discuss anything at all, as long as we use non-prurient language, and as long as our intentions are to be educated. The students are so avidly awaiting this information that I have had few violations of this guideline.

I then turn to explain that the term Eros, (Greek erasthai), is used to refer to that part of love constituting a passionate, intense desire for something. It is often referred to as a sexual desire, and thus we have the modern notion of "erotic" (Greek erotikos.)

Eros as a Greek god was an ageless, bisexual deity who could grant virtue and blessing to humankind, whereas Ken Wilber pointed out alternatively that the conception of Eros "operates in biology by uniting bodies, in the mental realms by uniting people and ideas in a community of discourse and in spirituality by seeking to unite the universe." Yes, history's arrow, the energy that demands that we succeed and move forward, that change occur, is all part of the concept of Eros, and that quality permeated Pleasantville and its denizens with the sweet mystery of the sexual act.

Reese and her newly inquiring persona of Mary Sue takes us back to Plato's ideal, that there is a transcendental appreciation for Beauty, and that we also exist as love when our heart is unguarded and opened:

"In love, you allow yourself to relax your sense of separation, so that you become one with whomever or whatever you are contemplating, whether a child, a lover or the Grand Canyon. Love is unity, openness to the point of oneness, ultimately. And there is no limit to the number of people, things or places you can love."

So Reese transformed when she opened up to the Love that is beyond the mere sexual act, which is an aspect that my students had never truly held as a possibility in their hyper-sexualized culture. Toby transforms when he defends what he has done in the town in taking it beyond the status quo. What kind of love does that represent? Agape.

"Agape arguably draws on elements from both Eros and philia in that it seeks a perfect kind of love that is at once a fondness, a transcending of the particular, and a passion without the necessity of reciprocity... The universalist command to "love thy neighbor as thyself" refers the subject to those surrounding him, whom he should love unilaterally if necessary."

And thus, at last, my class has been opened to the mystery of Toby and Reese's transformations. There is concern for self, concern for other, and unity consciousness in a relationship, both platonic and physical. Toby had shown a general sensitivity and loving-kindness toward all those in Pleasantville, but his most consistent desire was to keep the status quo for them so that their world remained untouched. He had idealized the benefits of this modern-era life, the lack of overt antagonisms, the absence of uncertainty and chaos, and the soft lull of daily predictability.

He finally came to see the drawbacks of this fabricated modern-era society, with the absence of open questioning, or the expression of physical or creative output, the thin edge between the Pleasantville patriarchs who kept order and who could also turn into the oppressors stifling the urging of healthy Eros. He made his stand in court, out of love for all the people.

Reese, on the other hand, came to appreciate the harmful aspects of licentiousness and directionless hedonism. To balance her polarities, she chose to grow up and take on some of the routine responsibilities that all mature souls understand are necessary for their own Eros to unfold in a healthy manner. The insight that they both saw was the necessity for Agape to be as available to them as Eros. Agape, often seen as the divine, unconditional, thoughtful and self-sacrificing love, a "top-down" encompassing of the world, while Eros is the upward-thrusting aggressive love, is but one manifestation of LOVE.

Roger Walsh, a brilliant writer and reviewer of Wilber, notes that Wilber saw that it was critical for personal transformation and growth that both Eros and agape be available to the individual:

The process of ascent, according to Plato, is driven by Eros, the drive to find greater and greater unions. Complementarily, for Plotinus, at each stage of ascent the lower has to be embraced so that Eros is balanced with agape (love and concern for the lover). The vision of a multidimensional kosmos...interwoven by ascending and descending currents of love...would exert a profound influence on thought up to and beyond the Enlightenment. But according to Wilber both Eros and agape can go astray when they are not integrated in the individual.

This one day, this one flash of understanding about what constitutes Love, that there must be a balance of Eros and Agape, what constitutes the difference between sexual activity, romance, and caring love for another, literally transformed my class. I had not really seen the film through their psychosexual developmental level, and needed to expose them to the Integral understanding of Love.

They shifted that day. Finally, sex had a broader context, beyond current mores. Sex could have meaning beyond the physical. The act could be transformational when placed in an understanding of gross, subtle, and causal bodies, of care for self, other, and their unity.

My students were so hungry for this very lesson. They were able to make the Subject of their physical needs into an Object that could be examined, discussed, deepened, appreciated, as well as enjoyed. I never taught this lesson without this Integral understanding again.

My students rented "Pleasantville" and shared it with their parents. I cannot say how much conversation it generated, or whether understandings deepened among them. What I do know is that whenever I have dug into the AQAL tool kit to figure out how to broaden, deepen, and enrich my teaching, the results rippled outward with astonishing power.

I could easily reproduce my lesson plan below, but it would create a flatland rendering of the interactions that sparked my Integral response. In an Integral classroom, every moment is "teachable".

6

Botany in All Dimensions:
The Flowering of Integral Science

John W. Gruber

Some years ago, I was offered the opportunity to create a program of science instruction that would be truly compelling in its content while opening doors to new ways of thinking. This experiment came up as a kind of unexpected gift, and I chose botany as the focusing theme to develop a new course. My goal was to design a class that could serve as a pioneering foray into the realms of what is possible in a secondary school curriculum. So imagine for a moment that you have been given this gift, that someone has come to you and said, "Why don't you invent a class on anything at all, something you love, and take some time to make it the fullest possible expression of what is possible when an impassioned educator is given all the resources, support, and imagination needed to create a learning experience that is truly inspiring…" This has been my gift, and I would like it to be the gift each of you receives and passes on to generations to come.

Though I chose to design a course in botany, I recognized at the outset it could have been a class in anything—history, psychology, photography, or language. Botany was simply familiar to me and it tastes great, too.

At the heart of this botany class has been the development of a keen awareness that each subject, each question, each reflection we bring up is ultimately infinite in its complexity, reaching out in widening circles and across holonic levels to touch and connect with everything else. "Nothing exists truly in and of itself but requires everything to be what it is" (Cook, 1977, 9). In this way, we inherently recognize the sense of the all-quadrant terrain of integral education, or the nature of every subject tetra-arising as we adopt different perspectives through which we examine each question. By its very nature, botany, like the natural and physical sciences in general, lends itself quite easily to right hand quadrants and the description of What Things Are Like (Upper Right) and How Things Work Together (Lower Right.) The intricacy of these perspectives is vast and has occupied many researchers for a lifetime. Our goal in creating a more integrally minded approach has been to light up these quadrants with the interiors that add the fuller depth of meaning to the truth of what is.

When I speak to students who remember biology or botany classes in their own experience, they often recall the weight of half-forgotten details, particulars of mitochondria or xylem and phloem that have somehow fallen out of the context of meaning and remain only as names. So, among the questions I wanted to address in designing a course were these:

- What might an integral course of study look like in the sciences?
- How do you build a curriculum that is based firmly in science education and simultaneously honors the fullness of all that is present in the universe?
- How might a detailed study of intricacy in the natural world lead to the broadest possible reflection on our sense of self and our place as observers of our own awareness?

Importantly, our integral approach to botany does not abandon the careful, thoughtful study of detailed knowledge about plants. We are eager to gain as much insight as possible into structures, processes, and evolutionary and ecological relationships, just as one might do in a traditional biology course. Those details and facts are by no means the end of the line, and we do not limit ourselves to the leaves' chlorophylls, the flowers' anthers, or the Latin names of plant families. Our goal is to light up that knowledge in the fullest possible appreciation of its meaning, its social significance, and its beauty.

Without trying to provide a complete account, I want to share a little about what we do in our class, then look briefly at some of what makes it integral, and finally speak to what this experience has done for me as an educator.

What We Do: Eight Elements of Our Practice

In the botany class, we have a context that is nearly ideal for engaging a multidimensional approach that allows a deep exploration of the learning field. Most of these elements of practice can just as easily be taken up in any subject area. While these strategies may be uniquely contextualized in our class with respect to the ways they relate to plant studies and evolutionary ecology, they also are broadly applicable and any educator can adapt then to a specific learning situation.

1. Engage the body and the senses as fully as possible as often as possible. Get out of the classroom to look, see, and move through the living world; explore the taste of apples, chocolate, and peppers; investigate our sense of smell, our perception of color; and connect all of these to the realm of plants as organisms uniquely evolved to thrive in a complex world of change. Work intentionally with state experiences as part of the learning environment.

2. Build a community of inquiry. Using online forum discussions, in-class dialogue, question generating, and reflective writing, we engage in an ongoing effort to bring voices forward. We work to explore differences of opinion and practice listening, and whenever possible, encourage the practice of examining how and why people have arrived at the perspectives they are holding.

3. Mix it up. Methodologically, change styles, approaches, and media, using project-ed images, writing, discussion, debate, and brainstorming to vary the nature of the inquiry. We also move back and forth between lightness and intensity, finding enjoy-ment and fun and intrigue in some topics, with a good deal of laughing, and holding the seriousness and significance of other issues with more gravity.

4. Ask "so what?" Again and again we try to examine the opportunities for mean-ing-making: Why is this particular idea, information, or perspective relevant to you? Why should you care? And then allow individuals to try to offer a convincing case! The different kinds of meaning-making and the many different rationales for wanting to understand add a remarkable layering of experience and interpretation to the col-lective interpretation of course material.

5. Make it personal. Wherever possible, we find value in connecting ideas and obser-vations directly to our own experience. Memories, experiences, insights, and connec-tion to outside sources take the learning experience at hand and connect it to the rest of our lives and experience.

6. Seek out paradox and controversy in and around our subject and engage it. While connecting ideas and reflecting on their significance, we actively look for places where paradox presents itself, where the complexity of a situation presents multiple, simultaneous truths that lead in different directions. At these moments, we invest time and thought to explore the paradox and how it influences our previously held beliefs and understandings.

7. Actively seek (and offer) feedback. In our writing, our use of time, and the general approach we take in the course, we frequently pause to check in and get feedback: "How is this working?" "What could we do better?" "What could we do more of or less of?" "How can we continue to refine the learning experience?" Formal written feedback also is collected at several points, and we practice how to give and receive feedback to make it direct and constructive.

8. Recognize the different types of learners in our group. By diversifying our tech-niques and approach, we seek ways to allow a balance between introverted and ex-troverted styles of learning, masculine and feminine energies, and the many different personalities that come together in the classroom. We recognize that while each has something to offer, our collective learning is best served by moving toward one particular style for a given moment or day.

A Short Case Study: Botanical Food

Among the many different plants we use to explore the dimensions of integral science, the most appreciated for many students are the numerous food species. Beginning with the evolutionary history of a food plant and the structural role of its fruit or other plant part, we start out by thinking in the plant's perspective about the physiological and ecological purpose of the food parts. From this perspective, the bright red color of hot peppers advertises ripe fruit to bird dispersers, who successfully carry seeds far and wide. The intensely pungent, fiery heat of these peppers serves the plant as a defense against non-target species who might want to move in on the birds' nutritional reward system. Ecological advertisement, color perception, genetics of inherited heat, and the chemistry of the waxy organic oleoresin that makes peppers burn are all readily available subjects that allow complex and detailed study. Coming to know these principles and truths in their right-hand quadrant manifestations is undertaken in large part through first-hand experience. Tasting sweetness in all its different dimensions or watching a bumblebee orient itself on the hanging flower of a jewelweed plant both offer direct apprehension of experiences that can then be explained or explored in ecological or cultural terms.

The pepper, the tomato, and broccoli also offer opportunities to ask questions that move away from the descriptive natural science of the plant parts. By changing the question set to move from asking what these foods are like to asking who grows these foods, who harvests them, how they grown, and how they get to us, we open a very different inquiry into the same plants and our relationship to them. Labor conditions and the role of immigrant farm workers in the produce industry are soon part of the inquiry. The use of pesticides and organic growing methods, the advent of genetically modified organisms in the food industry, and the embodied energy of transporting food items across global hemispheres raise questions about the social and ethical dimensions of the food plants we consume. Again and again, students report that they never knew, and had in fact never thought about, how foods they consume were brought to them. Suddenly, a personal dimension is opened up that directly links their own behaviors and choices to broader structures of production and consumption that may be at odds with their own values and beliefs. The questions are no longer just impersonal and objective, but directly engage students in our own lives.

At the same time, the dialogue typically shifts from seemingly indisputable facts (e.g., the part of an apple we eat is a specialized floral accessory tissue called a hypanthia) to layered and multidimensional issues for which students may arrive at very different conclusions. As we learn about many different purposes for genetically modifying organisms (GMOs,) students often confront a disorienting dilemma in realizing they cannot decide whether they support or oppose the practice. They encounter a real case of conflicting truths, of benefit and harm that accrue differently to different entities. Students recognize that, from one perspective, the use of GMOs in food species is an unethical tampering with nature, or that some organisms may be irreversibly harmed by the application of GM technologies. At the same time, they may see that GMOs in foods could offer humanity a way to care more fully for all the residents of the planet by producing more food for more people or more nutritious food with less environmental impact in pesticide use or water consumption.

Finally, we work to turn the inquiry back to the individual interior and find ways to reflect on why we hold the opinions and values that guide us in our thinking, how we experience the relationships between our body and the food we choose to consume, and what arises that we find dissonant as we examine beliefs and choices in our individual lives. Much of our written work is offered in a community forum in a way that lets students hear and respond to each other's perspectives. This provokes both collaborative building on themes, whereby one student picks up on and builds on ideas introduced by another, as well as feedback and alternative views, whereby a student might recognize one way of looking at something, while also offering a very different angle that illuminates other facets of the question at hand. Through that shared workspace, we also come to know each other much more fully and have a stronger sense of a shared process of thinking and learning.

What Makes It Integral?

Our work to make the botany class an integral science course is based in part on the nature of what we choose to examine and how we think about questions that arise. It is also grounded in the ways we try to approach the process of learning and working together in an educational community. Because the school where this course was created is a Friends' school, with its own philosophy regarding a holistic approach to education, the class is well situated in an overall school community that emphasizes reflection and is open to world-centric views in all subject areas. Although that particular setting has provided a particularly supportive environment for the course, it could certainly exist in a wide variety of other, broader educational settings.

Here are some observations on ways that the botany course works specifically to be integral as an educational experience.

- We take an all quadrant approach to ideas, seeking different dimensions of the subjects we are exploring by examining both interiors and exteriors, and individual and collective aspects.
- We engage multiple lines of development and assessment in the work we undertake together and in the work that is assessed to measure student growth and engagement in the class.
- We strive to maintain recognition of verticality. There is a clear sense we are all walking the path, and we create a community that offers support and care to each person right where they are, while continuing to encourage both individual and community growth.

• We acknowledge the coexistence of multiple perspectives and appreciate the different dimensions that are illuminated through them.

• We work to cultivate a deep awareness of the ground in which learning arises.

• We take time to intentionally check in at the beginning of a class or the end of a week, to pay attention to our state of being and how it affects the learning experience: "How are we?" "How are you feeling?" "What currents of enthusiasm, curiosity, fatigue, or anxiety are present?" Taking just a moment to check in that way reminds us that the inner states we bring to the learning space are themselves an integral part of what transpires in the time we take together. Stepping back to acknowledge our inner states often helps us to settle into a place where we can listen more fully to the many voices that are present and give our attention more completely to what is at hand. Perhaps most importantly, these few moments also establish a connection of caring about each other. As we enter into the space of learning, we feel a genuine sense of care for our wellbeing in a way that clears a path for better understanding.

What Has This Done for Me?

Whatever it has been for the fourteen years of botany students, I can write most directly about what it has meant to me to have the chance to teach such a course and share the experience each year with a new group of enthusiastic learners.

First, the experience has been absolutely liberating in the sense of moving beyond any limited set of expectations or outcomes. It has opened me up wide and allowed me to embrace a set of possibilities and potentials in myself and in my students that I would not have imagined possible when I first began teaching.

Second, because of the nature of our shared experience and the depth of the questions we take up together, the course has engendered an uncommonly deep and cherished connection with the students, one that often lasts well beyond our years together in the school community. I find myself having ongoing dialogues with students through and beyond their years in college. Often these simply are deepening extensions of the conversations we began in and around our botany class.

Finally, the opportunity to teach this particular class in this way has fostered a genuine and abiding love for the work in which I am engaged. I love coming to class each day; I look forward to each exploration and line of inquiry; and I am always stimulated by the newness, the different-ness, and the variety of experience that is brought forward through the shared endeavor.

So, wherever you are, think for a moment about all the things you love to explore, whatever it is that excites your imagination and thinking in a way that you want to share with the wider world. Now begin to imagine what that looks like in a community where you can use that excitement and energy to illuminate the process of connection and self-awareness. Bring that very taste of the mystery of genuine discovery into a course that is waiting to be created. Let the experience lead you where it will!

7

Presencing the Optimal We: Cultivating Collective Intelligence in the University Classroom

Olen Gunnlaugson

> *One of the zones that have taken forever to get going is the lower left quadrant and the connection people have. In a way we're talking about collective intelligence and thinking more in terms of pre-personal and post-personal. So we had collective intelligence back in the caves, but that was pre-personal. We got through individuality and now maybe we're ready to have collective intelligence in a post-personal context?*
>
> —Allan Coombs in conversation with Andrew Cohen

Coombs and Cohen's conversation raises a pressing educational question of our time: what would it mean for instructors across different academic fields to be ready to cultivate collective intelligence in their classrooms? Post secondary education has and continues to be for many students and faculty the last place they might expect to encounter a collective post-personal experience. Within most academic settings, it is not uncommon to encounter a public mood of skepticism, cynicism and restraint when voicing questions that pertain to spiritual, existential or consciousness matters—that is, questions that uncover the very heart of integral education. Bearing witness to and enduring countless hours of classroom life where this pervasive fragmentation and disenchanted ethos prevailed, in these occasions students and educator assembled with "the most minimal sense of we," or connection, possible.

It is a functional "we" designed to serve the interests of private selves. There are, of course, advantages to our modern self-centered "public sphere," allowing for freedoms that were not possible in the mythic membership societies of the past, but these freedoms come at a cost. The self, in winning and maintaining its independence, is cut off from the whole in fundamental ways, which are frequently difficult to identify. (Balder, 2007,1)

Given that we are living in a historical epoch where our personal, social and planetary challenges require a more advanced set of collective capacities than we presently embody as a species, I am persuaded of the need for educators to take seriously the importance of leveraging the conditions for an optimal "we" through an integral yoga of dialogue education. In terms of an optimal "we," I am referring to a classroom ethos that invites and draws students into a collective experience of deeper states of consciousness within the intersubjective dimension of classroom life (zone 4 of IMP) as a basis for generative learning and inquiry into the class subject. By directing our presence and attention to improving upon both the quality of the process and content of conversations with our students, an optimal we-space is cultivated through more highly engaging fields of conversation. Too often classroom interactions in academic settings are in bondage to the norms of Balder's (2007) functional we. I sometimes ponder what discoveries might await a university classroom if the conversations were being lead by a collective investment in attentiveness, curiosity and humility towards what is emerging from the class field of learning? By experimenting with pedagogical approaches that engage students in post-personal forms of collective learning, collective thinking and collective being together, it has been my experience that the classroom becomes a learning laboratory for exploring the potential of optimal learning experiences.

Evolving an Integral Yoga of Dialogue Practice

As a process method of collective intelligence, dialogue can be demanding. Much like learning how to stably access deeper states in meditation, do an intelligible ink brush painting or compose a haiku that exemplifies a lucid Zen moment, learning how to engage with the deep interior of group life requires ongoing committed discipline. Principles of engagement or conduct within dialogue sessions can offer helpful forms of upper right and lower right (Wilber, 2006) practice. However, perhaps more importantly students need to learn how to cycle between their own and the collective's interiors through upper left and lower left forms of attentional practice.

In the classes I teach on interpersonal communications, dialogue and collective leadership, often I work with "yoga" as my guiding metaphor of integral communication practice. The term yoga in Sanskrit means to yolk or bring together and integrate, which in the case of the traditional practice of yoga, fosters states of enhanced well being and integration of one's interior and exterior realms of body, mind, soul and spirit in a comprehensive manner.

Since I began teaching and facilitating dialogue, I have worked with a number of yogic practices of conversation in order to enact, bring forth and illuminate significant forms of collective learning and breakthrough. I have found many of these practices quite helpful in fostering experiences of collective intelligence, with each practice containing at its center a hidden key to unlocking the optimal we. The next section proceeds to address the specifics of presencing as a foundational yogic discipline that I believe instructors will benefit from in their efforts to bring about a climate of post-personal collective intelligence in their classrooms.

Presencing the Optimal We

We tend to live in an inner chaos of daydreams, partially digested notions, and half formulated plans. But the possibility exists for the development of attention, awareness, and intentionality, for the growth of presence.

—Wertenbaker

To date, instructors advocating for presence in the classroom have not written about the role, significance or implications of shared presence in terms of how this influences or engages classroom learning and conversation. Furthermore, dialogue educators have yet to address Scharmer's (2007) notion of presencing and its multidimensional roles in supporting the conditions for collective intelligence. To convey the richness of Scharmer's account of presencing, I often introduce a fractal definition in my courses. Like a fractal, depending on what context you experience presencing, there will be interrelated yet distinctive structures that help us recognize the underlying patterns or meaning of the term.

I draw the first dimension of presencing from Otto's analysis of the term. "Presencing" at its root is about presence. In this most fundamental sense, presencing is the practice of coming into presence, which might involve a) learning to make stable contact with the source of your experience while observing what is arising in your consciousness and b) being more viscerally aware of your students in the intersubjective field of conversation you share with them as you listen to their views and articulate your perspective. By practicing coming into presence in conversation, we are preparing the conditions for a state-shift and fundamentally different sense of self or self-sense to emerge collectively. Orienting from this presence-infused self-sense can at times feel foreign or a bit vulnerable for both instructor and students, however with ongoing practice and embodiment, we can begin to model a comfort and at-homeness with this orientation. In the work I do with presencing as a field of conversation, this presence-based self-sense takes on greater roles as we move into more complex and co-creative fields of conversation.

The second dimension of presencing is drawn from Otto's earlier notion that presencing also involves literally pre-sensing or intuiting something before it manifests in the world. Contrasted with clairvoyance and certain psychic traditions, I introduce presencing as a way of learning to access the most resonant form of knowledge that we intuit is significant and wanting to be expressed through us or the group. In other words, this dimension of presencing is about subtly sensing into a certain tacit order of knowledge or insight that has not yet been embodied or lived by us or others, nor is yet a reality or manifested in physical form but on a deeper gut level feels crucial to articulate. This second sense of presencing involves learning how to sense into and co-creatively unfold and manifest something with others through the medium of a generative conversational field.

Presencing, in addition to being present and learning to pre-sense what is emerging in the conversation and our lives is also connected to our third definition: as a way of learning. As a learning disposition, presencing involves a kind of surrender and humility to learning from the intimations of future possibilities in the present rather than simply downloading what has been said before. As one might imagine, learning from the future involves being more attentive to the emerging dynamics of the unknown and articulating the vital possibilities of a given conversation through a felt alignment with one's deeper core self-sense and its capacities for knowing in this way. In this third sense, presencing helps us develop a new learning disposition that is attuned to a fundamentally different order of knowing. Instead of leading from what has been done before, I encourage students to periodically explore being attentive to the subtle nuances of reading both "between the lines" and what lies "beyond the lines" in their inquiry into the class subject at hand.

Varella's Three Gestures of Presencing in the Conversation Field

Drawing from these three dimensions of presencing, in my Dialogue Processes graduate course that I teach through the University of Massachusetts (Boston), I have at different points adapted a version of Varella's (2000) research into the three gestures of becoming aware to help students further grasp the conversational yogic posture of presencing. For Varella, the three gestures take place through introspection. First suspend or take a witnessing perspective of what is arising in your consciousness. Second, redirect your attention to the underlying source. Third, let go of past knowledge and associations so a clearing can emerge and new knowledge can come forth. In the following section I will elaborate a bit on Varella's three gestures and illustrate my second-person adaptations to bring this yogic discipline into greater focus within the context of dialogue.

Suspension

The first gesture is suspension. In suspending our thoughts, we begin to notice that we have thoughts. When we suspend our thoughts as an introspective or meditative exercise, we are becoming more mindful of our thoughts from a third-person perspective as a means to observe our thinking mind and its conditioned content. Suspension here is not interested in the content of the thought. Within the context of dialogue, suspension becomes a practice to be more mindful of our thoughts, to slow down the habituated processes of thinking so as to glean insight into both the underlying assumptions and our deeper nature as humans having thoughts. Suspension then helps open the field of conversation, inspiring a shared willingness to be tentative, curious and ultimately less invested in either asserting our perspectives or refuting others' perspectives.

Redirection

Given our accustomed habit of making meaning from either the past or present, Varella (2000) describes the second gesture of "redirection" as involving learning to subtly move our attention away from the content we have "suspended" and to sense into the source underlying this content. Redirection involves a subtle but discernable change in the direction of our habitual mode of attending to our thought process. In the context of dialogue, if we are ordinarily going forward in conversation, suspension involves slowing down and redirection asks that we temporarily relinquish the need for horizontal direction and instead sense vertically into the underlying source of our intersubjective experience that gives rise to direction. Initially this can be confusing for students, insofar as distinguishing the locus of creative emergence is generally not clear to the untutored eye. However in learning to notice "the source of our mental process rather than the objects within it" (Varella, 2000), redirection can help students and instructor better identify the state of consciousness and gesture of awareness that is key to facilitating creative insight in class conversations.

Letting Come

According to Varella and Scharmer (2000), following redirection is the gesture of "letting come," which involves a recursive movement of attention towards articulating or being receptive to the formation of new meaning, knowledge and insights to manifest. For Varella, letting come is practiced with the intent of redirecting one's awareness to a receptive opening or clearing within one's self. That is, connecting with a felt-sense of heightened inner receptivity to what is emerging within and being with this experience in a way that allows for the insight or words to come forth on their own terms. In the classroom, I generally encourage students to experiment with relating to the intersubjective field as this fertile clearing and to open themselves to allowing different emotional, intuitive, imaginative and kinesthetic expressions of emerging knowledge through. Following redirection, the gesture of letting come provides a temporary portal for learners to indwell into the subtle textures and nuances of a fundamentally different order of knowing in their conversations, opening a new horizon of collective knowing that otherwise dwells dormant on the periphery of a group or an individual's awareness.

Closing Thoughts

Almost without exception, collective intelligence processes are contingent upon the post personal emergence of the optimal we. Until post-secondary instructors wake up to the unwholesome effects of perpetuating the status quo functional we in classroom life, the deeply creative and meaningful interiors of the lower left quadrant will remain an uncharted frontier obscured beneath a landscape of discursive chatter. As a means to recovering a key dimension of our human potential in the classroom, I encourage you to further experiment with evolving an integral yoga of dialogue, to test out my fractal definition of presencing and recontextualized account of Varella's three gestures. For it is my hope that this chapter will shed light on your classroom ILP and evoke a sense of urgency for moving this work ahead. As the post-personal radiance of being flickers much needed light into our classrooms via the second-person intersubjective window of consciousness, my hope is this work will not become an emerging future trend of integral education so much as an enduring tradition.

8

Integral Education: Community Building

Kyle Good, Ph.D.

As I sat in the "hot seat" during an interview for the principalship in 2003, I chose to answer each question through the lenses of Tiffany and Billy, two students in my first grade classroom my first year of teaching.

Tiffany was a very thin girl whose appearance was similar to someone from the Appalachians. When I met Tiffany's parents during Parent-Teacher Conferences, I found out that their family did indeed move to the Pacific Northwest from Virginia. Tiffany had bucked-teeth and a mildew smell. She also had a huge heart, and she was never afraid to show here teeth through constant, big smiles.

Billy was an insecure boy who rarely completed his homework. He was quiet, didn't cause any problems, and would have been invisible if the class and I had let him.

The interview question was about the characteristics that make a school a highly effective place for students. My mind slipped back to my first year teaching those six-year-olds. Tiffany took the spot light. Through daily class meetings that focused on positive characteristics such as being responsible, respectful, accepting... we had created an amazing community. We were known as Mr. Good's Courageous Cougars (voted on by the students.) Another first grade class had entered our classroom for a joint art lesson. No one from the other class would sit by Tiffany. There were whispers about how badly she smelled and how poorly she dressed. In less than two minutes, the Courageous Cougars had gotten wind of what was going on. They immediately sat around Tiffany to keep her protected. Later, I over heard my students reprimanding kids from the other class with words like, "How would you feel if someone told you that you smelled?" "Tiffany doesn't stink." "The next time you come to our class, you better be nice." A strong, caring community is what makes school a successful place for kids.

Then came the question about holding teachers and students accountable to reach high standards. Billy now got center stage. Call me old fashioned, but we had weekly poetry recitals in my class. Each week, students would select a simple poem and memorize it with the help of their family in preparation for standing in front of the class and reciting it on Fridays. Since Billy rarely did his homework, he was not prepared for the Friday recital. When I called his name, he refused to come to the front of the class. During recess, I privately told Billy that he would have to at least come up to the front of the class next Friday whether or not he learned a poem. The next Friday came, Billy did come to the front of the class but had no poem. Again, in private, I gave Billy the line that he would speak in front of the class the following Friday and told him that he could read the words from the paper I had given him. That next Friday, Billy hesitantly came up to the front of the class and read, "Jack and Jill went up the hill." Those weeks that turned into painful months of pulling Billy's "poetry" teeth took us to Christmas break.

In January, Billy told me privately that he wanted to memorize "The Cremation of Sam McGee" by Robert Service. Wow! Was he pulling my leg or just out of touch with what it takes to memorize a poem? Thank God the good teacher in me spoke out. "That is a wonderful goal, Billy. You should memorize a line each week so that by the end of the school year you will be able to recite the entire poem."

Billy did memorize a line each week, and at 10:00 am on June 15th, the entire class stood up and applauded Billy (with some hoots and hollers) for just reciting, from memory, the entire "Cremation of Sam McGee." Reaching high standards is achieved by believing in each person and not giving up. There were a lot of questions asked during that interview, but none of them seemed as relevant as being reminded of these two precious souls, Billy and Tiffany.

I guess we all have known Tiffany and Billy…poverty, insecurity, support, success…embarrassment, pain, care, and generosity. My own first grade school year with Miss Stanton was one during which I was just like Tiffany and Billy. My parents had divorced that fall. Our electricity was shut off that winter. The Mattson's, our next-door angels, had run an extension cord from their home to our electric heater so that there was some warmth in our house. I wore black-rimmed glasses that were broke in the middle and held together by black electrical tape. I had little self-confidence. Students avoided sitting next to me. I didn't understand that letters made words. Like Tiffany and Billy, I had success. Miss Stanton knew how to build a community within a classroom. I knew I had to be a teacher when I grew up ever since I was in Miss Stanton's 1st grade class.

Integral Education explicitly addresses the intuitive sense we get from the "goodness" of the Billy, Tiffany, and Ms. Stanton stories. Teachers have access to two particular tools that support integral education: example and influence.

Rather than just "pouring in information," teaching through example is a more powerful tool because it is about inner motivation. "Influence" is also an important concept in integral education. Outstanding teachers are perpetual students themselves. They are learners teaching learners. In this era of No Child Left Behind (NCLB), society is creating a school culture of test-givers and test-takers. The value of developing understanding is giving way to the importance of memorizing. NCLB does not emphasize the development of imagination as much as it emphasizes the power of knowing facts and piece-meal information. The inner domains of the human spirit and the classroom culture are being pushed out of the educational system and society in general. The Tiffanies and Billies of today are the ones who lose.

It is important to acknowledge that the NCLB test-giving legislation does not serve our society well because it places itself (by the very nature of its rules) within the two upper quadrants (holons) of the AQAL, focusing solely on the individual. This imbalance has overshadowed the two lower quadrants, the collective. NCLB has also inhibited elementary age students from fully being able to take a first-person perspective which is a critical beginning step that is necessary to eventually integrate all four quadrants. Egocentrism drives are repressed by the test-driven curriculum which restricts elementary age students from developing a magical worldview and a type of creative impulsiveness. Prior to NCLB, students were encouraged to express their ideas through magical insights and imagination. This type of development is fundamental for any and all new tasks, thus enabling youngsters to eventually move toward take a 2nd-person perspective with a capacity to take the role of an "other."

An activity that may counter the negative effects of NCLB and its back to basics approach and may encourage an integral educational experience is a type of laughing meditation. Laughter as a form of meditation might surprise many educators. Yet laughing meditation is a very powerful and simple tool that promotes a balanced education. The physical act of laughing is one of the few actions involving the body, emotions, and the soul. When we laugh, we become one with the present moment. We also are able to momentarily transcend minor physical and mental stresses. Practiced in the morning, laughing meditation can lend a joyful quality to the entire school day. Practiced after the lunch recess, laughing meditation is a potent relaxant that has been known to inspire creative thinking and focused learning. Laughter also can help children open their eyes to previously unnoticed silliness that can make school life seem less serious.

There are three stages to mindful laughter. Each stage can last anywhere from 5 to 10 minutes. The first stage involves stretching the body like a cat and breathing deeply. The stretch should start at the hands and feet before moving through the rest of the body. Stretch out the muscles in the face by yawning and making silly faces.

The second stage of the meditation is pure laughter. Imagine a humorous situation, remember funny jokes, or think about how odd it is to be laughing by yourself. When the giggles start to rise, let them. Let the laughter ripple through the belly and down into the soles of the feet. Let the laughter lead to physical movement.

The final stage of the meditation is one of silence. Sit with eyes closed and focus on the breath. Laughter brings with it a host of positive effects that operate on both the physical and mental levels. It is also fun, expressive, and a way to release tension. If students learn to laugh in the present moment, they will find that joy is always there.

In addition to a laughing meditation, community building is also fundamental to integral education. Norms and agreements are critical. These include respecting ourselves and others, being responsible for our community, and working together to be the best we can be.

High behavior expectations are also conducive to a positive community of people. Responsibility is encouraged more than dependence. Likewise, assigning students jobs is a wonderful way to give them a sense of pride and ownership. In order to provide equity, every student should be assigned a job. One of the jobs should be that of a job monitor—someone to check on all of the other jobs to make sure they get done.

Community meetings are also a great community building tool for problem-solving and decision-making purposes. The goal is to empower students while developing a variety of critical thinking, problem-solving, and interpersonal skills. These meetings encourage students to set goals and reflect upon their progress in achieving these goals. They also enhance students' sense of belonging and responsibility to the community by providing opportunities to express opinions and contribute to group decisions. They help students gain an understanding of the meaning and importance of fairness, kindness, and responsibility. They also help students gain greater understanding of themselves and others by providing a supportive environment in which they feel "safe" expressing themselves. In other words, community meetings address all four AQAL quadrants.

For example, the Upper-Left Quadrant "I" (interior individual) is represented in community meetings by students brainstorming ideas around the community meeting's topic. Individuals reflect and write as they think of ideas and record them before sharing with the larger group. The Lower-Left Quadrant "We" (interior collective) is represented by small group discussions or partner chats and then bringing ideas back to the large group. Ideas are collected by asking partners or groups to share one idea, then asking all others with similar ideas to raise their hands, then asking another team or group for another idea, and then asking all with similar ideas to raise their hands, and so on until enough ideas are collected. The Upper-Right Quadrant "It" (exterior individual) is represented by students using the consensus process where all agree on an idea that everyone can live with. The Lower Right Quadrant "Its" (exterior collective) is represented by students listening with empathy, suspending judgment, being respectful, and having a cooperative spirit.

The Tiffanies and Billies in our society can definitely benefit from an AQAL approach within our educational system. By focusing on a balance of all four Quadrants, classrooms can give students the tools necessary to become integral human beings both in school and throughout their lives.

9

Homeschooling from an Integral
Point of View

Chris Nichol

When our children were young and we first thought about keeping them out of school, I wish that I had had someone to put their arm around my shoulders and told me to *trust*; trust my instincts, trust my ability, and trust my children to love learning. As most of us come from a background that includes formal schooling, it is difficult to imagine how this can happen. In our experience, much of our learning has been constructed by forces beyond our control; really there is no escaping this because soon after birth, our mother tongue and culture begin to shape us in deep and lasting ways. By taking the risk and carrying the responsibility of homeschooling, we have a chance to carefully judge and choose the colors in the palette of our children's lives. Their learning is certainly constructed, but by forces that we ourselves have decided upon and in environments that we have chosen and created. We can incorporate their specific needs and loves into the day too so that what they learn is a natural extension of who they are. To let go of the idea that some form of regular school equals education is not easy because it is so deeply ingrained. However, there is a wonderful freedom in homeschooling because when the parents are managing the environmental cues, the kids can be left to explore, guided when necessary and trusted to learn.

Modern homeschooling has been a growing movement in North America since the 1980s but the families who choose it are incredibly various. Some come to it as a rejection of their own public education experience; some pull their children out of regular school when they see that their child is being bullied or is intellectually bored or creatively stifled. Some children are so passionate about a subject or sport or training that their time is better spent in concentrated study at their own pace rather than going at the speed of a larger group; some parents are high achievers themselves who take on home-education as another of many projects. Some homeschooling is highly structured with timetables, daily lesson plans and detailed curricula; some is so deeply unstructured that the child is only guided by inner reference points and desires for knowledge, and then either left to explore alone or supported by the efforts of the parents to meet those yearnings. Some parents wish to protect their children from external influences while others wish to expose them to more life experiences and immersion in society—many are actively doing both at the same time! Despite the variation, one common thread that I can see is that the parents are interested in taking personal responsibility for the education of their children and can somehow manage to commit the time and energy to being available.

From an integral perspective, there seems to be an intuitive sense in most families of balancing the four quadrants and a range of lines of development; the way that this happens, the different emphasis placed on different areas, becomes the color and texture of that family's culture. Parents make a great effort to fill in family gaps with classes and extra support. There is an ever-evolving rhythm between home based activity and involvement in the outer world. After the initial paranoia of pushing their children and themselves to do school-at-home, something relaxes into a trust in *Learning* itself. I have noticed that there seems to be much more time spent on "input" without any expectation of "output" from the kids. Endless hours of reading aloud, long conversations, free puttering, along with some focused work—these elements are part of the learning week.

In our family, homeschooling in the beginning was not strict or externally structured except by a myriad of lifestyle activities like making meals, cutting firewood, work obligations, music lessons or whether it was a good puddle day, garden day or beach day. As they grew older, I loosely carried a Waldorf curriculum in mind but the kids were mostly unaware of it. A few times, we did a concentrated study or Main Lesson block (that should have taken 3 weeks) over three months, and sometimes we would have a math spurt that would take them through a couple of grade levels in a few weeks. I found it helpful to use some published curriculum materials and old fashioned workbooks in some subjects. They brought a level of challenge and structure to areas that my kids weren't inherently driven to explore.

They were involved in music, gymnastics and choir and these provided a regular discipline; Jaya (who is now 14) loved to sew and would spend hours creating beautiful quilts, fabric bowls and dresses, Hazel (who is now 11) liked shoes and would make flip-flops from cardboard and string, or play business with discarded forms and an old adding machine. Their own interests grew and changed and we did our best to enter and explore each of them. We did not have TV when they were young and were picky about the rare videos they saw; we read a lot of great books aloud, went to concerts and listened to a wide range of music. We travelled and camped, rode horses; we played spelling bee and did oral math in the car. Each spring they spent hours in the sheep barn across the road where they helped with many births and were present for several deaths.

Our lifestyle was lovely but for me, exhausting too. I needed to hold and weave so many threads, creating the fabric of the kids' life and learning as well as living rurally, doing my paid work with a literacy program and having my husband travel for weeks at a time in his work as a sculptor. Family dynamics were generally good but there were some lasting scars from early mistakes with our parenting approach that we needed (and still need) to attend to all the time. Overall, homeschooling was a natural extension of our DIY ethic—homebirthing, attachment parenting, building our home on raw land, growing vegetables, canning—and feeling that our kids would share our own inherent drive to grow and learn all the time.

A main focus for me was to remain attentive. Because children are deeply imitative creatures, who we *are* in front of them is far more important than what we say or tell or teach. Our genuine warmth and enthusiasm, our presence within in the world as learners ourselves is a priceless model. Children are also finely tuned to learn about what it is they need to survive in the world they are given; we must notice what these needs are in our children's lives. We need to look at the adults who surround them; what are they teaching by just being themselves? What is the climate of the microculture that our children inhabit? The primary focus thus shifts away from what is to be taught to questioning *who am I as a teacher? What is the learning environment that I am creating?* By shaping the external elements of our behavior and the child's environment, we create the framework within which they can grow without needing to poke at them directly so much. This approach doesn't mean that everything must be perfect all the time. With time and reflection, even negative experiences can become rich opportunities for learning.

The term that best describes this idea for me is enculturation; for thousands of years humans have grown into the knowledge of their people in this way. Alternative education movements of all kinds (Waldorf, Montessori, Suzuki music, free schools etc.) use this type of immersion experience to convey what is to be learned as much as they directly teach anything. Any successful school teacher also has this ability to create an environment for learning and I remember with great fondness my own teachers who had this ability. In a shared culture warmed by affection, we bring children into alignment with our values and can also receive what lessons they have to share with us.

Obviously, we don't live in a traditional society any longer and it is a rare child who flows seamlessly from infancy to young adulthood without struggling within the bonds of the family or society. However, homeschooling allows enough time to be spent with your kids that their basic alignment is in tune with your own. From there, each outside experience builds on that foundation, forming concentric rings of membership in other communities but always coming from a core of connection that you as the parent have the power to construct.

While homeschooling parents are attending to the interior aspects of alignment and enculturation all the time, they are also responsible for the exterior part of learning—the what, the how, the materialistic part of education too. Sometimes this can make us overbearingly didactic, wearing out the Present by turning it into "teachable moments." Many become neurotic over not teaching enough or making the kids do enough and this is often what scares parents away from taking on the responsibility in the first place. I feel that this is a product of growing up in a world that under-stands education mainly in an acquisitive way, where knowledge is thought of as an accumulation of facts from a particular range of subjects. Rudolf Steiner noted this and commented that facts learned in isolation from imagination, creativity and beau-ty are like a collection of small, cold stones which rattle around in an empty vessel. Some homeschooling thinkers have gone on to reject the idea of any essential body of knowledge and advocate complete learning freedom for children. While this is an interesting thought experiment, I don't accept it as a healthy approach to education. There is always a frame of reference within which learning occurs and it is better to be conscious of what that frame is and to create it with intention. We call an unstruc-tured approach *Unschooling* but when this is done well, there is usually a rich invisible knowledge environment at work.

The luxury of homeschooling is that you can create a *meaningful* life for your child; what they learn can have true personal relevance. Following a genuine interest is one way, Steiner's imagination, creativity and beauty can be another, having an appropri-ate context and need to know something is a third. Our timing can vary depending on when those windows of relevance arise. In comparison, school teachers must deliver material in a set program schedule, whether every student is ready to receive it or not. At home, we can stretch the relationship between time and learning. Instead of taking measured steps in a regular pace through the year, we can absorb life in longer arcs and then *zoom* through material when a door opens in the mind. We also need not have our kids *do* something for everything that they take in. They may digest for years before anything is observed in external action but the learning is just as genuine as if it had been tested and measured. Sometimes it feels risky and experimental because it is hard to tell what exactly is going on. My hope was always that we were cultivating learning capacity even when it looked like no work had happened in a while. I held an image of gardening where, instead of cold stones we planted ideas like seeds.

In our family, studying music has fulfilled this whole balance of elements beauti-fully. We have been fortunate to have a warm and caring community of players; there is immediate, meaningful feedback when things are done well and beauty is earned through listening, practice and repetition. Excellence is expected. We struggle with it every week and create new strategies all the time but the kids have never wanted to quit as the challenges are well matched by the rewards. When they were young our question to them was "which instrument will you play?" so there was freedom to al-low for the soul's resonance with a particular sound and type of movement. However, music is valued and assumed as a family language just like English and French. This isn't easy as my husband and I do not play, but it will be a gift our kids can share with their own children or others. We have also not been terribly strict about practicing and take a longer view of it as a weekly average amount of quality-time spent rather than a daily task.

A big concern in the past was that children out of school would not be able to socialize but the opposite appears to be the case. Because they are often in small-er, mixed age-group settings, they possess an ease with a range of people that many school children do not. They also tend to be in alignment with more mature ideas of socialization, rather than being deeply peer oriented.

It feels both ironic and poignant for me to be writing about homeschooling now as both of my kids are at a Waldorf school this year. My younger daughter started last year for a couple of reasons; she needed more intellectual stimulation and variety in her day and wanted to meet more kids. My eldest began this fall. She had never wanted to attend school but I felt that she would benefit from a wider social context for her learning. Sometimes as we worked together last year, she would sink into an altered state and be like a bottomless black hole I was pouring my energy into. No matter how genuinely engaged I was, if she didn't somehow meet me energetically, I was left feeling drained. I saw that she would easily be carried by the group energy of a class, many kids engaged in doing something together. Tribal consciousness would be a stronger force than a maternal agenda. Also, an inherent motivation to work academically hadn't grown in her yet and no amount of creativity on my part could change that reality.

Both of our kids have a perspective on school that their classroom peers lack. They have an ability to see and name the dynamics of the students' behavior and the teachers' foibles. This doesn't mean that they are beyond getting embroiled but they seem know where they need to go eventually. They are fresh and enjoy the writing, painting and woodworking. I can't believe that the same girl who can disentangle the legs of a lamb at birth is now wearing red nail polish and purple eye shadow, but as she said, "I want to do this now before I am too mature to be this silly." Both girls are carrying all of their life experiences forward into this new setting, maintaining their core strength while exploring new ground. I am finding that I can trust them to be decent, hardworking and to choose good relationships with others. So far, the experience has been imperfect but positive. It has exposed them to a whole new variety of learning situations. In a weird way, it feels like only a short step from homeschooling in that I still feel that we as a family hold the responsibility for their education. The school itself is like a support system and extension of what we were already doing. It is not flawless but we can see how things go and decide each year what path we will take.

Homeschooling is not for everyone. There are so many great alternative education programs to choose from which balance the ideas of respect, attentiveness, alignment and trust against challenge and stimulation. Even public schools have wonderful, inspired teachers who bring those qualities to their work. If someone is thinking about homeschooling though, I would encourage them to take the risk. Given a healthy environment, we can trust that children will learn and trust that parents will manage. I know I could have done many things better over the last few years but it appears to have worked out all right for my kids. When I asked if they thought homeschooling had been a good thing, my youngest said "Oh yeah, I didn't have to deal with all those girl politics all those years." My oldest knows that she would not have been able to progress as far as she has on piano and violin just from lack of time. She would have struggled as a late reader when her developmental agenda was different from the norm. Entering now, she is doing very well and her marks are high.

Our homeschooling practice was not overtly integral; Ken Wilber's model was one of several that I found useful as a reference map. What I have appreciated about it and others is that they reflected my lived experience, in that way proving their relevance in our lives. From there, I could use them to see into new ground, areas that may not have come into my awareness otherwise. The four quadrant model also influenced me to give myself permission to let go of homeschooling for now. There is a subtle tendency within the homeschooling movement to see "going to school," any school, as giving in, a failure on the part of the parent (at least I have felt that way). I began to see that the external structure that school affords is right now a great benefit to my kids in their development. It is also a much needed breather for me.

Homeschooling brings with it a special set of challenges but it can give us insight into effective teaching practices too. In the balance of curriculum against individualism, the weight tends to shift towards the individual. Because of our intimacy, we have a chance as "the teacher" to be closer to the lived, subjective experience of the child as a learner. We can adapt our approach, alter the environment and meet them with our hearts open to hear what has sunk in, to notice what has glanced off for now and to understand why. The quality of caring, a sense of respect and the experience of deep affection is what makes the teaching relationship work for both parties. It is also what makes it possible to continue on through the inevitable struggles and grit of everyday life. When this foundation is in place, the surface may look very different, ranging from strict and structured to loose and open-ended. As a teacher, the focus is less on *telling* and more on holistic *listening*. Both become learners, engaged together in discovery.

10

The Cradle of Education

Miriam Mason Martineau

There is a humble and powerful thread that connects and underlies all the times I have been engaged with others as an educator—be this as a teacher, a parent, a counselor, or a workshop facilitator. I call it the cradle within which learning and teaching take place: it is the relationship. Sounds perhaps too obvious to make a big deal of, I know, but how much attention do we actually place on the health and quality and growth of the relationship? How much time do we give it in the wide variety of educational settings, from schools to lecture halls to home life? In educational seminars across the globe the focus is generally on curriculum, pedagogy, and technology; what is consistently missing are seminars and conferences on the relationship between student and teacher. By its very nature, however, our profession involves at least two individuals—student/child and teacher/parent—and thus, being able to do our jobs well rests on the health of the lower-left quadrant, the "We"-space we teach and learn within.

"Mama, look, look! Come see! Come, see!" 2-year old Adonia calls excitedly. I look up from my book and walk over to where she is, hanging lopsidedly from a hammock amidst four kittens—all five of them bundled in a mass of cuddles and contentment. "I see you," I say, with a big smile. She returns to her big job of tending to kittens in a swinging hammock, focused and content.

That's all it takes—just a present moment of acknowledging her, seeing her, and of her feeling seen, then she is ready to continue in her work of cuddling and learning.

Tears well up again, right at the end of a counseling session as we get up to go. "I feel exposed, I feel shame," Elizabeth says. Alas, there is no more time for words, as another client is waiting outside. What to do? "Come," I say, and offer a hug. There, in the silence I extend warmth, care, and a squeeze of assurance. We check in through eye contact, "OK for now?" I ask. "OK," she says, and then we part.

"No!" 4-year old Joanna states with absolute conviction, both in body language and speech. This is not an easy moment. I know deep in my heart that if I budge now, I am not doing her a favor. I must hold this boundary, even if it would be so much easier to let go. I check within myself to make sure I stay lovingly firm and don't tip into an exasperated reaction. In the midst of this "meeting of wills" —hers versus mine—I am struck by how, whilst I hold a firm boundary in the face of her desire, there is no fear whatsoever in her eyes of me, of who I am or what I might do. Frustration, yes, intense resistance to and dislike of the situation … but no fear of me. This feels so deeply right. Our relationship is not threatened, not for one moment. I know that I am not breaking her will, that sacred force in her. I hope I am helping shape it, so that she is not only accommodated by the world, but also learns to adapt to the world.

Facilitating a course for first-time parents on the theme of parenting as an integral practice, and trying to fit too much material into too little time, I look around at all the faces, following the stream of information eagerly, willingly. I also notice a slight tension or feeling of rush in the air… "Slow down, Miriam," I tell myself, "Let go of 'covering it all.' Be informed from the 'outside in,' not just from the 'inside out.'" This is a stretch for me to do, as I can easily get carried away with all the wonderful information and the articulation of it all. Still, the rushed feeling is nagging at me, and I have made this mistake enough times. So … I stop, I breathe. Cancel the planned agenda. I look around again and this time I ask: "How are you all doing?" "Any questions arising in you that you would like to share now?" A moment of silence, an almost tangible feeling of relief follows and then we enter into a more delightful conversation that is rich and meaningful.

There is "Me" and there is the "Other." Then there is that space, the energy and dynamic between us: the relationship. Ultimately the educational journey hinges on that, and especially on the quality and health of that "ship," which carries it all. I think many of us know this intuitively. Sometimes we get so consumed with figuring out where we are heading with our ship—was it Africa or Spain? —that we quite forget to take care of, let alone notice, the leak in the bottom of the ship, the water pouring in, and the underlying sense of unease as the ship goes off balance.

Think about this: Who were your favorite teachers in school—the one(s) you remember, the one(s) who inspired you? Think back to that one particular teacher who really did it for you—and write down what it was about him or her that made the difference.

As you take a look at your list—isn't it basically a list of relationship attributes? Our favorite teachers are the ones we trusted, and were not afraid of. We wanted to listen to them because they listened to us. They are the ones who inspired us, were passionate about something real. The ones who embodied something we wanted to become. They made us feel good, we looked to them for guidance and direction. They provided a realistic, enthusiastic challenge. They are the ones we went to for help and enjoyed spending time with. The ones we liked to do good things for or wanted to please, not because we had to, but because we wanted to. They are those we wanted to share with because they truly cared.

Over two millennia ago Socrates articulated the secret to his teaching method, the Socrates method: Students need to love their teacher in order to really learn. They also need to feel safe, accepted, and loved. When asked why one of his students was not learning and making any progress, he answered simply; "He does not love me." When students are busy defending themselves, their attention and energy are split.

In holding the health of the relationship with awareness and intention, we can give special care to that which is so foundational. We can explore ways and perspectives with which to nurture and support this cradle upon which every educational experience rests upon, actually depends upon. So what does taking care of this "We" look like in practice? In the remainder of this chapter, I will share a few examples, perspectives and suggestions on how we might do this.

Getting Our Priorities Straight

This is a simple, profound step. If we understand that the relationship we co-create with our children and students is what any healthy educational process rests upon, then we can simply put our attention there first and foremost.

Getting back to the water pouring in the leak at the bottom of our ship. What do I do first? Fix the leak or figure out where I am heading and what instructions I need to give to my crew? Fix the leak first, silly! Funny how I tend to forget that part so often…seriously, even as I sit here writing this article and having spent a fair bit of time reflecting on this topic as well as seeking to put it into practice on a daily basis, I catch myself time and time forgetting to put it first. Goes to show how fully we can get involved in and taken over by our own subjective "bubbles of experience and existence." Integral education invites us to break through that bubble, to reach into the space between ourselves and the other, to honor both our self and the other self, as well as that third element, the intersubjective field: the "We." So, first of all, we do whatever it takes to connect authentically FIRST: Connection before direction and instruction!

If I want to get my 2-year old daughter's attention, I begin by getting down on my knees, I make eye contact, I put my hand on her arm and we connect. Then, I speak.

As I enter the classroom in the morning, I first gauge the relational temperature in the room. If it is low, I take time to connect, to bring everyone together. This could be with a story, a question, or an exercise. Only when the temperature is warm, do we proceed as a learning community to engage with our day's learning materials.

When I begin a workshop session I allow time for a check-in circle, for each participant to share how they are doing, what is alive for them today, and express questions they carry into the session. Once we are connected as a group, we enter together to engage with the course material and experience.

In a heated disciplinary moment when I am fuming, frustrated, or impatient, I reach out to my child or student and say, "Hey, let's talk about this later, and take care of our connection now, in whichever way it needs. Shall we take some space apart? Do we want to sit and read a book together, or spend some time together in stillness? Or do you have another idea?" Later, we talk about the disciplinary direction or correction when I can express myself from a grounded, non-reactive place, listen to the other person's perspective, and when my child or student is also more receptive to the conversation.

The relationship is not threatened, ever. It is not used as a card to play. Often, this is easier said than done. We intuitively know how important relationship is, and can find ourselves using it as a leverage point before we know it. With my young daughter there have been a number of evenings when I am so tempted to say "If you don't fall asleep in the next five minutes I am going to leave the room and you'll just have to do it on your own!"

Some might say that would be a good idea. I believe there is another way, one where I don't play with her uncertainty about being alone as she transits from awake to sleeping state. Instead I can say: "Adonia, I am here and close to accompany you to sleep. I also have a lot of work to do tonight. So, if you would like me to be with you as you fall asleep I need your cooperation." Then I go on to repeat our simple "sleep formula" of "close your eyes; be still in voice and body." This usually works.

Another way to honor the relationship while also honoring a boundary is to implement some "quiet time," which never implies emotional separation and does not necessarily involve physical separation (although it can, if that is helpful and agreed upon by both parties.) Thus, the relationship is not threatened as part of a disciplinary moment, but space is created for both individuals to calm down, to ground and center. With a very young child quiet time can happen in the mother's arms or in silent play. With an older child some suggestions can be offered for activities that s/he can engage in during the quiet time. Afterwards, it is important to go back to the conflict and sort it out in a relaxed, loving, firm manner.

When we understand that relationship is the foundation of any educational moment, we can begin imagining and implementing what can be done differently if trust and integrity are viewed as social imperatives in any educational setting. The benefits would be multiple…not only would the student truly learn the material more fully and thoroughly once the relationship "vessel" is healthy; s/he would also learn about how to relate; how to resolve conflicts; how to navigate in the world where we are relating with others on a daily basis. There is something deeply satisfying about getting our priorities straight, aligned with what makes intuitive sense and offers authentic empowerment to both teacher and student.

In viewing the relationship as a central dimension of education, and understanding that, much like a plant, this dimension requires care and attention, one ongoing question we can bring to our work as teachers and parents is: "What would be sun, rain and humus to this particular plant?" With an older student, this could even include getting together and having a conversation about the "plant" and what it needs. In very stuck relationships, where a lot of tension, mistrust and resentment have developed, a third person, such as a mediator or counselor, can accompany the involved parties in finding out what their "relationship-plant" needs, and help them implement this. By bringing awareness to the relationship as a "plant" that needs nourishment and care, as something between two individuals rather than attached to each of them, we already begin to untangle and create some breathing space in the dynamic.

By asking questions together about what could nurture the relationship, we move away from an accusing/defending stance and basically become a team, inquiring together into what is going on and what could shift: How is our relationship doing? What do you think it needs? How could we help it thrive? What could it grow into? Tending to relationships is an art that requires ongoing inquiry, patience, practice, and commitment.

In this way teaching, parenting, and their many tasks, such as providing instruction and guidance rest upon an authority that is gained through respect, trust, firm love, and care instead of fear and threat.

So, in summary, we put the relationship first: we check the temperature of the relationship, and if it needs some extra care, we offer that. This happens at the beginning of our time together, and may also be necessary every once in a while as the day/workshop/interaction continues. Ultimately and ideally there is an ongoing awareness in us as educators to gauge the intersubjective field and tend to it.

Meeting Self and Other as "Evolving Wholes"

This perspective was gained through two "Aha" moments. The first was over a decade ago, in a conversation with a father of six. We were speaking about meeting and interacting with children, whatever their age, as a whole person, a full human being, however little he or she may be. This resonated so deeply, and was an articulation of one of the keys I had intuitively brought to my relationships with kids since I was a teenager. I recognized it as one of the reasons children liked to hang out with me, and why I was fascinated and so enjoyed spending time with them—simply because I treated them as real people. Children can tell, they notice immediately whether we treat them as "just a kid" or as a full-fledged human being who deserves respect, attention and integrity regardless of their age.

The other insight came a few years later—after observing many a time that one-sidedly viewing and interacting with a child as a "whole person" and not considering their young age and still developing capacities can lead to overestimating a child, to accommodating them, but forgetting that they also need to learn how to adapt to the world and its social expectations.

Bringing these two dimensions of each human being together as we interact with our students and children facilitates healthy relationship. Try it out. Think of a student of yours. Or if you are not a teacher, think of any person you know and relate with. Close your eyes and imagine them sitting before you.

Now bring your awareness to the fact that they are a whole person. That there is an essential dimension to them that doesn't need fixing or changing. That is sacred, sovereign and perfect just as it is. Be present with them in this way. Notice what arises in you as you view them in this way. What might you want to say to them? What hand gesture might express this way of seeing and relating to them?

Next, bring your attention to their evolving nature, to that dimension of their being that is partial, that is developing, learning, making mistakes, and requires guidance. Be present to this aspect of their being—the "becoming" part of them. Notice what arises in your awareness as you perceive them in this way. What might you want to say to them? What hand gesture might express this way of seeing and relating to them?

Now bring these two perspectives together—allow them to exist simultaneously. The other, a student or child, as "evolving" and as "whole." Right now, right here, both dimensions present: the being and the being-in-the-becoming. How does that feel? What arises in you in relation to them when you hold both perspectives together?

If you discovered hand gestures to express each perspective respectively, offer one gesture with your right hand, the other with your left hand, and feel the dynamic energy between the two. Holding them together is not just adding one to the other. A "third" emerges. By joining them, they inform each other, and bring forth new possibilities. The opportunity and challenge to do so presents itself in every moment as we engage with each other.

We are late, the roads are snowy and I feel my anxiety level rising as my 5-year old daughter once again dawdles (whose perspective is that?) Looking at her you would never guess that we are supposed to be getting dressed to drive to town for her music class. She is standing in front of the mirror, contentedly viewing herself in a variety of positions, when, as I ask her for the fourth time, with a slight increase of impatience in my voice, to please get her boots and coat on, she remembers that she absolutely has to pack her dollies to bring along. "Adonia, that's enough, just get dressed and let's go!"

She looks up surprised, as if I just woke her out of a dream, her eyes looking worried, "But Mama, I can't leave without my dollies, they have to come too." So, here we are, I can go along with my current track of, "You don't get it, love, we are really late, and we must go NOW" which means forget the dollies, just get dressed and off we go, whether you like it or not, this is just the way things are. Or I can go with the opposite one of "OK, you can take your time, and we will get there when we get there, even if half the class is over..." Or I can take that third option, and bring the two perspectives together simultaneously to form a new path forward...I sit down, make eye contact, and lay my hand on her arm: "Hey, honey, listen for a moment. Class starts in an hour, it takes us almost that much time to get there and with snowy roads probably a bit longer. We had an agreement when you wanted to learn to play the harp and take music lessons that this involves practicing each day and attending your weekly lesson. I also understand that your dollies are important to you. So, can you run as quickly as possible, get the dolls, get dressed quick as lightning, and jump into the car?"

As soon as I kneel down, the energy changes, she feels I am seeking a solution with her that could work for both. "Yes, as quick as lightening!" she laughs as she races upstairs. We have fun with our breathless whirlwind of getting dressed and then, when we are finally driving to town, we go over what happened, what we can do to be less rushed in the future, and also that as soon as we park the car in town, we will be as quick as lightening again to make it to her class just in time! In this way we become a team, working together to navigate the various realities and perspectives present.

As you can see in the above example and as you reflect on the myriad daily situations you encounter with students, spouse and children, friends and relatives, a one-sided perspective of seeing the other as "evolving" likely gives rise to an impulse to provide direction, feedback, a firm boundary or correction. The perspective of seeing them as a "whole" on the other hand, enables us to feel a sense of honor, appreciation, and respect as we regard them. One-sided this can also lead us to be too lenient, to ignore unhealthy behavior. Then, as we bring the two perspectives together we can offer firm love, or loving firmness. Instead of delivering one or the other (love or firmness), the two responses can join and allow for a fuller meeting of and engaging with the other. The duality of being too strict/harsh or too lenient/soft can make way for a third path, one that consistently meets the other with respect and dignity, while also, in understanding the stage of development they are at, neither over- nor underestimates their capacities and thus can offer a healthy balance of support and challenge, which is what human beings thrive on.

Depending on the age of your students or children, what this balance will actually look like will vary. The developmental stages a human being grows through (one of the five basic elements of the integral framework) means that what our students and children need, in order to grow and learn, changes as they grow up. The fact that each of them is also a "whole," a subject, never an object, means that as we engage with them they always deserve respect and integrity, from the newborn to the teenager and adult.

When we also view ourselves as "evolving wholes"—as human "becomings"—we can both challenge ourselves to continuously improve, to stretch and grow in our work as teachers and parents, and we can offer kindness and compassion when we fail. Because integral education involves bringing more consciousness to everything we do as teachers and parents, we may eagerly aspire to achieve new ideals, but when we fall short (which each of us will undoubtedly at times,) we may fall into either giving up or feeling guilty. Offering kindness and forgiveness, while aspiring to do better allows us to continue onward and upward.

Awareness Practices

In the following I would like to share two awareness practices that can help us be in right relationship with our students and children.

One is to become increasingly aware of who we are (ultimately) and where we are coming from as we relate to our children and students. This is both a spiritual and psychodynamic practice, as it requires awareness of self and shadow.

Who am I, truly? Am I "Miriam," who grew up in Switzerland, was home-schooled and went to university in Zurich, loves dancing and singing, is a counselor, mother etc.? Yes, and … what is under all that? What lies beneath the various experiences and labels I identify my "me" with? What glimpses do I catch of myself in moments when I plunge deeper into my being? What is my true nature? When I am most authentic and present, who am I? Perhaps there are no, or little words to describe what we discover in those precious moments, but there is a self-sense, an experiential knowing. There are symptoms, "ingredients" to the recipe of dropping into our authentic self. The voice drops pitch, contraction in the body releases, awareness expands, self-concern recedes, presence increases...

As we learn to notice the difference in ourselves between our constructed frontal self and our deeper nature, we can increasingly choose "who" we bring forth in our teaching and parenting work. The more we can rest in our authentic self, the more present we are to others, and to our relationships with them. The more we remain in our egoic self, the more self-absorbed we tend to be and distracted from being fully present to who is before us in each moment.

The second practice is closely connected to the one above. It is a practice of being present to another by allowing ourselves to bring real awareness and attention to the other. To see them as if for the very first time with all our senses acutely present, heart and mind included. Leo Tolstoy says the most important person is the one you are with, in the present moment.

Try this—go find an exquisitely-smelling flower. Sit down with it, and simply smell it. Let its fragrance draw you in, forget yourself for a moment, let the fragrance take you over and in, inviting you to break through your habitual self-bubble. Notice how in doing so, you lose nothing of yourself that is truly you. Your unique "you" remains, better still, it expands as it is given space to be.

How often do we already formulate a response to a student before they are done speaking? What if we practice listening so fully and deeply that when it is time for us to speak we may ourselves be surprised by what we say? Or we might just be silent for a while...

Just as I was pausing, wondering how to bring this short article to a close, my daughter called me outside into the garden. She wanted to show me a surprise—a newly emerged snowdrop flower! I stooped down to smell it—exquisite indeed, a good one for the exercise above. We wandered through the garden and sat on the bench between the apple and plum trees. As I sat there with her, nestled close and listening to her merry account of afternoon adventures, my awareness toward our relationship was sharpened by my afternoon writing, and I noticed how viewing relationship as a cradle for education and for parenting invites us to become more present in mind and heart to the one before us. It is as much a mental focus that shifts, as it is a heart opening. It felt good. We got up, she squeezed my hand and skipped...yes, it felt good and right all around.

11

Classroom Conversation:
How to Move beyond Debate and Discussion and Create Dialogue

Jonathan Reams

One mark of an extraordinary class is great classroom conversation. Educators and students alike live for moments when the degree of engagement with whatever subject matter is at hand reaches an intensity and quality that is palpable. These "teachable moments" can take diverse forms, each offering different capacities for inquiry into truth. Experience has taught me the relative merits of various types of classroom conversation, and in this brief chapter I would like to offer some reflections on distinctions between these, focusing on the theoretical foundations of dialogue and a simple structured technique for creating a space for dialogue to emerge.

I will begin by briefly framing three notions of conversation that can be used in the classroom:

- debate,
- discussion, and
- dialogue.

Debate is a well-honed form of discourse in our society. For instance, the legal system is built upon the premise that advocating for opposing views can reveal the truth of matters. Students are often trained to use the techniques of debate to be able to advocate for a position, with a larger purpose of finding the truth through the weeding out of weaker arguments. This kind of advocating requires the student to have the capacity to take a perspective on the topic. It does not require, but can also benefit from, the student's capacity to take a perspective on how another person relates to the topic. Yet as Plato noted long ago, debate often falls prey to a kind of sophistry, or aiming to make the weaker argument appear stronger. Good lawyers defending their clients do this all the time. A kind of truth may emerge from this form of conversation, but not always, and not necessarily the kind of truth we may be looking for.

Discussion can offer a less adversarial approach to conversation and inquiry into truth. It can allow for more of a give and take of views on the topic, a degree of reflection on relative merits without the need for one's own views to be totally right. This more reflective capacity is contingent upon a greater degree of ability to take a perspective on one's own views. Thus at some point a person matures they outgrows an identification with views on a wide range of subjects. A person begins to realize that their views can change without them losing their sense of self. This often occurs in early adolescence, but also much later or never in some people. The broader scope of choices that emerge from this maturation process allows for a quality of discussion that can transcend the limitations of debate, and offer a different quality of truth to emerge.

Eventually, either through personal growth or exposure to other forms of conversation, students can find themselves feeling that there is even more to be learned, or that discussion is not the best way to get there. There can be a kind of flatness to the quality of conversation in discussion, an ability to inquire about factual truth, and even into a relational truth, but not an ability to get deeper under the surface of things, into the kinds of assumptions that are generating the views that we inhabit. At this stage there is not always much support for neither a deeper quality of inquiry, nor recognition of truth that is not merely factual or propositional. The norms of conversation in our society do not provide structured opportunities to direct our attention to the sources of our views, or our assumptions. A kind of inertia prevents us from being able to look inwardly for too long.

It is in addressing this need to counter such inertia and inquire into truth in a deeper way that can lead to <u>Dialogue</u>. As in the transition from <u>Debate</u> to <u>Discussion</u>, there is a further requirement involved for dialogue—an ability to entertain, or take a perspective on the constructed nature of our perception. To get a better idea of what is involved in making dialogue different than normal forms of conversation, I will outline some of the key elements that are foundational to the notion of dialogue I use.

Though the term dialogue is used in many ways today, I want to distinguish a very specific meaning of the term. Because this specific meaning is not common in our everyday language, it is easier to begin by contrasting what is not meant. Dialogue can be used to describe the linguistic aspects of performances such as plays, television shows and movies. It can be used to describe parties in conflict simply talking to one another. It can also be used to point to a more refined quality of conversation in a general way, indicating less of the adversarial positioning driving conversation. It can even be used to describe how an interest in mutuality can shape conversation. While there are areas of overlap between some of these other uses of the term dialogue and my intended meaning of the term, I will focus on what I have learned to be some of the more profound differences.

Dialogue, as explored by the late physicist David Bohm, (*On Dialogue*) and more recently carried forward by Bill Isaacs (*Dialogue and the Art of Thinking Together*) and Otto Scharmer (*Theory U*) is premised on a view grounded in understanding the essence of reality as unbroken wholeness. From this wholeness, thought makes maps, or abstracts limited images of reality, as it cannot comprehend the unlimited nature of reality directly. These images or maps then enter into perception. However, thought forgets that this process is happening, and takes instead its "perception" of the world as being "reality as it truly is." This process is ongoing, operates faster than we can normally be aware of, and leads to an assumption of perception being true, or coherent with reality.

Bohm perceived this unchecked functioning of thought to lead to fragmentation, wherein our perception of such wholeness becomes less and less coherent, and we see the world as fundamentally made up of pieces. Identifying with these "pieces" (such as an image of "self" that thought creates) tends to concretize the initial maps, images or assumptions of thought. In turn we then defend such perceptions, leading to all manner of incoherence, fragmentation, conflict and violence easily seen in the world at large today. This identifying with and defending of the perceptions of thought is what drives the intensity of debate and entrenched positions in discussion.

It is from this understanding of the operation of thought that Bohm proposed dialogue as a means to slow thought down sufficiently to bring direct and conscious awareness to this process while in operation. The images or assumptions that thought creates are part of an ongoing process. They become embedded with emotions and physiology, and develop complex layers of reflexes that reinforce and defend the process. We can temporarily reverse this by suspending what arises in thought, allowing ourselves to reflect on it and relax the defensive reflexes. We can do this anytime during the process. It is more important to change the direction of the process than to worry about how deep we might be into it at any given moment.

Once we begin this practice of suspension, we can start to peel back layer upon layer of reflexes and assumptions that mask clear or coherent perception. Our initial experience with noticing an assumption arising and then suspending it can jump-start the growth of our capacity to notice the reflexive process of thought at work. This experience can allow for an orientation of self-transcendence to emerge, building momentum in the transformation of consciousness.

So how can this transformative potential of dialogue be engaged? While there are not many possible routes into this process, and a number of pre-conditions that are not easy to articulate, nor are likely all known, I will mention two things I have found to be important orientations, and suggest a structured process for engaging in dialogue.

The first pre-condition is to have an attitude of humility of mind and openness to not knowing. It is the mind's certainty of knowing anything that stops genuine inquiry cold in its tracks. Knowing in the deeper sense is not a mental process, but a deeply spiritual one. It is this spiritual essence of our being that is able to pay attention to or witness thought in action, and is thus the source we cultivate through dialogue. A mental certitude about its own perceptions hardens the system of thought, and sets up its reflexes to defend that certitude against all perception to the contrary. Being open to not knowing allows the dialogue to be held in a state of inquiry, and makes it possible to question assumptions with the support needed to counter the defensive reflexes of thought as they engage.

The second issue around pre-conditions relates to the introductory remarks around the capacity to take a perspective on the process of thought constructing perception. The act of suspension, the ability to hold thoughts out in front of your perception and a central aspect of dialogue, can be more readily accessed if one has sufficient internal perspective-taking capacity. Engaging in a structured exercise can allow one to temporarily access deeper levels of perspective taking and enable this suspension.

Given these pre-conditions being met to the degree possible, I will describe some steps for introducing dialogue to a group of people. If it is a small group, it can be done all together. If there were more than six people involved, I would break them up into smaller groups of four to six.

I begin by explaining the basic principles involved around listening, both to who-ever is speaking and to what is arising internally within each participant. I introduce the practice of suspending what initially arises in thought to be able to reflect on it. I also introduce the use of taking deep breaths to anchor the process for suspending the reflexes of thought.

I then ask one person from each group to volunteer to answer a question that I will ask. Upon hearing the question, they are to take two deep breaths before an-swering. During the first breath, they are to notice what arises in thought, the first thing that comes to mind in response to the question. By simply noticing it while taking a deep breath, you are suspending it, as it were hanging it out in front of you to perceive it as something separate from your awareness of it. While taking a second deep breath, they are to direct attention to their solar plexus and become aware of what kind of sensation is present. While breathing and noticing this sensation, they are to allow a response to the question to arise from this place within them, and then to articulate the response to the group. The response may be the same as what first arose (and hopefully with a deeper quality of energy to it from the second breath,) or something new may arise to be spoken of to the group. When vocalizing, they are to speak to the center of the group, the collective, rather than to any one individual.

The group is to listen intently while the first person speaks, not allowing any re-flexes of thought that arise within them to be voiced. Instead, their aim is to simply notice these reflexes and allow them to flow through their awareness without letting them take their primary attention away from the speaking that is going on. When the first person is finished speaking, they are to take two more deep breaths and ask some other specific person in the group a question that arises for them. That new person will then take two deep breaths and go through the same process outlined above.

This procedure is repeated until everyone in the group has spoken. Once everyone has spoken, the process can continue on with this same structure. The group may find itself in a quiet and reflective enough space to move from asking specific people questions to placing a question and responses to it into the center of the group, and allowing responses to be guided by the movement of attention and awareness upstream to the source of what is arising in the collective space. The early practice of taking two deep breaths before speaking to the group can continue, building in a structured capacity for suspending assumptions and the deepening of the quality of presence and participation in the dialogue.

My experience has been that it can take a group of four people up to an hour to simply move through the first round of everyone speaking. The opportunity to speak uninterrupted to a group who is intently listening is a rare one in our society and classrooms today, and people often find it very liberating. Once what we have spoken is "out of our system" so to speak, there is space for new insights to reveal themselves to us. It is also common to have insights arise while listening deeply and observing the flow of conversation. The method described here is not the only way for dialogue to happen, nor is it essential for it. It is one way to create a "liberating structure" for students to experience a quality of conversation in the classroom that can link them with deeper aspects of themselves and truth.

In my experience using this method in the classroom I have found several signs of how it has enabled students to move beyond debate and discussion. Beginning with the contrast of when a group struggles with the process, it is easy to notice their conversation moving quicker as they go along. The pitch and tone rises in a more staccato like tempo. The momentum of the conversation carries it forward so that participants drift into the kind of discussion that is more the norm of conversation.

For those groups who are able to engage this process, a number of shifts can be observed. The conversations often shift to a more reverent tone. There is more silence. There can be a palpable feeling of quality, depth and authenticity to the energy in the room. It often opens up new insights and spaces for reflection. A brief example arose when one student reported that while listening to another student speak of some difficulties in her life, she assumed that she needed to voice her feelings of support in order for them to be felt. However, upon describing her feeling around this (rather than simply voicing her support), the student who had been speaking said that this was not necessary, that the feeling of support was clearly present for her without it being voiced. From this the group saw how suspending the reflex to act on the assumption of needing to voice her support allowed the space for reflecting on this reflex and having its truth disconfirmed by the other student.

Moments of conversation like this, with the qualities of authenticity, reverence and openness that can arise from using this method for dialogue can make for extraordinary classroom experiences. Students can come away with not only new information and knowledge, but also insights into themselves and the world around them that can transform their capacity for coherent action in the world. In this way dialogue can help classroom conversations transcend the limitations of debate and discussion, and open new spaces for learning.

12

The Peace Bench:
A Kindergarten Class Adventure

Nancy Simko

With over fifteen years of teaching experience under my belt, it came as no surprise when the thirteen five year olds who comprise Blue School Kindergarten began arguing, having difficulty turn-taking, being traumatized by sharing, and basically relentlessly saying that life was not fair. We spent many morning meetings talking with the children about their disagreements, and helping them discern between "small problems" (those which they could solve independently) and "big problems" (those which require teacher intervention.) We found that the children could usually tell the difference between the two types of problems, but that there was often no place to go, nowhere sacred and quiet and special, to work things out with a friend. The children decided that they needed to build a Peace Bench.

These particular children are a community of builders, so the prospect of actually constructing a piece of furniture filled them with excitement. They wanted to begin right away! It became immediately evident that their excitement led to even more arguments, as they each tried to share their plans for the bench. It was decided that we needed to research the topics of benches in order to see how they differ structurally and aesthetically. We used the computer to find benches made of everything from recycled pencils to iron to plastic. With these ideas in their heads, the children arrived at school one morning to find clipboards and a wide variety of wood planks and blocks in the center of the room. Their task was to construct a temporary bench from the wood, and sketch the plan for future reference. This activity led to many discussions about the shape of the bench. Should it have arms? How many legs did it need? How about pillows? We instituted a democratic voting process to decide on a bench with sturdy legs, a plank for sitting, and no arms.

It would have been easy to simply build the bench from this moment, but as an educator I decided to use this opportunity to introduce the mathematics of measurement. The class was asked how big the bench needed to be to seat two kids comfortably, and each child was given masking tape to lay down the length he/she felt necessary to make an appropriate sized seat. The children then pondered how to measure their individual tape strips. Some suggested measuring with their feet, others suggested measuring with hand spans, and one child even wanted to measure with his head! Over the course of several days the class measured each other's strips using various body parts, only to find that they came up with different answers. Apparently, feet, hands and heads are not standard units of measure!

Rulers were then introduced to the class and we spend several days introducing the concepts of inches and a foot, and we practiced using these new tools to measure everything from our shoes to paper snakes. When the children were then asked to take their rulers and measure their tape strips, they found them to be too small, and hence we introduced tape measures. It was great fun to see the class venture out into the school, tape measures in hands, to measure the kitchen, the cabinets, each other, and even try to measure floor to ceiling!

Finally, they were able to measure their tape strips. I found the children, as a whole, to be extremely perceptive to the correct measurement of the bench. They could tell which tape strips were too short and would crowd the sitters, and which strips were too long, giving the children too much space to resolve conflict. It was a good day indeed when the children unanimously agreed upon a bench that would be 32 inches in length. On that day, I remember thinking that this form of collaborative exploration, experimentation, and discovery was not only a wonderful learning tool, but also empowered the children as they worked toward a greater good.

During the weeks spent measuring, the children also became adept at using tools. We introduced hammers and a tree stump, and were amazed at the children's hand-eye coordination, along with their sheer determination to get nails in the wood, and to get them in straight. Anyone observing their class could see how the children assumed roles of importance as they donned safety goggles and used real tools. In addition to hammering, they practiced using a level and sawing.

The big day came, and we were thrilled when our art specialist arrived at the door with a gift: two small tree stumps. She asked if we needed them for our bench. The class immediately opted to use them as legs. Later that day we took a trip to the hardware store to get the rest of our wood. As other projects progressed, the children did all of the work. With adult supervision, they measured the plank of wood, and sawed it to the right length. They sanded, and found it to be hard work. They nailed the legs on, and made sure the seat of the bench was level. Plus they did it all without fighting. They took turns, they shared, they helped each other, and they had fun doing it!

The bench was complete, but it needed to be painted. We asked the class, "Does peace have a color?" They responded with beautiful answers: peace is light yellow like my mommy's tummy when I rest my head on her; peace is blue as the ocean, peace is green like a new leaf. The children had so many wonderful ideas. It was difficult to decide which color would be best for the Peace Bench. Finally, one girl in the class suggested we paint the seat with rainbow stripes so that everyone would feel happiness when they sat on the bench. The bench was painted, and the children were so very proud of the work they had accomplished, and in a spirit of giving, they made the choice to present the Peace Bench as a gift to Blue School.

The Peace Bench: A Kindergarten Class Adventure

Inquiry:

After several days of small social conflicts among the Kindergarten, we asked: Can we build a place where two children can come together to talk, solve problems, or agree to disagree?

Integrated Learning:

Emergent Curricular Unit includes research and planning, representational drawing, expressive and receptive language skills, mathematical concepts of estimation and length, emotional development, gross motor skills and hand/eye coordination.

Skills:

- Scientific research, observation and documentation
- Utilizing mathematical skills involving estimation and length
- Internalizing vocabulary associated with research and math
- Exploring conflict resolution
- Individual and collaborative work
- Engaging in woodworking
- Artistic expression
- Emotional exploration
- Songs, stories and poems associated with peace keeping

Learning activities:

1. Using books, magazines, and the computer, research the different ways in which benches are constructed.
2. Build prototypes of benches out of blocks and wood planks.
3. Document prototypes with representational plans.
4. Introduce mathematical concept of estimation. Using masking tape, children estimate how long bench needs to be to seat two children.
5. Introduce mathematical concept of measurement.
6. Explore different ways to measure tape estimations (with hand spans, feet, heads).
7. Introduce rulers, and accompanying vocabulary (inches, foot).

8. Practice utilizing rulers by measuring paper snakes and shoes.
9. Introduce tape measure, and practice measuring each other, different areas of school.
10. Democratically agree on length of bench.
11. Introduce tools. Practice hammering, sawing, using a level.
12. Class trip to a local hardware store to purchase wood planks.
13. Woodworking: saw plank, hammer onto legs.
14. Explore emotional concept of color in relation to what color the bench should be painted.
15. Represent colors and emotions through paintings and storytelling.
16. Introduce voting process. Hold election to determine color of bench.
17. Collaborate on painting bench.
18. Discussion, documentation, and recording of children's emotional relationships to the concepts of giving and getting.
19. Present Peace Bench as gift to school.

Understandings:

• Communication is often the best way to resolve social conflict

Editor's Commentary

While I acknowledge that there are twenty elements to the AQAL Framework in an educational critique, this brief analysis will emphasis the four quadrants, developmental levels, and learning types. Given the early stage of development of these learners, the most salient aspects of the activity light up in these areas.

From an integral perspective, this story about the children at the Blue School contains all four of the elements that comprise the four quadrants. In the upper left quadrant, the individual interior aspect of an educational lesson, Nancy provided the kids with an opportunity to reflect on a question, otherwise called contemplative inquiry: "Does peace have a color?" They responded with beautiful answers, "Peace is light yellow like my Mommy's tummy when I rest my head on her. Peace is blue as the ocean. Peace is green like a new leaf."

The children also engaged in critical reflection, to discern between "small problems," those that they could solve independently, and "big problems," those which would require teacher intervention. Nancy reported, "We found that the children could usually tell the difference between the two types of problems, but that there was often no place to go, nowhere sacred, quiet and special to work things out with a friend. The children decided that they needed to build a peace bench." Thus, they had the opportunity to gain an awareness of each other's opinions about this idea for a bench.

The kids used experiential knowing to gain insight about the nature of measurement, using their new tools, body parts, and masking tape strips. They learned how to consider their options about the use of various materials, tools and strategies.

In the upper right quadrant, where one would consider the educational behavior of the educator, we can easily observe the decision making process that Nancy facilitated. She described a democratic process for deciding: what was needed, how to build it, what materials to use, what color to paint it, and where to put the bench. She characterized the process in this way: "It was decided that we needed to research the topics of benches in order to see how they differ structurally and aesthetically. We used the computer to find benches made of everything from recycled pencils to iron to plastic." Following this the class constructed a model and sketched a plan.

In the lower left quadrant, the domain of the collective interior or cultural meaning-making system, we can observe the ethical participation, perspectival embrace and the connective encounters that this lesson expressed. Ethical participation in a kindergarten class would sound something like this: "... one girl in the class suggested we paint the seat with rainbow stripes so that everyone would feel happiness when they sat on the bench. The bench was painted, and the children were so very proud of the work they had accomplished; and in a spirit of giving, they make the choice to present the Peace Bench as a gift to Blue School." The values expressed in this statement reflect sensitivity to each individual child's creative expression, while considering the overall goal to create harmony for the whole class in the path forward.

Perspectival embrace, the capacity to include the input of multiple perspectives, is expressed in the same statement, in that each child's preferred color is included in the final color choices for the bench. There is a consideration for everyone's perspective, and each child is part of the collective whole. This example of perspectival embrace is limited to the community of students, while a wider embrace would also include the school, the local societal community, the global community and the universe.

Connective encounters in this class's experience are characterized by the collective decisions made by the children, the trips to the hardware store, and conversations that inevitably occurred while building the bench and painting the bench.

The lower right quadrant, the domain of the collective exterior, includes the *systems* in place that support an educational experience. This quadrant is characterized by the functional fit of the social system/s and the environment, to include the physical arrangement. One could say that the Peace Bench itself is an addition to the physical arrangement of the school, while simultaneously being a result of the values, behavior and insight enacted by the class and its teacher, Nancy.

The children's developmental levels were incorporated into the task. They were given the opportunity to engage in an experiential lesson with the appropriate level of supervision, support and challenge, resulting in a sense of ownership for the bench that was collaboratively created: a delightful discovery process!

Learning types are a particularly helpful addition to curriculum design and activity facilitation by the AQAL Framework. When we can include the particular methods that captivate an individual child as well as a small group by providing a multisensory learning opportunity, the potential for creating a state of flow for more than one type of student is exponentially higher. Generating multisensory learning experiences is the fine art of an educator, and the peace bench is an extraordinarily good example of tapping into logical-mathematical, kinesthetic, spatial, social, linguistic, interpersonal and intrapersonal forms of intelligence. Howard Gardener's theory of multiple intelligences points to eight ways of knowing, and at least seven of these are clearly represented in this single task.

Seven kinds of intelligence would allow seven ways to teach, rather than one. And powerful constraints that exist in the mind can be mobilized to introduce a particular concept (or whole system of thinking) in a way that children are most likely to learn it and least likely to distort it. Paradoxically, constraints can be suggestive and ultimately freeing.

—Smith

Ultimately, freedom is what that most of us desire, while teaching and while learning.

13

The Invisible Children:
A Parable in Which the Invisible Become
Visible, and the Visible Invisible

Sue Stack

"It is all your fault," Tracey shouted angrily at me. "You have given me writer's block, you have made me look stupid in front of my boyfriend, you have..."

It went on and on—a litany of all my wrongs throughout the whole year. We were standing privately in the corner of the large graphics room. Tracey's histrionics were largely ignored by her classmates who were busily working on computers. It was just another episode in the life of a drama queen, and by now everyone had experienced being the brunt of one of Tracey's projections of blame.

A wave of angry twirling energy was hitting me and, despite my past experiences with this kind of an attack, I could still feel myself shaking, low on resilience today, trying to breathe, trying not to get sucked into Tracey's drama, trying to see deeper and find a path forward. However, that transformative position was beyond me, and I found myself simply struggling not to react to all of her outrageous claims. I admit to trying to calm her down. Perhaps another strategy might have taken her out of the contracted moment and space, and enabled her to see herself more clearly. For while she seemed highly visible to us, with her contradictions laid bare, she seemed to be largely invisible to herself. She was equally dismissive of those aspects of self she could be proud of as well as those more negative aspects that lead to her blaming others.

It was the Year 11/12 Journalism—Media Production class and we had just put the yearbook to bed (it was at the printers.) Now the students were working on the launch extravaganza and getting their folios up to date. I had been going around to each student checking in with them to ensure they met all the criteria before the end of the year, which was only three weeks away.

Going through my checklist, I had said to Tracey that she had yet to show evidence on Criteria 9 "Taking something from an idea all the way to final product." Perhaps there was an article that she would like to finish (she had started many) and put on the class e-zine? Maybe I could have predicted her eruption and had that conversation privately, or tried to say it in a different way. Yet what was remarkable about this class was their growing meta-cognition skills: their ability to reflect honestly about their performances, to name their strengths and weakness, give useful feedback to each other, and to reflect on how their thinking and being was changing and growing. I wasn't saying anything about her; it was about her folio, wasn't it?

But Tracey had yet to reach this sense of detachment and maturity that the others had gained. Her sense of self—who and what of herself she could see—seemed to be deeply entangled with her behaviors and her products. Sometimes she seemed to lift above it with the aid of meta-cognitive processes and see herself honestly. Other times she seemed entrenched in her own perspectives and dramas, working herself into a state, regressing deeper and deeper, black and white, unaware that others had different perspectives and experiences of the same event.

I was still shaking from my "moment" with Tracey when I sat down at one of the classroom tables next to Jillian, my student teacher. I put my head in my hands and sighed. Jillian seemed really angry too, as she exclaimed, "I would like to throttle that girl, I just can't stand her. She is the most self-centric, egotistical girl I have known. She shows absolutely no respect, she needs to grow up! I don't know how you put up with it."

"Maybe I should have throttled her!" I said smiling wryly. "What I am currently doing is not working!" I sighed. Tracey and I had a year-long history, which no doubt had contributed to this "moment." Tracey had been quite depressed over the previous few months, dealing with feelings of suicide. She refused to see any counselors and I had been giving her quite a bit of support. There was a fine line here between my role as her teacher, or as "a significant other," or supportive friend, or someone who perhaps can help "lead her out" from diminishing behavior patterns or cultures and help her into healthy ways of being. Perhaps the breakdown in our relationship was a blurring of those lines, with Tracey not understanding which role I was playing.

What is my role as a teacher and what is my locus of care? Surely it is more than just asking, "How can I best help this student pass this subject?" Do I have responsibility to come to know my students and to see beneath their surfaces? And once I do, what then? Gordon (2008) suggests 8 key roles for integral teachers:

- The gardener ("I" inner): facilitating the inner flourishing of students—developing fallow, healthy line, state, and quadrant potentials; introducing the learner to life-enhancing knowledge, insights, frameworks, "stories," and metaphors; helping the learner to extend these and current line abilities across AQAL domains; helping the learner to incorporate the partial truths of split-off lower levels and exclude the limitations of these levels; and creating a climate of psychological safety.

- The alchemist ("I" outer): drawing forth the inner evolution of students into new levels, especially, eliciting higher stages of the cognitive, perspective-taking line; preparing the ground for the transformation of lines; and moving lagging lines and type up to the level of the learner's current cognitive development.
- The health ally ("IT" inner): supporting, encouraging, or directly enabling the health and healing of the various levels of the learner's body, including the brain.
- The coach ("IT" outer): stimulating the learner's stretching to optimum bodily functioning and the next stage of body and brain development.
- The initiator ("WE" inner): initiating learners into their culture(s)' unique, interior ways of inhabiting AQAL world spaces and honoring the life-enhancing aspects of these.
- The liberator ("WE" outer): releasing students from exclusive identification with their culture(s)' unique, interior ways of inhabiting AQAL world spaces by helping learners transcend the limitations of these perspectives.
- The citizen ("ITS" inner): reproducing the unique, exterior ways the learner's society (e.g., societal institutions, systems, and roles) inhabits world spaces; helping learners to embody life-enhancing societal aspects.
- The activist ("ITS" outer): freeing students from reproducing the life-diminishing aspects of their society's unique, exterior ways of inhabiting world spaces by empowering learners to transcend the limitations of these in embodied ways.

Was I trying too hard in being the "alchemist" with Tracey, helping her to rise to new perspectives beyond her capacity to do so? How do I walk the path of being an Integral Teacher with ethical tactfulness? (Stack 2007) Am I overstepping the mark when I take these roles on? How do I ensure I am not making too many assumptions about my students (their learning and being) or taking on roles, which are not wanted by them? How do I pay attention to my own states and development? What might it mean for all of us to make the invisible visible and thus to liberate ourselves?

Yet, for many in my class, they had already experienced a key liberation moment that had set the tone for the rest of the year. Mid-way through the year, I asked the students to reflect upon their audience for their e-zine: "Who are they, how might we demarcate different audience groups, and how do we profile them?" What came out initially were two key categories— "normals" and "alternatives." All my students saw themselves as "alternatives" and felt alienated from "normals." In fact many of them felt invisible in their other classes and around the school. When I asked the class to look at the sub-cultures within the two groups they came up with a list: emos, Teenie-Boppy-Plastic (TBP), alienated TBP, musos, jocks, hippies, ethnics, Christians, stoners, Goths, nerds, teachers' pets, gays, deep thinkers, comedians. They were at first quite derogatory about some of the cultures, particularly the teenie-boppie-plastic, which they saw as shallow consumers trapped in media images of themselves.

I then gave each student a profile sheet to fill in, and each one selected a category, which they most related to. They made comprehensive profiles on what people wear, watch, eat, read, how they relate to others, aspirations and issues they have, what they are most afraid of…etc. In the course of filling out the profile questions their derogatory comments transformed into more compassionate and insightful ones. We discussed how much they identified with the culture they had chosen… and a sense emerged that these were stereotypes, yet which held an element of truth. To what extent were they captive to their sub-culture and could they move outside of it?

The immediate effect was that one girl ("Christian" and "teachers' pet") started to find her own voice and search for alternative perspectives. Another boy ("comedian") immediately stopped his disruptive behavior and set goals for what he wanted to achieve from the class. Am I playing the "liberator" role here or perhaps orchestrating an opportunity for students to liberate themselves?

The cultural metaphors then became a springboard for stories for the e-zine, they informed students' thinking when writing articles, enabled new ideas for articles to be generated. I realized that my students had a deep need for meaning and soul expression—to dive deep into the invisible layers of the world and to be creative with what they found. When we were asked to take on the yearbook I realized how the conventional form of collating teachers' stories and information would be soul destroying for us all and we needed an opportunity to express our creativity. We decided that the notion of school culture should become the creative concept underpinning the yearbook. So rather than the yearbook recording what college students had done throughout the year, our informing question was "How could a yearbook capture school culture, of which the student "sub-cultures" were just one aspect?" What did we value in our college culture and how could we express this in creative ways?

The yearbook evolved into 24 pages of vibrant color and graphics with a distinctive "mood," complete student voice and an accompanying DVD. Students created stories, interviews, student sound bites, and graphics. They used unusual and engaging photographs (e.g. of zombies, the principal with a spade burying students.) They used game metaphors to express the journey through two years of college. They also created a photographic comic of a girl "LOST" who explores the different sub-cultures before she decides to just be herself. They owned the yearbook, and they wanted to launch it in a spectacular way…

So here I am now, sitting with Jillian, as students around me are creating the signage, planning the balloons which will fall from the balcony of the school theatre, looking at the DVD footage that will launch the book, and practicing with the megaphone their sales pitch for when the other students will leave the theatre "Don't miss out on your yearbook…imagine looking back on school in 50 years' time…laugh at your friends…laugh at yourself…and look at how far you have come…!"

Jillian is still talking angrily. "And I also can't stand Samantha; I would like to shake her as well."

I am completely thrown. "Why?" I ask.

"She swans in an hour late, no apology, smug, superior…"

"But Samantha is one of my success stories...You should have seen her at the beginning of the year. She has been very ill, and has a long way to get to school, having to get up at 5:30am to get here on time. She used to try to be invisible, hiding behind a veil of hair, disappearing into the wall. Yes, she was late today but she came in full of energy, asking what she could do. That is a complete turn around from the lethargic person she used to be. The yearbook has provided something meaningful for her to be involved with."

"Oh! When I saw her picture on the front cover of the yearbook I just thought she was an exhibitionist..."

The picture on the cover of the yearbook was carefully constructed after much thought and discussion. We wanted to represent the experiences students had in their rite of passage during their college years (years 11/12). Samantha is standing naked facing a mirror, her arms crossed in front of her breasts—we only see her back. The picture we see facing us in the mirror is Samantha in her own individual clothes—standing tall and strong. Samantha was perfect for this picture because her own rite of passage was about visibility and seeing, searching and becoming.

"You know," I say to Jillian, "It sounds strange, but for me teaching has a lot to do with personal development. You can't be a teacher without opening yourself to growing, to learning...particularly when you see your students—not just as students, but also as your teachers. It is those students with whom you have the most emotional relationships who are often the most significant for you. When I am all stirred up by a student, I ask myself what is it in them that they are mirroring for me about my own insecurities, weaknesses, or aspects that I might be suppressing (whether good or bad.) One reason I don't throttle Tracey is that I am trying to understand what buttons she is pressing in me (perhaps calling up my own relationship with my mother?) Deep down, she is very insecure and frightened. There is an aspect of me which is also unconfident, and when I hear her negative self-talk it reminds me that I tend to do the same to myself."

Jillian looks at me, but doesn't say anything. A student calls to me, asking for help, and I stand up and move away.

Next lesson, after the initial start-up, there is a bit of quiet time, and Jillian comes over to me.

"I decided to do a reflection based on the last lesson," she says. "I have written it down and would like to read it to you."

"Go on," I say, surprised but becoming aware that what Jillian is about to do is actually going out on a limb for her. We sit quietly and she reads. She reflects on why she got so upset about Samantha. She picks up on the theme of invisibility.

"I realize now that I am essentially invisible to this class. This is basically what I wanted, to sit in the background and just observe, but now I realize I resent this. I want to be seen by the students and be part of what they are doing."

There is much more, and I listen hard. I know this is a significant teaching moment, a healing moment. I ask Jillian what she would like to do now. She decides to work with Samantha on creating the banners. Over the next week our conversations about pedagogy, the nature of teaching/learning and relationships grow in depth. Students give feedback on what they want in a teacher-student relationship. Jillian comes back especially for the launch, even though her practicum is finished, because for her it is now also a celebration of her rite of passage, not just the students'. She too has become visible.

A few days after the highly successful launch, my students have taken on an energy and visibility that I haven't seen before. For the first time they seem like a coherent team with a purpose, rather than individuals doing their own thing. The yearbook has created major contention within the school. Many teachers hate it, and one boy says that a teacher said, "What are you carrying that piece of rubbish around for—the only place for it is in the bin!" As the other students hear this they get riled up, "Tell him to f$%k off!" However, at no time is their confidence in what they have done shattered. I am really surprised because I admit to having serious doubts about whether we had gone too far. But no, they tell me how they have seen students all over the school reading the yearbook, how so many of them have said how good it is. "It is a generation thing," says one student patting my shoulder. They are standing tall, loud and proud. I admit to being astonished. It is their moment and they have grabbed it.

This is just one peak experience—an opportunity to glimpse what you can do and how you can influence others (changing the world had become an articulated intention of the class during the year.) Have they now discovered the "activist" role? But where does it lead? Is it sustained? What happens when the invisible and visible support disappears? What happens when it is not so clear what to fight for? What happens when the mundane overcomes the creative?

One thing I learnt was how much these students craved for creativity, for expression of their souls. Many were deeply spiritual and felt suppressed, marginalized and worn down by the grind, boredom, triviality and lack of meaning of their usual classroom experiences. How can education inspire, and help our invisible students shine? I also realize how important it is to artfully integrate authentic experience with metacognitive processes. It was so important for these students to try on the different identities and roles that creating an e-zine or a yearbook gave them. In doing this in a safe, playful environment they were then able to name other "identities" and roles, and actually move on from them. Well, most of them. Tracey was still very much trapped in the roles she played.

What happened to Tracey? The following year her reputation preceded her into her new classes. Teachers withdrew their emotional availability to her as she continued her dramas, projected blame and took no responsibility for herself. The highly visible has now become invisible. Who cares? How much can a teacher take on? Whose responsibility is it? Yet Tracey is still a human being, someone who deserves to be seen. How might you help Tracey "lighten" up the dark patches within her soul and help her glimpse that deep, invisible self and claim it?

And what of me? Have I resolved any better the dilemmas I face in adopting multiple roles and responsibilities in the classroom? Am I trapped by my expectations of the roles of an integral or holistic teacher? Can I walk lightly, dance across many identities, and continue to stretch and grow, and forgive myself for the imperfect being I am, for the students I fail to help or fail to connect with? But I am not walking the path alone. When I sit quietly I know that the gifts I have to offer will connect with some, not others, and their gifts may lie unseen by me but seen by another. Perhaps the failure (if there is such a thing) is in not making the effort to look.

14

A Frothy Edge

Andrew Suttar

Do you remember the moment you first saw a soap bubble—that fascination, that wonder, that awe?

I'm Andrew Suttar, aka Dr. Froth, a bubbleologist and integral educator. My involvement with bubbles began when I was in 11th grade and our physics class had the opportunity to choose any science topic for an in-depth self-directed investigation. I chose to investigate superior soap bubble recipes. At that time, I had a vision that everything in the universe, from microscopic atoms and cells to macroscopic stars and galaxies, was made up of bubble-like structures. As I came to understand the principles of energy conversation that explain a soap bubble's minimal surface form, I began to recognize those principles in other, apparently unrelated phenomena. You could say I began to see bubbles everywhere.

It was a paradigm shift. My new paradigm was bubble shaped, with me occupying the center. I experienced myself as a bubble, with an inner world, a skin or membrane, and an outer world. When I felt confident, my bubble expanded. When I felt vulnerable, it contracted. When I felt open, it became more permeable. These days, I play with these terms to create new words, such as expanda-bubble, vulnera-bubble, contracta-bubble, permea-bubble, and invinci-bubble to help simplify and clarify these concepts for people from all walks of life.

I thoroughly enjoy playing with meaning-making and I firmly believe this playful joy accelerates my continued learning. When I was young, my dad often said, "You never really realize how much you know until you have to teach it to someone else." Over the past 15 years, I have been exploring and extending my bubble model, using it to teach and seeing how far it can reach. This has become my life's work. I have developed a broad spectrum of products and services; on any given day, I might perform a show for children in the morning, write educational science investigations using soap bubbles in the afternoon, and address business people about "how

135

everyone lives in his or her own little bubble and the difficulties this brings to communication" in the evening.

In this chapter, I describe how I have appropriated the integral framework into this bubble. Having adjusted components of the framework here and there to bring the two models together, I offer bubbleology to you as a fascinating example of integral consciousness. I hope you enjoy and find it useful in your work.

Principles of Bubbleology

I began to put bubbleology and integral theory together after I read Ken Wilber's *A Brief History of Everything*. Wilber describes the 20 tenets shared by all holons, and I found these to be almost identical to the bubble principles I had discovered. The term *holon*, first coined by Arthur Koestler in his 1967 book *The Ghost in the Machine*, is anything that is simultaneously a whole and a part. For example, an atom is both an individual whole unit and also part of a molecule. In fact, everything can be thought of as a holon. I would say that the structure of a holon is simultaneously microcosm, membrane, and macrocosm; that is, the same as a soap bubble.

A wonderful discovery for me was the term homo bulla, or "man is a bubble," an idea popularized by Dutch vanitas painters during the 17th century, who used bubbles as a symbol for the brevity of life. The vanitas tradition continues today and circles around the theme of the impermanent nature of vanity. Similarly, Buddhist sutras state that the body "is like a water bubble, not remaining very long," and advise the wise person to regard life as they would "the appearance and disappearance of a bubble of water" (Thurman, 1976).

This, then, is the essential principle of bubbleology: the bubble structure (i.e., microcosm, permeable membrane, and macrocosm) is the basic structural unit of life. From biological cells to ecosystems to housing and stock market bubbles, all units are subject to expansionary and contractionary forces that find a resolution through some kind of dynamic balances. Although at first it may appear that these dynamics involve quite complex principles, when a lay person learns about and experiments with bubbles, and then looks for bubble-like phenomena in the world around, these principles become readily accessi-bubble.

My approach, in a nutshell, is to teach students the principles of soap bubbles and then show them that those principles are manifest everywhere. No matter the topic, if students understand and can identify the bubble principles, they can orientate themselves quickly within the given context. The result is that they have a cornerstone of understanding from which to approach a new topic or discipline. The process involves a simple translation and extension of their current understanding, rather than a complete uptake of something new or abstract.

Bubble AQAL: Using Bubbles to Frame Perspectives

Bubbleology can be used to better understand each of the four AQAL quadrants. I have developed specific exercises and techniques to help students in this process of exploration. A summary for each quadrant follows.

Interior Individual (Upper Left). Applying the bubble paradigm led to a richer experience of my inner world. I began to think of the way I perceive myself, my self-image, as the inside surface of the me-bubble. I saw the way others perceive me as the outer surface of the me-bubble. I realized that the bubble model offers a great tool to frame a healthy, flexible, and resilient self-image and ultimately a greater understanding of one's psyche.

To this end, I developed a bubble meditation that leads people through a vivid experience of their sense of self. Meditators begin by visualizing themselves inside a bubble. Then they experiment with adjusting the size, permeability, color, temperature, and texture of their bubble and experience the incredible malleability of their internal state. I have also incorporated some neuro-linguistic programming (NLP) techniques to help meditators anchor positive internal states.

Interior Cultural (Lower Left). Bubble visualizations and analogies can help us understand collective holons, particularly with respect to culture and relationships. In both cases, we develop a relational identity; that is, as part of a group or in a relationship.

To extend the bubble-membrane visualization, I use a well-known children's toy—a plastic sphere with circular-, triangular-, and square-shaped holes on its surface through which children put circular-, triangular-, and square-shaped pieces. The triangular piece fits through the triangular hole, but not the square or circle, and so on. This serves as a simplified model for how our bubble-membrane, or meme-brane, filters information. The shapes that fit through the holes are *memes*, units of meaning specific to a particular culture (or relationship); to derive an accurate meaning (i.e., within that culture), we need to match the shapes and holes. If the match between the information and our filtration system is not exact, some of the intended communication is lost.

Collective Exterior (Lower Right). The phenomenon of the stock market bubble is a superb example of a social holon. Seen from a lower-right perspective, a stock market bubble is created by over-inflated perceptions of value within the market culture (lower left.) Sudden contractions in the shared perception of value can cause the stock market to collapse, as we have seen. The techno-economic and social effects (lower right) of these contractions demonstrate the interrelationship between the interior and exterior of social holons in a most fascinating and dramatic way.

Exterior Individual (Upper Right). The correspondence between the physical and chemical properties of soap bubbles and those of cell membranes is well established in the field of biological science. The structural arrangement of detergent and water molecules in soap bubbles is so similar to the structure of cell membranes that bubbles are regularly used as a simple model to introduce students to the field of biological membranes. The differences between soap bubbles and cell membranes present an important starting point in developing an understanding of the complex inner workings of modern biological cells and even of abiogenesis (the study of the origins of life.)

Soap bubbles are wonderful for numerous upper-right quadrant science lessons. I frequently use an exercise that looks at the permeability of membranes. Because it is heavier than air, carbon dioxide sits at the bottom of a glass aquarium. When I blow bubbles into the aquarium, they float on top of an invisible sea of carbon dioxide. After a few hours, students see that the soap bubbles sink. This occurs because carbon dioxide is able to leech into a bubble through its soap film wall, without popping it.

In another activity, students blow the largest hemispherical bubble they can (on a table) with a single lungful of air. After fully expelling their lungs, they pop the bubble. Left behind is a ring of suds, showing the bubble's perimeter, which they then measure. They calculate the volume of air in the bubble, which gives them their lung capacity. Students then run around the school track or engage in some other form of cardiovascular activity, after which they repeat the bubble blowing experiment and discover a startling increase in their lung capacity. Variations on this activity include tracking the results over time and tracking the results in conjunction with heart rate measurements.

Yet another activity consists of adjusting conditions (e.g., humidity) to improve the sustainability of soap bubbles. With some simple household items and a little systems science, students can create bubbles that last for days.

Levels

Many developmental theorists agree the stages of human development are largely universal. In general, most concur everyone begins at an egocentric level and progresses through ethnocentric and on to world-centric levels. I view these levels as existing in the psyche of all humans as potentials, much as electron-shell potentials surround an atom's nucleus. As we accumulate experiences, they fall into electron-shell-like orbits (i.e., our memory.) Our mind sorts these experiences and organizes them into an array of associations. This is how I understand what constructivists call *scaffolding*.

For example, in March 1997 I had a dream about a car accident that was so strong it woke me violently 10 minutes before my alarm clock was set to ring. I remember using that extra 10 minutes to reflect on my dream over toast and coffee. Four months later I had the accident exactly as it appeared in my dream: same car, same road, same distractions. The moment I realized it was happening, I popped out of my bubble. I had been very confident in my understanding of the world and knew science well, particularly physics, yet the experience of the accident did not belong to that world. For the first time in my life I had a completely real experience, one that was utterly illogical. I spent much of the next three months in a wheelchair contemplating it. I distinctly remember my mind's attempt to make sense of the experience. The only frame of reference I had was déjà vu, yet the logic required for me to understand *déjà vu* was insufficient to interpret the experience of having the car accident I had dreamt.

Toward the end of a bubble session, after showing a tetrahedron, cube, and dodecahedron-shaped bubble, I usually run an activity that demonstrates levels. I say, "Okay folks, it's time to go inside a bubble. But the question is, who gets to go into the bubble first? To answer this, we are going to a have quiz with just one question. You have seen the tetrahedron, cube, and dodecahedron-shaped bubbles; now tell me, how many surfaces does a spherical bubble have?"

So far every time I have done this, the answers have come in the same order and pattern. A second after I ask the question, someone answers, "One." A second later, I receive two simultaneous answers: "None" and "It's infinite." Usually, after a six-second pause, someone quietly offers, "Two?" This person is the first in the bubble.

The ability to perceive the inside surface of a bubble requires a fascinating advance in cognitive development that is the hallmark of the concrete operational stage of cognitive development—the ability to see from someone else's perspective, or in this case, to perceive the view from inside the bubble without ever having been inside it.

Lines

I see lines of development as trajectories out from the center of my bubble. They are vertical potentials for scaffolding, such as the potential to develop kinesthetically through levels, or emotionally through levels. Concentrating development only along favored lines eventually results in shaky foundations, blind spots, and shadows.

For example, intellectuals who especially focus their growth in the cognitive line of development, but remain relatively underdeveloped in the kinesthetic line, often receive criticism for being "too much in their heads." Their lack of body awareness is a blind spot, a form of shadow. Incidentally I believe there are two forms of shadow: repressed awareness and underdeveloped awareness. Instead of saying people are "too much in their heads," I think it would be more constructive to say they could be more in their body.

Developing lines simultaneously is akin to horizontal development across a level. I speculate that focusing on multiple lines allows us to develop holistically at each level, thus increasing our chances of reaching and maintaining flow.

States

I am a clown. When most people hear the word *clown*, they think of someone wearing a costume. Those are not what I consider authentic clowns; they're merely people in clown costumes. In the sense to which I refer, a clown is a state of consciousness. Think of stand-up comedians, such as Robin Williams or Eddie Murphy. Their humor is based upon their exceptional insight into human nature, coupled with stinging critique. Even without a script, they can go into a state of mind that sees hilarity in everyday things. Comedians and clowns are wise fools. The wise fool sets aside all of his or her previous experiences and assumptions and maximizes receptivity to experience as it unfolds in the moment.

Seeing (and seizing) opportunities to expand students' state of consciousness is central to the integral approach. Comedy is a superb way of quickly and effectively changing one's state of mind. I use comedy as a way of putting myself in a peak state of consciousness and bringing others into a similar state. Peak performance states are those in which we perform best. In these states, people generally report feeling both supported and exhilarated. The feeling of support comes from having access to multiple lines of development simultaneously, resulting in a sense of resourcefulness.

Working as Dr. Froth (my clown alter ego) in an educational context, I guide my audience into peak states. The beauty of a clown alter ego is that it grants me permission and provides me with the skills to access any state immediately. A clown-like character also allows me to use bizarre methods, free of reason, to state-train my audience. For example, during a bubble-making activity in which students make really huge bubbles, if I see a large bubble floating more than 5 meters above the ground, I might shout in a tone mimicking that of an angry teacher, "Hey, Bubble!"

This grabs everyone's attention because the bubble is an inanimate object, and yet I am shouting at it as if it were a person. Out of curiosity (curiosity stimulates cognition), everyone turns to see me pointing at the bubble with an accusing gesture and then pointing at the ground demandingly. I always continue with, "Come down here this minute, or you'll fall!"

At this, everyone always laughs. As a result of my making an obvious and absurd error in perception, they experience a rush of joy that shifts them into a peak state of consciousness. Furthermore, through my example, I have granted them permission to be more playful, absurd, and creative in their bubble making. Students immediately start talking to their bubbles, giving them names and treating them like pets, even crying when they pop.

Prior to my outburst, the students already were kinesthetically and cognitively engaged in bubble making. The absurdity of my angry outburst stimulated their curiosity and rewarded it (training the state) with humor. The result was the activation of the dramatic and creative lines of development. This is but one example of how I use clown-like comedy to lead my students into a peak state of consciousness.

A flow state of consciousness is a perpetual peak state, wherein one can maintain that state, performing exceptionally while flowing on to address new situations and circumstances. A prerequisite for flow states is the ability to reframe. Reframing is changing the way something is perceived. For instance, most people feel the blood literally drain from their frontal lobe at the notion of having to untangle something. They contract.

Being a clown can help with this situation. For example, if I am surveying my outdoor giant-bubble-making activity and spot a child holding a tangled rope-type bubble blower and frowning, I approach and say, "What's up?"

Generally the frown intensifies as the child replies, "Mine's tangled!"

I reply with, "Can I have a look?"

After the child passes the blower to me, I lift it up and inspect it closely. I frown briefly. Then the child sees my expression change to relief as I say, "Oh cool, this one's not tangled, it's just a puzzle!" This constitutes a cognitive reframe.

The child looks at me curiously. Curiosity triggers a state shift.

"I love puzzles!" I enthusiastically announce. We lay the bubble blower down and I explain, "The trick with puzzles seems to be to just make the whole thing look simpler by moving one part at a time. Whatever you can do to make it look simpler, do that first."

I move at least the first piece to get the student started. There is no problem and we are not missing out on getting to blow bubbles because we are getting to solve a puzzle. Each step simplifies the puzzle, and as soon as the end is in sight, the student shows genuine anticipation and even excitement. I make sure the student does at least the last few moves so he or she can own the triumph. By reframing the situation, I maintained my flow state, while at the same time reframing and training the student's state toward flow. Clowns deliberately misinterpret the otherwise unambiguous. In other words, we deliberately and strategically get everyday things wrong.

Types

Imagine you arrive at a party and the only person you know is the host. How does your bubble feel? Would you tend to contract your bubble in order to protect yourself (introvert type) or would you tend to expand your bubble and readily meet new people (extrovert type)? There are many different types beyond just introverted and extroverted. One's type is one's predisposition to favor and develop along certain lines (trajectories) easily. This fact has been made clear to me by working at language development schools for children who require extra assistance with communication. I have met some children who ask superbly constructed, very articulate questions about bubbles, but who cannot pay attention to the answer. Others really struggle to formulate their questions, but listen astutely to the answers. What has fascinated me about these children is that they frequently seem to be exceptionally sophisticated in at least one line of development and very underdeveloped in at least one other line.

Conclusion

I hope you enjoyed reading this account of the workings and playthings of an integral consciousness. I promise I will continue to explore consciousness and shed light on life with these amazing bubbles.

15

High upon a Mountaintop:
Teaching, Doing, and Being

James Wheal

We scooted along on our butts, crawling across the narrow rock ledge to our "classroom," on the side of a steep mountain. This was our first backpacking trip of the semester, and students from all over the country had gathered together in Colorado for four months of learning and adventure at the Rocky Mountain Semester (www.hminet.org). Not a desk in sight, we found ourselves scrambling across a granite shelf to find the perfect spot to begin our studies.

As we made it past the narrow squeeze of the cliff, the ledge opened up enough for us to sit in a tight semicircle of stunted pine trees and look out over the vast Arkansas River valley and snowy peaks surrounding us. For many students, this was their first overnight adventure, their first extended time away from home. For all, it was their first academic class held miles from civilization and nearly thirteen thousand feet above the sea.

First, we made sure that everyone was comfortable—changed into dry clothes after our hike, and armed with a full water bottle to replenish what we had sweated away—now sitting on a sleeping pad to keep the rocks from sucking away body heat. (In the absence of a four walled classroom, teaching in the backcountry forces an instructor to pay attention to details we often overlook "on campus," and frustrates any attempt to force our audience to perform. Sun shining in students' eyes, a chill descending or blood sugar dropping all trump the familiar structures of obedience and authority when you're a two day's hike from the principal's office or the snack machine.)

We pulled out our folders and notebooks along with dog-eared copies of environmental historian William Cronon's "The Problem with Wilderness: Getting Back to the Wrong Nature." This thoughtful piece had created a stir in environmental circles because in it, Cronon argues that "wilderness," or what we mean when we refer to what lies beyond civilization, is really just a construct, and therefore the wrong thing to try and preserve. From Pilgrims seeing the forest as the haunt of the Devil, to 19th-century industrial barons seeing it as board-feet and mineral profits, to contemporary students from New York and Los Angeles, seeing it as their prep-school hippie "Big Adventure" away from home—Cronon maintains that all of us have projected what we need to see onto these assorted rocks, trees and creatures, often obscuring their intrinsic nature and enduring value.

Then we discussed the article, following a Socratic line of questioning and close reading of the text—teasing out the shy students, encouraging the early contributors to expand on their initial thoughts, pushing to move beyond the standard call and response of well-trained performers and into the beginnings of true inquiry.

In choosing this essay to launch the term, our faculty deliberately wanted to kick the stool out from under the assumptions of students still cradling some pretty romantic visions of wilderness themselves. We hoped that by prompting what Harvard's Bob Kegan calls the Subject—Object shift (Kegan maintains that what we are subjectively immersed in at one stage of development, we become objectively aware of at the next), we could pop these young learners out of their usual frames and into a place of greater self-awareness and responsibility. Combined with the fact that all of their prior personas, roles, and "personal brands" had all been left behind—we had a rare opportunity to skirt the notorious twin teen defenses of arrogance and insecurity, and actually get to the heart of their hearts with what we might call Super-Egoic Distantiation.

Just like Bertoldt Brecht had done almost a century earlier with plays like Three Penny Opera and Mack the Knife, and like Woody Allen had continued in his own filmmaking style—suddenly breaking the illusion of the illusion by turning and speaking directly to the camera and distancing the viewer from his own subjective experience—we might be able to get around the Super Ego of teen culture. By leaving malls and media behind, we could then use that forced separation to shine a more informative light on the impact of norms and culture on self.

For the rest of the semester, we would be hammering on the question of "When you merge with the Wild, do you find yourself, or lose yourself, and how can you tell the difference?" Drawing on Ursula LeGuin's short story "Vaster than Empires and More Slow" about an empathic member of a space voyage who jumps ship to merge with the consciousness of a rainforest planet, Tim O'Brien's haunting piece "Sweetheart of the Song Tra Bong" about a G.I.'s high school girlfriend who visits him in Vietnam only to ditch her saddle shoes and willingly lose herself in the heart of darkness, and Gary Snyder's peerless poems on Turtle Island—North America—we would unpack line by line, our relationship to the blank canvas of Nature—both terrible and Sublime.

As we continued to explore the wilds of the Colorado Plateau for the following months, hiking, climbing and skiing through that stunning landscape, our students would have the chance to process their own emotions, impressions, and analyses in real time, and begin to articulate their emerging adult worldviews.

But before any of that would unfold, before some insightful comment by student or teacher could crack open that spaciousness of perspective, the sun on that particular autumn evening began to set.

Not just a regular, John Denver Rocky Mountain sunset, either, but a show-stopping explosion of light and color that rendered the most meticulous lesson plan moot.

The sun had dropped behind the mountains, dripping liquid gold alpenglow down from the tops of the peaks, and lighting up the high cirrus clouds in purple and orange streaks. September snows dusted the higher mountains of the Mosquito Range that separated our valley from Breckenridge and South Park. Gold leafed aspens carpeted the flanks of Mount Elbert, the tallest peak in the Rockies.

And above it all, there we sat.

I made a few more efforts to return the conversation to the good Doctor Cronon and his Important Essay, but felt like a Scholastic debating theology at the Rapture. Yes, it was still important for us to get our heads around four centuries of American thinking of wilderness. Yes, it was still important for us to scrutinize our own perspectives and see them for the utterly human creations they were. Yes, it was still important for us to complete our scheduled lesson plans and return to campus with checks in all the right boxes.

But for that fifteen minutes, they were all inarguably less important than simply showing up, shutting up and opening up to that rare and visible intersection of the everyday and the ineffable.

"If Enlightenment is an accident," queries the young monk in the familiar story, "then why do we meditate?"

"Ah," responds his seasoned teacher, "to make us more accident prone!"

It's not too much of a stretch to extend that concept to Scopes and Sequences, ILPs, assessments and every other construct of the educational industry. In the end, they have nothing at all to do with true Learning—that sublime moment where a student's curiosity is sparked, and as Plato describes "travels from one soul to another." At that moment, like with the accident of Enlightenment, all of the structuring and planning and practicing melt away as clunky form, even as the shining formless moment comes alive.

Just as with contemplative practice, we would not serve our students to ignore the form, the practice, and simply wander around waiting for those happy accidents to happen. We need to create the structures to guide, the handrails to steady, the assignments to hone—and at the same time, be willing to cast them aside, the instant they inhibit rather than help.

For me, that moment on the mountainside etched this "pedagogical non-attachment" into my brain. As a teacher and curriculum designer, I couldn't have been more chuffed with what I'd put together for that class. I'd refined it over a couple of semesters, and felt that it represented my absolute best and most authentic transmission as an educator. But as a lover of the wild and open, I could not deny that that evening (and most days) Ma Nature had me beat, hands down.

The most skillful thing for me to do was to ask everyone to close our notebooks, swivel our camp chairs 180 degrees, and take it All in. There was nothing to add, nothing to delete or amend. We had found ourselves transported by Grace and dumb luck to our destination even though our journey had barely begun.

"Good jazz," reflected Miles Davis, "should be tight, but loose. Tight—but Loose." That's a helpful dictum for those of us interested in exploring the emerging edges of integral education. On the one hand, quadrants, levels, lines, types, states and stages can serve as useful benchmarks, just as advanced chord structure and music theory can inform a genius blowing his horn.

On the other, obsessing over the educational equivalent of minor 7ths and sub-dominant harmonics can leave us composing pieces so avant garde that their technical mastery cannot compensate for their lack of humanity or spontaneity. We can become so entranced with the idea of the sound that we miss the opportunity to drop into the pocket, and swing.

At times, particularly within large and bureaucratic learning organizations, we're not playing jazz at all—our "music" sounds more like the restrained precision of a classical orchestra or the military compulsion of a marching band. Even in more alternative settings, where philosophies such as Waldorf, Montessori, Reggio Emilia, Sudbury and others hold sway, we, and our students, can find ourselves hostage to the notes on the page of the founder rather than to the songs in our own still-beating hearts. If our project in integral education is to create what Kegan describes so simply as "Self-Authoring" individuals, then surely, a little bit of improvisation, and ability to play (or not play) the perfect note for that perfect moment, remains an equally valuable skill to train as those of recital?

Like every suburban family who forces their kids to practice the piano, in the earnest hope that they will discover "a lifelong love of music" and inadvertently turns what could have been a gift into a chore—we can miss the mark when overbuilding and overprescribing the delicate transition from innate curiosity to acquired mastery.

At the same time though, the aphorism that "it is far better to be prepared for the chance that does not come than to have the chance and be unprepared" encourages us and our students to practice those scales and notes precisely so we are ready to set them aside when the music slots into a groove and begins to play the band.

That sunset evening on the mountainside taught me more in a few moments than I had learned in a career before it. I was faced with the stark choice of being Right or Effective. I could have kept on lecturing and explicating, chiding students rubber-necking at the splendor behind us, and driving to the completion of assignment and assessment—and I would have been Right. Assuredly, professionally, didactically correct. Or I could have realized that those efforts, while technically right, would have been practically wrong—missing the gift that lay right in front of us.

That day, I had little choice in choosing to be Effective—to make a difference and get out of my own way. The majesty of the Mystery showed up so fully that it left no room for anything beside itself. After soaking in the splendor of that evening, we returned to it again and again throughout the term, as we discussed a teenage girl gone feral in the jungles of southeast Asia, as we read aloud the poems of Gary Snyder on Dharma and Coyote, as we wrote in our journals reflections on Wilderness and our American Minds. It anchored all of our subsequent discussions of text and verse.

There, at the ever-shifting intersection between Planning and Riffing, between Doing and Being, that Teaching and Learning most authentically emerge. Had we not started that essay just in time to lay it aside, the mountain sunset would have lost much of its transformative impact. Had we not reinvested the gift of that spontaneous fifteen minutes of silence back into a deliberate semester of related reading and writing, many of its greatest insights might have remained buried.

We are not always so lucky as teachers, nor are those choice moments between Rightness and Effectiveness so clearly defined. Sometimes, it's the decision during a lecture on quadratic equations to digress into an anecdote about Isaac Newton's secret career as an alchemist, or in a literature class to explore the connection between Mary Shelley's monster and today's slasher flick, or in a science course to demonstrably connect fried chicken and roofing shingles in less than six steps. Sometimes, it's encouraging a student to veer out of the bounds of an assignment and give them room to roam, or to offer credit and encouragement to an apprenticeship or crackpot web startup for an Econ class.

So while we cannot predict these moments, when our best laid plans yield to a more Implicate order, one thing is for certain whenever they arise—they require us to humbly face them, free of the clutch and grab of presumed Knowledge, and to stand, with heads bowed beside our students, in the face of something—in the face of Everything, and trust that it is enough.

"Taste all," wrote Gary Snyder in a poem we read that semester, "and hand the Knowledge down."

Conscious Teaching Practices

16

Cultivating Integral Awareness in the Classroom

Willow Dea

My hope is to about holding the clarity of the integral framework, or 'the map' while facing the daily challenges and opportunities of the territory, and finding your way through the proverbial forest with the aid of an integral perspective. Imagine that someone is taking you on a tour of a nearby forest. Your attention will be directed to the treetops, the flora and fauna, as well as the stream, soil and stones. Each heading in the chapter could be seen as a trail guide—a helpful set of pointers for easing the way. The focal point of the chapter is the space between the map and the territory, which lies in your heart and mind. You know the way. These words are just a pointer to your way of knowing.

We'll explore the practice of cultivating integral awareness in an educational context. We'll consider several aspects of integral awareness as they relate to your inner state. We'll also review the distinctions of the integral model, their relevance to education, and the need to address the darker aspects of the psyche. Here a quick overview of the trail guides we will explore:

- Cultivating Integral Awareness
- Quadrants
- Using the Four Quadrants to Make a decision
- States
- Levels and Stages
- State-Stages
- Lines
- Types
- Environment Impacts Behavior
- Shadow

Cultivating Integral Awareness

Think of your awareness as the aperture of a camera. The aperture can open, and it can widen again, enough to let more light in. We're training the aperture of our awareness to take in all that's going on: in your own heart and mind, as well as your surroundings. Have you ever noticed that when you take a walk in the woods you may become more aware of the sounds, the sunlight, your chattering mind, your heart or the thud of your boots? Maybe you feel invigorated by the cool air, and aware of your thirst. Perhaps there's a group of people walking ahead of you, and you can hear their voices, faintly. You may also be aware that it is a park in which you're hiking, reflect on the history of the land, and the fact that the local government protects it. This is integral awareness. One has the capacity to have a balanced, inclusive experience of all these (and more) elements of one's experience. An integral framework is a theory of "everything," a map. Yet the direct experience of using the map while hiking in the woods is like having a GPS with you in the forest, letting you see exactly where you are, and where you might like to go. Ken Wilber's Integral Theory provides a higher altitude from which to view the surroundings. From the top of the mountain, we can see all the terrain, the contour of the valley, the river's curves and the bare areas where urban growth has occurred. The whole picture comes together to inform us more accurately. Every skill is honed through practice. Cultivating an integral perspective is no exception.

Quadrants

Let's take a look at the quadrants, now, to gain four new perspectives on your experience. Remember, the quadrants are irreducible. They represent the simplest way to see through a particular lens of one's experience. Take a moment to put each pair of glasses on! Each quadrant offers a distinct facet of reality.

Upper Left, (UL): The "I" of the upper left is all about one's thoughts, feelings, intentions and psychology. The UL contains one's sentience, sense of self, sensations, and even inner voices. It represents our direct, internal experience from a first person perspective; that which is subjective to us. It is the domain of the singular, interior, subjective space.

Lower Left, (LL): The "WE" of the lower left quadrant refers to the collective interior, or in our case, the cultural experience of a class. The culture is experienced as a social phenomenon, and is shaped by the participants and the systems that act upon it. The shared values and ways that the groups make meaning of their collective experience are part of this lower left quadrant. The lower left quadrant refers to the relational space of being with a friend, a student, your spouse, a family member, or a group of people.

Upper Right, (UR): The "It" of the upper right quadrant refers to the physical body and behavior. The UR is the perspective of the surfaces of reality: the individual, objective, exterior domain. Observing your students working, from the second person perspective would be accounted for in the upper right. Sciences are predisposed to occupying the upper right when utilizing objective observation. The "physical behavior, material components, its matter and energy; and its concrete body; these are all items that can be referred to in some sort of objective, 3rd-person, or 'it' fashion."

Lower Right, (LR): The "Its" of the lower right quadrant refers to the collective exterior, the environment, social structures of our environs, and the legislative or governing systems that uphold the collective arena. The lower right includes such considerations as the arrangement of room, the laws that guide the behavior of people in a school, city, state or country. It also refers to the way that architecture has the power to influence the behavior of its occupants.

Using the Four Quadrants to Make a Decision

Remember, the quadrants are merely a lens through which we can look. These four lenses are present together all the time—each aspect is arising simultaneously, which is called "tetra arising" in integral lingo. They facilitate the capacity to view discrete phenomena through four lenses. Within each quadrant there are levels of development. Within the interior, Left-Hand quadrants there are levels of depth and within the exterior, Right-Hand quadrants there are levels of complexity (Esbjörn-Hargens, 2008).

The Four Quadrants

Try this exercise: Think of a professional decision that you may need to make. If it's helpful, draw the four quadrants and jot down your thoughts as you proceed.

1. Consider the first-person singular perspective (UL)—my intention, feeling, motivation, self. Where am I coming from? What do I intend, desire or know? Consider paying attention to your dreams, meditating on the decision, connecting with your intuition, and/or journaling to access information from your subtle body.

2. Consider the third person singular perspective (UR)—his or her behavior and or action: What will I do, given the opportunity to try to view myself more objectively, as an "it"? How will that person respond? Consider noticing your physical sensations in relation to the different possible decision outcomes. As well, make sure that you are well rested and fed as you make a decision.

3. Consider the second person plural perspective (LL)—shared meaning, resonance, and the mutual feelings: What will our experience be? How will this decision affect our sense of connection? Consider engaging in dialogue with a friend or mentor, or speaking with people who may be affected by your decision.

4. Consider the third person plural perspective (LR)—shared action, systems, and observable connections: Consider the impact to the whole system, or the common good. How does my decision effect the environment, or system? How does the system effect my decision?

5. Take a moment to consider the primary factors from each perspective. Write a sentence or two about the way that you now view the outcome of your decision: Summarize your decision taking all four quadrants into consideration. What did you notice about this way of approaching a decision?

6. What factors affecting your decision had you not considered? Did you discover a missing question, insight or perspective?

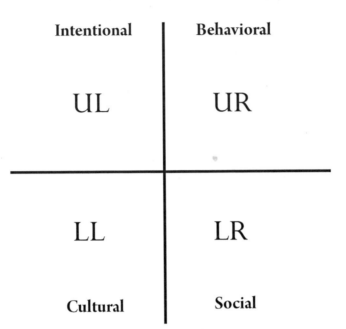

John Gruber, an integral teacher from Philadelphia, PA, uses the four quadrants routinely. Here's what he offered about a curricular component in four quadrants: "In my science course, I have reflected on what each of the four quadrant perspectives has to offer about what we are doing in a lab exercise—if we are going to set up a laboratory investigation of colored light and atomic emission spectra, I might reflect on how it will engage all four quadrants or how it will show up through all four quadrants. What are we doing in the physical space? What are we seeing? How are the time, movement around the room and activity structured? What do the leading questions we have composed, ask students to reflect on? How will the experience potentially involve both interior and exterior elements? How much open space is here and how much directed structure? What will the students find inspiring or what has "wow" factor? What will be grounding and give insight? I see our behaviors and the facts in right-hand quadrants, as well as the materials, activities, and ways we structure space, time and movement. I see our goals, inspiration, motivation and desire to listen to each other as left-hand aspects of the same experience."

Inquiries for Taking the Map into Your Classroom

These inquiries are designed to lend you the lenses of an integral level of awareness. They are simply ways of considering the elements of your experience, through the elements of the integral framework: states, stages, state-stages, lines, levels, types, shadow. Let them assist you in unearthing the missing questions. Feel free to extrapolate and expand upon them!

States

States are fleeting, temporary aspects of phenomena that arise in our direct experience in all four quadrants. States are universal, and common to your ordinary experience. Three general categories of states include narrow, phenomenal states of body or mind. Waking, dreaming, and deep sleep are examples of broad, natural states of consciousness. Obviously, when we drink alcohol we're bound to encounter altered states! As well, deep meditative practices will induce non-ordinary states.

In an educational context, we might consider the state of our students when they haven't eaten breakfast, or if they are enduring a divorce at home, or are charged with the responsibility to work while attending school. Attentional states are also worthy of consideration in a classroom, as the ability to learn is clearly facilitated by one's ability to be alert enough to focus on the task at hand, or to be able to self-regulate one's attention for long enough periods to be able to receive the material.

States arise in our gross, subtle and causal bodies. By this I mean we experience the world at several levels simultaneously. The gross body may be sleeping, while the subtle body is dreaming, all the while both of these experiences are occurring within the causal level, wherein the non-dual nature of reality is always and already arising. Here are a few words that evoke states, while physical circumstances also evoke states—feeling tired, or euphoric, relaxed or frantic etc. Take a moment and feel each of these:

- A sunrise in the mountains
- The holocaust
- A blooming rose
- A child's laughter
- A woman mourning
- The thrum of a large city at midday
- The birth of a child
- The death of a close friend

The sensations that are evoked by each phrase are undeniable influences upon our ability to learn, teach or be calm. Consider adding experiences to your curriculum that include intentional state changes for your students to enjoy, or gain access to deeper levels of information. Questions about states, for you:

- How am I? (Sleepy, hungry, angry, lonely?)
- Did I get enough sleep and a good breakfast?
- What's my intention for the day?
- Where's my edge—where can I stretch today?
- What can I do to bring myself into greater balance each day?
- What need I attend to, to further cultivate integral awareness today?

Questions to ask about your students:

- How are they? Check the vitals: sleep, emotional state, nutrition, illness/health.
- How does their level of attention/engagement look?
- Do they appear distressed or stressed?
- Does anyone appear to be in an altered state, as a result of medication, alcohol or drugs?

Questions to ask your students to get them thinking:

- What's a state?
- Why is your state important to learning?
- What facilitates your best state for learning?
- How is your ability to attend compromised when you're really upset? Stressed? Well-rested, tired, or sick?
- What's an altered state, and how does that affect your ability to learn?
- How do think a meditative state would affect your ability to learn?

Questions about or to the administration/system:

- What state is the building in?
- What could be improved to optimize better academic performance, emotional wellbeing and overall function of the school?
- Considerations: lighting, airflow and temperature, arrangement of seating?
- Are there aesthetic changes to be made?
- Do we have effective equipment and strategies for supporting our students struggling with special needs?
- Does the school have effective programs and/or policies for dealing with drug and alcohol abuse?
- What preventive programming or curriculum could be offered to educate our students about health, social awareness and/or financial fitness?

Levels and Stages

Levels and stages of development are exactly the same thing. Stages and levels are structural, in that they are permanent developmental milestones of higher, deeper or broader potentials. The word "level" isn't used as a rigid structure, but rather as an indication of a higher order of discrete qualitative change or of complexity. Stages are enduring—one may inhabit a stage for five to 10 years, or for the duration of a lifetime. One cannot skip a stage, to attain a higher level of development. For example, when a child learns to walk, it is a permanent acquisition. She can transcend the ability to walk by acquiring the ability to run, but she will always be able to walk, and she must have learned to walk before running. As well, consider that we develop along multiple lines in stages, such as the cultural, spiritual, moral and cognitive lines of development. There are many developmental models that use stages to describe development. For example, Kohlberg describes moral development as moving from a preconventional stage, in which one's awareness is largely self absorbed, to a conventional stage of development in which society's rule and norms are enacted, followed by a postconventional stage of moral development which is characterized by the expansion beyond the rules and norms to include the higher concern for the world and all her people. "Thus, moral development tends to move from "me" (egocentric) to "us" (ethnocentric) to "all of us" (worldcentric)—a good example of the unfolding stages of consciousness." (Wilber, Stages and Levels of Development, 2008)

In the context of education, we can look at levels as forms of development such as:

1. Vertical or "up"—transformation, development along specific lines that allow for greater capacity in that one line. For example, one could develop their cognition and not the physical body.
2. Horizontal expansion—acquiring new skills or knowledge at the same personal stage. For example, one might learn to speak Portuguese, which does not develop the ego.
3. Regression—temporary or long-term regression from one stage to a lower stage. If someone was gravely ill, and lost their physical ability to remain autonomous they might regress a level or two.

Developmental Altitude refers to the levels or stages of consciousness, and their relative sphere of care. As one ascends through the levels, one has an increased ability to consider others and is motivated to care for even larger circles of people, and eventually all beings in the Universe.

Levels and stages reflect what motivates us—the unseen drive to act a certain way, especially with respect to the values line of development. For example, we might observe a colleague describing two opposing political candidates and their differing perspectives in such a way that demonstrates the ability to hold both perspectives as partially true. While this behavior is outwardly observable, what motivates that person to vote a certain way would vary, depending on their values, and relative level of development? Thus, we can't assume that we understand everyone by means of his or her actions. Rather, a skillful way of understanding another is to inquire about why they might make the choices they do.

The concept of levels and stages are highly relevant to education in that one can better communicate with colleagues, parents, administrators and students if you can identify the "center of gravity" from which their values are enacted, and what they are actively listening for. I cannot overstate how practically useful and effective it is to utilize a solid understanding of the stages so as to best effect your teaching practice, or influence change within the system.

State-Stages

We know that states are brief and transient, like a cloud passing before the sun. They are also exclusive, in that we can't be jubilant and furious, or stoned and sober. We also know that stages are more structurally enduring and inclusive, each new stage building upon the last, acting to filter our perception and experience in very definitive ways. For example, when the momentary state of grief arises in someone at a conventional stage of moral development; there is a particular flavor and tone or texture of expression that an integral framework has helped to articulate for us all to understand(Wilber, States Stages and Skillful Means, 2006).

The conceptual advantage of the distinction between states and stages is the synthesis of the Eastern philosophies that articulate varying universal states, while the Western philosophies have brought forward a clear measurement of our growth and maturity.

Individuals necessarily interpret any state experience from the stage of consciousness they are at. One is never outside one's context; no matter what sort of experience one has, their altitude is the lens through which they will understand the experience.
—Wilber

The distinction of the state-stage concept is helpful in that we can better understand what we're experiencing, anticipate other's perceptions and responses, and understand the complexity of the human experience with greater humility. We can create the conditions for change on a personal, organizational or global level when we're equipped to engage in the dynamics that the state-stages point to.

The utility of the state-stage distinction lies in the abiltiy to use skillful means to understand the many ways that the truth is experienced, understood and expressed, at any given moment in any context. Accepting this, we can better open our hearts and minds to each and every person without hesitation and will full acceptance.

Questions about state-stages for yourself:

- What is my sphere of care? Do I care about my people? Do I care about the world?
- Can I expand my awareness to include the whole universe?
- Can I see that my perspective is merely partially true?
- Am I comfortable holding more than my own perspective as valid or at least partially true?
- How does my stage of development impact my students?

- How does my stage of development impact my relationships with other teachers?
- How does my stage of development affect my relationship to the system that I serve?

Questions to ask about your students:

- What is the range of awareness of their selective perception?
- What are their preferred defenses? How do they hide?
- How do they make sense of their experience?
- What is the logic behind their perspectives on the self and the world?

Questions to ask your students to get them thinking:

- How do you cope with difficulty?
- Are you aware of other people's feelings, motivations and perception?
- How invested are you in other people's perceptions? Why?
- What do you do when you feel defensive?
- What do you do to gain mastery in your life?
- What are your strategies for doing so?

Questions about or to the administration/system:

- What is this school's administration's sphere of care?
- Does the administration embody policies and procedures that address the needs of the students, the staff, the community, and/or the world?
- How does the administration interact with each of these groups?
- How does the administration solve problems?
- Is there anything you'd like to offer to your administration in terms of new ideas, perspectives, solutions or strategies?
- What is the philosophy guiding the school?

Lines

Lines of development are areas in which one can be more or less skilled. We all know that we have strengths and weaknesses —areas of ourselves that are more developed than others. One may have great cognitive development, but have less moral development or more ego development and less social development. Likewise, one may have greater or lesser kinesthetic abilities (physical, cognitive, morals, values, spiritual etc.)

Inquiries for yourself:

- How do I use my strengths to overcome my weaknesses as a teacher?
- What type of learning style do I tend to favor?
- What type(s) of learning styles do I have the most trouble relating to teaching?

- What qualities do I embody when in my essence?
- What qualities do I regress to?
- How can I communicate with my students to help them to understand me better?
- How can I communicate with my students to help them understand them selves better?

Questions to ask about your students:

- What are their individual strengths and weaknesses?
- Who's introverted or extroverted?

Of the multiple intelligences, as described by Howard Gardener, which type of intelligence does each student demonstrate most frequently? The multiple intelligences are linguistic, logical-mathematical, kinesthetic, interpersonal, intrapersonal, and spatial and nature intelligence. See the section below for further insight.

- How can I include that style in my approach to the material?
- Who has a natural proclivity for leading? Managing? Details?
- Who is the visionary, the artist, or the technician?

Questions to ask your students (get them thinking):

- What do you feel is your learning style?
- What are your strengths? Weaknesses?
- Do you know how to capitalize on your strengths and secure support to evolve your weaknesses?
- Do they know what areas their challenges are?
- Do they know how to access support to address and change them?

Questions about or to the administration/system:

- What are the strengths or well-developed aspects of your school system?
- In what areas could the system develop to provide better education for students?
- Consider the areas of interpersonal communication, values, morals, aes thetic, and the emotional impact of the school in the community.
- How does the school add to the sense of the true, good, and beautiful in the community?

Types

Types are styles or orientations available at any level within the quadrants. They intimate differences in the expression of a trait. Learning styles are paramount to an integral approach to education, as we must include the perspective(s) of each type of learner when conveying a lesson. Consider that one student may primarily access her world through vision, while another may learn through his auditory system. Yet another could best understand the material through direct contact, manipulating the materials in space. Utilizing all of the senses while teaching will allow each student to experience multiple aspects of the material, and it will optimize their direct understanding more efficiently in the long run.

In Howard Gardner's *Frames of Mind: Theory of Multiple Intelligences*, he proposes that there are seven main areas in which all people have special skills; he calls them intelligences. The multiple intelligences are linguistic, logical-mathematical, kinesthetic, interpersonal, intrapersonal, spatial and nature intelligence. "(The theory of multiple intelligences) has helped a significant number of educators to question their work and to encourage them to look beyond the narrow confines of the dominant discourses of skilling, curriculum, and testing. For example, Mindy Kornhaber and her colleagues at the Project SUMIT (Schools Using Multiple Intelligences Theory) have examined the performance of a number of schools and concluded that there have been significant gains in respect of SATs scores, parental participation, and discipline (with the schools themselves attributing this to MI theory)" (Smith, 2008).

Howard Gardner viewed intelligence as "the capacity to solve problems or to fashion products that are valued in one or more cultural settings" (Smith, 2008). Given the increasingly complex demands of a global economy and job market, one would imagine that this form of culturally relevant intelligence would be wise to consider!

The most important point is that we need to include a more comprehensive approach to teaching. We need to acclimate ourselves to the fact that our educational models, to this point, have been biased toward one or two forms of intelligence, verbal and mathematical—with a strong emphasis on memorization skills. This is no longer acceptable. We must adapt our current approach to include the natural intelligences that arise in our students, to enable them to carry out their innate purpose in the world using their native forms of intelligence.

To this end, the multiple forms of intelligence are but the beginning of our greater understanding for moving forward. I challenge you to learn the types, and find ways to convey your material to a myriad of learning styles/forms of intelligence.

What if your classroom was designed to:

- Include your hearing to learn math?
- Include your eyes to learn music?
- Include the taste buds to learn philosophy?
- Hands to learn spelling?

Many of us are familiar with the Myers-Briggs personality types. These represent four ways that teachers and learners might encounter each other, based on their personal style. For example, introverted people tend to listen deeply, process information silently and enact their new understanding without necessarily needing to talk to other students or the teacher. Providing time for quiet reflection during class time might support an introverted learner to learn more efficiently. In contrast, extroverted people tend to "talk it out" in order to process new information. Partnering extroverted students together and providing structured time to process information in a given class time might facilitate faster integration of new material in the classroom.

Girl or Boy... Health and Unhealthy

We're all intimately familiar with the differences that gender brings. Girls can be quite different from boys and vice versa. Let us jump right to the point: recognizing the difference between a healthy boy or girl and a sick boy or girl. Each type has a healthy expression and an unhealthy expression. We all intuit the difference, so without belaboring the point, let's move on to the finer points: the inner experience of more subtle qualities of being.

As we develop and evolve, we may become aware of the differences between the expressions of femininity among different women, or the varying qualities that men exhibit along the continuum from feminine to masculine. Feminine qualities tend towards an emphasis on communion, embrace, immanence, agape or descending, or an "embodying" type of spiritual path. Meanwhile, masculine qualities tend to express agency, autonomy, transcendence, Eros, or an "ascending" type of spiritual path. That being said, we each have access to both sides of the continuum: the feminine qualities of receptivity, communion, immanence, and radiance as well as the agency, autonomy, and ascension of the masculine. Ideally, we're able to identify where we could express ourselves more fully in either direction, so as to further cultivate the mastery of our own embodied expression. Possessing the fluid agility to enact from either the feminine or masculine qualities, in the appropriate contexts or modes of being, can be exquisitely skillful.

Questions about types:

Questions for yourself:

- What is my personality type?
- How does it affect the way that I teach? Learn?
- Am I aware of my particular personality style? Teaching style?
- What could I include, from other perspectives that might allow me to widen my experience?
- How do I use my strengths to overcome my weaknesses as a teacher?
- What type of learning style do I tend to favor?
- What type(s) of learning styles do I have the most trouble relating to teaching?
- What qualities do I embody when in my essence?
- What qualities do I regress to?
- How can I communicate with my students to help them to understand me better, and therefore themselves better?

Questions to ask about your students:

- How do they process events?
- What strikes you about their learning style?
- What are their individual strengths and weaknesses?
- Who's introverted or extroverted?
- How can I include that style in my approach to the material?
- Who has a natural proclivity for leading? Managing? Details?
- Who is the visionary, the artist, or the technician?

Questions to ask your students, to get them thinking:

- What are your strengths? Weaknesses?
- Do you know how to capitalize on your strengths and secure support to evolve your weaknesses?
- Do they know where their challenges lie?
- Do they know how to access support for working with them?

Questions about or to the administration/system:

- What are the strengths, or well-developed aspects in your school system?
- Where could the system use some consulting to develop?
- Consider the areas of interpersonal communication, values, morals, aesthetic, and the emotional impact of the school in the community.
- How does the school add to the sense of the true, good, and beautiful in the community?

Environment Impacts Behavior

When students are welcomed into a sunlit lobby on a new school day, filled with uplifting art, fresh flowers and a welcoming atmosphere they are more apt to feel nourished, respected and inspired. One could argue that students feel more ready to learn. Bill Strickland, the founder of the Manchester Craftsmen's Guild in Pittsburgh, Pennsylvania has demonstrated the power of aligning the learning environment with the higher ideals of the True, Good and Beautiful. As a result, he has created a visionary educational organization called the Manchester Craftsmen's Guild, a highly successful job training center and community arts program.

Remember I'm the black kid from the '60s who got his life saved with ceramics. Well, when I decided to reproduce my experience with other kids in the neighborhood, the theory being if you get kids flowers and you give them food and you give them sunshine and enthusiasm, you can bring them right back to life. I have 400 kids from the Pittsburgh public school system that come to me every day of the week for arts education. And these are children who are flunking out of public school. And last year I put 88 percent of those kids in college and I've averaged over 80 percent for

15 years. We've made a fascinating discovery—there's nothing wrong with the kids that affection and sunshine and food and enthusiasm and Herbie's music can't cure. For that I won a big old plaque—Man of the Year in Education. I beat out all the Ph.D.s because I figured that if you treat children like human beings, it increases the likelihood they're going to behave that way. And why we can't institute that policy in every school and in every city and every town remains a mystery to me.

—Strickland, 2002

Questions for yourself about the physical plane, senses, and embodiment:

- Do I have clutter to discard?
- How does the quality of light and airflow affect me?
- Have I created a space that reflects my core values and aesthetic, and that serves the class?
- Do I feel a sense of beauty in my classroom?
- If not, how could I shift this?
- Are the ergonomics correct for my desk, monitor and chair?
- Have I designed organizing processes to keep papers stored easily?
- Could I customize my space to better suit my body? A comfortable chair? A standing desk? A particularly supportive desk chair?

Questions to ask about your students:

- Do they have adequate storage space for keeping the room organized?
- Are the ergonomics correct for their workspaces?
- Does the room have supportive equipment for those with special needs or differing learning styles?
- How could they help to improve the space?
- What roles might they take responsibility for in maintaining the aesthetic and function of the room?
- What do they think adds beauty to the room?

Questions to ask your students to get them thinking:

- Are you comfortable at your desk?
- Does your chair fit the height of the desk?
- Do you have a good system for storing your books, pens and papers?
- What would make this room more beautiful?
- If you could use more senses while you're learning, how would you design it?
- What's missing for you?

Question about or to the administration/system:

- How could the administration allocate funds to support improved ergonomics for workstations for the teachers and/or the students?

Shadow

Taking responsibility for what we impart to our students also includes taking responsibility for what we unconsciously bring with us to the classroom. Our engaging in a regular practice of addressing our emotions and/or parts of our self that need attention allows for a natural, conscious evolution. That which we reject, disown, dismember and refuse to look at and love in our self has a way of being expressed, usually inadvertently. Why create unnecessary mess or confusion? Facing these parts of ourselves takes courage, yes, yet these feelings tend to pass quickly once they're directly experienced. Find out for yourself!

Try this: Get a piece of paper and a pen. Pick a nasty judgment about someone in your work environment; a colleague, student or administrator, or write down a whole slough of judgments. For example, "For the sake of the exercise, suspend the belief that you may not possess these qualities in your Being. Now, that it's possible to include and acknowledge those parts, find out if you like those parts of yourself. Review the list of judgmental statements that you've written about that person or those people (whomever is convenient for the sake of the exercise) and inquire with yourself:

1. Am I like that in any way?
2. If yes, even if just slightly, can I accept that part of myself?
3. What am I feeling as I do this? (Repulsion, shame, embarrassment, "bad ness," grief, frustration, fear, anger, anxiety?)
4. Feel it, fully! Take a few minutes to notice the sensation in your body, and to fully express that emotion.
5. See what happens when you bump into the opportunity to judge that person again. What response do you have to them now?

The power of handling and integrating one's shadow can emancipate your teaching practice, as much as learning about any new methodology, such as integral education. In other words, learning about and exploring an integral perspective is only one way of freeing your mind; shadow work can free up your heart, and break up hidden patterns of behavior, to your advantage. Both are part of an integral practice. When we look squarely at the ways that we avoid feeling, or avoid being with inner conflict, there is an opportunity for a wider perspective, and new, more constructive choices can be made. We can forge new pathways when we take a step back, feel our way through the icky hard stuff, and clear ourselves to be more whole and healthy, and in this way meet others more fully.

Shadow Inquiries:

Questions about shadow; issues that get ignored, suppressed, repressed, rendered taboo:

Questions for yourself:

- How is my spiritual practice or lack thereof contributing to the field, the collective felt sense, in the room?
- What are my spiritual limitations, my arguments with God/Spirit, re sentments, disappointments, frustrations, and stuck places?
- How do those internal conversations and positions and attitudes shape what's possible for these students?
- What are my unresolved sexual issues?
- What aspects of sexuality could we discuss that would make a difference for these students?
- Where am I projecting onto my students in an unhealthy way?
- What are my top three addictions?
- Notice how you consciously and unconsciously promote those in the classroom.
- How do you talk about them? Celebrate them? Repress them? Avoid them?
  Examples: I'm addicted to being right, to resisting feeling my feelings, and to going quickly though my days, in order not to be more intimate with my immediate experience of the sensations in my body and emotions in my being.
- What are my physical addictions?
- What are my psychological addictions?
- What are my mental addictions?
- Do I assume my students will understand the classroom material in the way that I do
- Do I expect others to emulate my learning style?
- Can I teach to other learning types? (Kinesthetic, visual, linguistic, musical, auditory, mathematical?)
- How? Take a few minutes to consider this. Write about it.
- Do I judge students by their sexual orientation, or race?
- Do I judge students based on their body type?
- Do I judge students based on their religious or ethnic background?

Questions to ask about your students:

- Do you students have a relationship with Spirit, God or a Source greater than himself or herself?
- What could open up further for them?
- What practices, prayers or inquiry might support that process?
- What are they struggling with?
- What are they curious about?
- Are they aware of sexually transmitted diseases?
- How can I better prepare them to be responsible sexual partners?

- Are they aware of their sexual orientation?
- Do they need support to develop in their personal expression of their sexual identity?
- What alcohol or drugs have they tried?
- What are they currently using?
- Why? What are they running from, if anything?
- Are there actions I need to take to intervene, educate or support them?
- How do they feel about their body?
- What are they doing about it?
- Is there a risk of bulimia, anorexia or obesity?
- Do any of my students suffer from severe self-esteem issues affecting their wellbeing?
- What are they not accepting about themselves?
- How are they projecting onto their peers? Onto you?
- Could you address this in a conversation?

Questions to ask your students to get them thinking:

Regarding Spirituality:

- Do you have a relationship to a force greater than yourself/God/Spirit?
- What scares you the most about God/Spirit?
- Do you have time in your life to be nourished by God/ Spirit? If not, how could that shift?

Regarding Sexuality:

- What are you most scared to talk about?
- What's most compelling to you in your sexual life?
- What are your greatest hopes?
- Where might our conversation support your growth?
- What action can you take to access more information or support for your sexual life?

Regarding Addiction:

- What's most compelling to you about drugs?
- How are you different when you are in an altered state?
- If you were addicted to two things, what would they be?
- What action can you take to get more information or support around us ing drugs or drinking?

Regarding Projection:

Think of the two people that irritate you the most. Write down two or three things that really bother you about those two people. Now, imagine that they hold a great gift for you. Accept that they are reflecting parts of your personality that you may have difficulty accepting or loving. Now, say or write, "I am ..." and jot down the same qualities that you've just written about them. Feel your way through each one, and really look inside yourself for how this is true about you. Try to love that too!

Questions about or to the administration/system:

- Are there counseling services or programs that support staff and/or students with spiritual issues?
- Are there programs or resources available to support staff and/or students with drug and alcohol abuse?
- If not, what action could be taken to change that?
- Are there programs or resources available to support students with health and sexuality issues?
- If not, why not?
- What could be done about it?

Concluding Points

The goal is to empower yourself and your students to be able to hold multiple perspectives, use a multi-systems approach to learning, engage multiple senses when teaching or learning, include an awareness of your own state, their state, developmental stage, types, strengths and learning styles, and assist them to enjoy states of flow while learning. Remember that hierarchy is a necessary aspect of holding an integral perspective. There are higher levels of achievement, or development, and lower levels of achievement and development. Demonstrate examples of healthy hierarchy in your lessons to encourage greater accomplishment and leadership, and expose students' to the height and depth available to them. Discernment is essential to evaluating any particular topic or student, though each piece is considered in its partiality. Ideally every voice is heard in a conversation, and included as part of the collective truth, yet there may well be a few voices that hold greater weight because of a more comprehensive and/or balanced perspective, or a higher stage of personal development. Cultivate discernment. Deliberate about why something is more noteworthy.

- Open the doors of perception by slowing down.
- Cultivate integral awareness.
- Consider using as many sensory inputs as possible to convey the lesson plan, to include multiple learning types.
- Make use of all four quadrants when making a decision.
- Include the larger systemic perspective and the cultural implications for any topic at hand.
- Tracking the energy in the room informs our next move—listen for the subtle signals: body language, level of engagement, emotional tone, and level of response.

- Holding an intention is a great way to enjoy the process and let go of expectations.
- Hold your everyday practice as a teacher as sacred.
- Aim for a state of flow, by listening to 'what wants to happen' in the Field and responding.
- Create opportunities to clear the air, and do any necessary shadow work for yourself and with your class.
- Don't confuse the map with the territory! Enjoy the ride.

17

Learning from Assessment: A Story of a Journey toward Integral Education

Nancy T. Davis

Although no quick fix or even best practice exists as an answer to the dilemmas faced in education, an integral framework allows those of us seeking change a place to stand. Integral theory provides me a direction to take, a way of understanding individuals and events I encounter. It provides clues to understand how others are experiencing events and ways I may be able to "speak into their understanding." When I better understand others' perspectives, it helps me to communicate with them and to offer them a more complex vision of the world around them.

In this chapter, I propose using elements of the integral framework, specifically quadrants and lines, to reflect on my own practices and to better understand my students and their perspectives. Suggestions are made to guide readers in using these elements to develop their own integral teaching practices.

Educational Reform and Assessment

Schools are institutions of society, created to reproduce the values and traditions of the dominant culture (Pinar, Reynolds, Slattery & Taubman, 1995). Education, however, can be transformational. It can lead the culture to evolve in a direction that assists in moving the culture to a more sophisticated level. A question to be addressed when thinking about education is "What is the world we want to create?" In schools, do we want to duplicate what is or do we want to create a better world? Schools provide an opportunity for society to re-form itself. In schools, participants in society can acquire images of the possible. If we want a society that values diversity, then schools should reflect that valuing. If we want a democratic society, then schools should model the democracy we wish to create. If we want students to be critical thinkers who are responsible for their own learning, value their own and others' contributions, and continue to improve, then our practices in schools should reflect that goal.

How Does Assessment Fit with These Goals?

One primary purpose of assessment is accountability—to make sure students, teachers, and even schools are responsive to the purposes for which they are created. A second purpose, as important (some would say more important), is to assist the learner to develop or improve. These two purposes often are conflated and tend to work against the other. For example, accountability includes value judgments when an individual is measured against a standard or a population. The focus on value judgment sometimes results in the learner developing such a level of fear about grades that they get in the way of learning (Pringle, 2000). Most teachers can relate stories of frustration as students focus more on their grades than on the concepts taught. Students often ask, "Is this going to be on the test?" to determine if they should put forth effort to learn. If we could separate out the purposes and the methods to achieve the goals of assessment, perhaps we could develop a more productive way of thinking about assessment that could accomplish all the purposes.

The process of assisting students to make sense of critical notions of assessment helped in framing my own sense-making (Davis, Kumpete, & Aydeniz, 2006). Four very different but equally valid purposes of assessment can be delineated: (1) accountability, (2) comparison within and between populations, (3) building communities of learners, and (4) individual continuous improvement. Applying Wilber's (2000, 2006) notion of integral knowing to assessment provides a way of constructing assessment to account for the various purposes (Table 17.1).

The upper left quadrant is the individual's assessment of himself or herself. Using feedback from others and looking at how he or she measured against criteria or a population, what does he or she need to do to improve and show learning?

The upper right provides the standards against which students are measured. Many state performance or content standards fall under this quadrant. Much of society and political entities use these external measures to gauge the effectiveness of schools. Grades are used as a value judgment rating the individual against the knowledge or skills the tests are designed to measure.

The lower right shows where an individual fits within a population. How did others do on similar tests; how many scored better or worst? The move toward schools and states being rated and given grades (educational report cards) reflects thinking within this quadrant.

The lower left focuses on quality criteria established and judged by the group in forming a culture of learning. The ratings done by the group provide feedback to the individual about how he or she can improve. The purpose of assessment in this quadrant is continuous improvement.

The four purposes of assessment contribute to a model of integral assessment. Each quadrant is important and none holds a privileged view in education. Through the use of this framework, the various purposes of assessment can be differentiated. If classrooms can be created to be places where individuals come to learn, then this integral model of assessment could be used to enhance the learning environment and

	Interior Assessment for continuous improvement	Exterior Assessment for accountability
Individual	**Self-Assessment** How does the individual measure against standards for achievement?	**Criterion-Referenced Standards** What does the individual need to do to improve his/her own learning and products?
Collective	**Peer Assessment** Using the group's established criteria for quality—what can be done to help the individual improve?	**Norm-Referenced Tests** How does the iundividual measure against the population—where does he/she fit?

Table 17.1 Assessment in the Quadrants

assist in reframing the notion of assessment to include continuous improvement as an integral part. The external measures could continue to be taken and the information would become part of the community. Individual students could move through the school system with an electronic portfolio that included all of the assessments from the various quadrants. Assessment could be integrated back into the whole, with the focus of the classroom on enhancing learning and individuals able to demonstrate learning.

Learning from My Own Practices

What I am really afraid of is finding out that I can no longer function within the system and that I have to give up teaching in my high school.
—High school chemistry teacher

Attempting pedagogical reform within schools as they currently are poses many challenges, especially for those of us who wish to change the system without actually leaving it. Learning how to use skilful means to achieve our vision of the potential of education is part of the daily practice of teachers. For me, integral theory assists in my being able to function within the current system because it allows me to see where I am in relation to where others may be. Integral theory causes me to rethink many of the assumptions I have made about education. I studied these ideas for years and held many conversations both online and face-to-face as I integrated the ideas into my own notions about teaching and learning. In my teaching, I continually try to make my practice as consistent with my understandings as possible. A major dilemma that continues to surface is with assessment and grading. The system in which I work requires that I give grades. The students I teach expect grades. At times, grading seems almost "anti-paradigmatic," in that I wonder about the ethics of rating someone else's learning. I also wonder how I can continue to work within a system that prioritizes standards and testing. This chapter is an exploration of my attempts to make sense, and to have my practices reflect my beliefs. In this sense, it is an action research project on my own practice, using student dialogue to inform me about my actions and my students' interpretations. Integral theory acts as a locating system, a GPS of consciousness, because it allows me to enhance my intentions and align my actions, while being aware of how students are making meaning of their educational experiences. It is my hope that by accompanying me through my journey, the reader can use this to inform his or her own journey.

Context

The class that is the focus of this action research was a graduate-level class on theories of teaching and learning science. The class contained 17 graduate students in science education; of these, 7 were concurrently in a teaching situation, 8 had no teaching experience, and 2 had previous teaching experience but were currently full-time students. The students used Blackboard, a commonly used web-based teaching platform, to communicate with me and with other students, and all assignments were delivered through the internet. Data for this paper were taken from a discussion forum on the web that was assigned the topic of "assessment." This forum included more than 3,000 lines of communication. This chapter discusses the processes and procedures of establishing peer assessment, as well as an analysis of the learners' developing understanding.

Creating a Community of Learners

In order to better understand the usefulness of integral theory for me, I must first explain the goals I had for the class that is the focus of this chapter. In trying to form my own courses with integrity (Palmer, 1998), I strive to create learning communities. I believe that the future of institutions of education should be about creating schools as learning places, rather than work places (Marshall, 1990). My image of schools is that they are places where anyone can come to learn. Using Bruffee's (1999) notions of collaborative learning, the purpose of education is to introduce the novice into the discourse community of the discipline of which the course is representative. For the course on teaching and learning science, the purpose was to introduce the students into the ways of thinking and talking about learning science and to introduce scholars and current issues in teaching and learning science. Bruffee asserts that introduction of the novice into a discipline's discourse can be accomplished by establishing discourse communities based on problems of the discipline. Discipline discourse is best learned through critique and peer negotiation of the ways of thinking and talking within the discipline. The role of the teacher or instructor is to establish a safe environment for the students to try out their new understandings and to check that understanding with the community. I needed my assessment practices to align with the goals of community I wanted to accomplish. Part of establishing community meant the power inherent in assessment needed to be distributed throughout the community as well.

The "learning" part of the community focuses on the evolution of thinking of the individuals enrolled in the course. Another way of describing learning is "continuous improvement." The term continuous improvement comes from new business metaphors about learning organizations (Senge et al., 2004) (if classrooms aren't learning organizations, what are they?) and from management psychology (Torbert, 2004).

Theoretical Frames

Although integral theory is far more complex, in this chapter, I use two aspects of integral theory to inform the interpretations: (1) Wilber's (2000) 4-quadrants and (2) developmental levels. The developmental levels are based on the work of Cook-Greuter (2002) and Torbert (2004), and action logics are used to identify the levels of complexity in learners' thinking. "The model refers to stages as action logics because it focuses on how people tend to reason and act in life" (Cook-Greuter, 2002, p. 1). Cook-Greuter delineates nine levels of adult development. The six levels summarized in Table 17.2 are the most prevalent within our culture.

The two further levels are rarely found in the general population and are not salient to this discussion. These levels of unfolding are "permanently available capacities and coping strategies that can, once they have emerged, be activated under the appropriate life conditions" (Wilber, 2000, 47-48). Individuals evolve through levels of development as their thinking becomes more sophisticated and previous ways of thinking no longer work as well. Earlier action logics are still available, and when individuals encounter stressful or strange situations, they may revert to previous action logics. "Although people may use several action logics throughout the day, they tend to prefer to use the most complex action logic they can produce automatically. Under pressure and rapid change conditions, they often resort to behavior patterns from earlier stages" (Cook-Greuter, 2002, 1).

Cook-Greuter's developmental model was selected because it was derived from sentence completion tests and thus relies on individual's use of language to determine the level of development. Because this study relied on written postings to a class discussion board, analysis of conversation was the primary data source.

Developing Criteria for Assessment

As I sought to establish communities of learners to inquire critically about the nature of teaching and learning science in schools, dialogue was the primary component of the class. Learners needed to develop the skills necessary to communicate their learning clearly to their own learning community as well as to the larger community of educators. The students needed to experience the sorts of reforms about which they were reading and that are promoted in much of the literature. Before they could create learning environments in their own contexts, the prospective and practicing teachers needed to know what it was like to participate within a community of inquirers and to experience shared power within the classroom.

Within the course structure, one primary experience shared by the community of learners was to have common readings. Texts were selected to enhance reflection on classroom practices and the larger political structures of science and science education. The students were assigned weekly readings and asked to create critical reviews of those readings, to be posted on the web. In addition to posting critical reviews, learners were required to assess their peers' reviews. Each learner assessed two other reviews. Functions within the website allowed the peer assessments to be assigned randomly and blind, so assessors were not aware of whom they were assessing or of who assessed them. Developing technologies have made the use of peer assessment manageable. Previously, the hassles created by trying to have blind and random reviews prohibited use of these techniques. Having all the assignments posted to the web made them easily accessible to the participants of the learning community.

Self-assessments also were required, and learners took into consideration the comments and suggestions received from their peers and from the instructor. In the self-assessment, the learner had an opportunity to defend his or her writing and to reflect upon improvements that could be made.

Criteria for assessment of the critical reviews were first introduced in the course syllabus. Further negotiation occurred in the notice boards on the web. To begin the conversation, the class used criteria established through consensus in previous graduate classes and were asked to negotiate the learning community's criteria by accepting or rejecting the proposed criteria. These criteria were explained in class, and questions that helped indicate the criteria had been met were provided and posted on the web for the students' reference. The areas suggested for assessing critical reviews included (1) criticalness, (2) scholarship, (3) connections to experience, and (4) professionalism. Peers used these criteria to guide their assessments of others' writings.

Criticalness involved looking at the underlying assumption in the article and posting a critique that made explicit these assumptions. Questions to help focus the assessment included:

- Is the text examined critically looking at the implication of what is written and discussing both positive and negative contributions?
- Is the discussion provocative, does it raise questions in the readers mind?

Scholarship involved showing that one was a member of the learning communities. Two specific communities were involved: first, the professional community

Level and % of US Population at Level	Perspective Taking Ability	Description of Level	Language Clues
Opportunist **4.1%**	In Person Perspective Later Rudimentary 2nd Person	Win/lose mentality Manipulative/ exploitive Others are blamed Anger projected outward	Use of I perspective Foreground self-view as only legitimate view Simple dichotomies: good/bad; right/wrong
Diplomat **11.3%**	2nd Person Perspective Later Rudimentary 3rd Person	Concrete operational Dependency on authority Suppression of Anger Acceptance of norms without question	Short stereotypical phrases Concrete description Use of "shoulds" and "oughts"
Expert **36.5%**	3rd Person	Ability to Introspect and compare self to others Competitive High Moral Standards	Know the answers or correct way things should be done Yes-but syndrome
Achiever **27.9%**	3rd to 4th Person	Formal reasoning, decisions based on evidence Ability to consider alternatives Look to root causes and explanations Intellectual skepticism	Analysis of causes and reasons Acknowledgement of others' views; "agree to disagree" Complex argument— rational thinking Sense of unique "I"
Individualist **11.3%**	4th to 5th Person	Systems thinking Holistic thinking Tolerance and appreciation of others	Acceptance of paradox "And" replaces 'but' and "or" Cognitive complexity in sentence structure
Strategist **4.9%**	5th to 6th Person	Acceptance of complexity Tolerance of self and others	Complex flexible syntax Acknowledgement of complexity of life in verbal expressions

Table 17.2 Summary of Six Levels of Development
Based on Cook Greuter's (2002) Levels of Ego Development

of the course content and second, the learning community of the class. Questions included:

- Does the writer show membership in the community of the text writing through connection to other readings?

of the course content and second, the learning community of the class. Questions included:

- Does the writer show membership in the community of the text writing through connection to other readings?
- Does the writer show membership in the class community through referencing of others' contributions?

Connection to experience included experiences as a teacher and as a learner that illustrated ideas discussed in the readings to the teachers' "real world" of teaching and learning. The questions asked to guide the assessment of this component were:

- Does the writer connect to his or her teaching/learning experiences?
- Does the writer connect to his or her research experiences?

Professionalism was a term derived to address technical issues such as appropriate grammar, spell checking, and posting styles. An important component of professionalism was timeliness—was the posting on time? Timeliness was particularly important because others' involvement in writing peer assessments depended on the posting being available in a timely manner.

Initially during the semester, I modeled the assessment process by providing students with suggestions for improvement using the criteria above and by building on the conversations started in the critical reviews. However, as the semester progressed, my role in the initial critical review assessment process faded. My role became to assess the assessments. The criteria I used in my assessments were:

- Did the peer assessment help the peer to improve?
- Did the peer assessment continue the conversation?
- Did the self-assessment reflect critically on the comments provided by others and reflect learning?

Experiences with Peer Assessment: Reflections on the Process

As the class had opportunities to engage with the process of peer assessment, several themes emerged. One that had an effect on this action research was the issue of rating each other, or providing a score. Students were reluctant to score their peers, doubting their own ability to assess.

I do not think we should rate each other's work; I thought that the point was to help improve and I don't see where a rating comes into play. I would like to critique but not give a "grade." I would prefer to leave that to Nancy.

This view that the teacher should be the one who assesses is common within traditional schools where teachers represent the authority and content experts within the class. This view is widely held and needs to be addressed openly in order for learners to understand the intents and purposes of assessment. Even with open explanation, those who are at a diplomat or expert level are unable to understand the intentions of higher levels of development. So, in this particular class, I acquiesced to their reluctance for two reasons: (1) my own struggle with grading and (2) a desire to let students know they had a voice in the decision-making process in the class. In subsequent classes, I maintained the requirement that students rate each other, for several reasons: (1) as professional educators, they are required to rate others constantly, and this is a practice they need to develop; (2) the rating system enhanced the responsibility that some learners had toward posting serious contributions; and (3) the focus of peer assessments included the evidence the raters used to make their decisions. This all fit with my intentions to help the learners focus on the process of assessment rather than rating. This focus assisted the learners in articulating their rationales, rather than focusing on the expectations or emotional reaction they might have toward individuals.

Competing Perspectives of Assessment

Analysis of the notice board discussion revealed that the students thought about assessment primarily from two differing perspectives. These two views (i.e., value judgment and continuous improvement) tended to clash and caused frustration in the learning community. Additionally, in the analysis, we can see levels of Cook-Greuter's action logics revealed in the students' words. If competing values are present within a classroom, resistance and stress often result unless the leader (i.e., teacher) is well aware of the contrasting values (Davis & Blanchard, 2005). Even with this awareness, the students may be unable to overcome their resistance. In this section, an analysis of both the contrasting perspectives and the levels of development are explored.

Assessment as Value Judgment

One of the primary purposes of assessment in our current culture is to prove to individuals external to the classroom that time and resources are being well-used in the schools and that the students and teachers are "working." This accountability is judged by measuring the students' knowledge against an external standard of knowledge to be gained. The result of this measurement is often translated into grades that represent the knowledge a student has achieved. The intent is interpreted within a work metaphor for schools (Marshall, 1990), and grades are interpreted as measures of effort.

Learners in the class reflected this view of grades using payment and credit meta-phors.

> *If I understand everything, the peer reviews have no weight whatsoever. I think that it is important that we get some credit for it. The age-old argument is we should learn for the knowledge, but my feeling is if I am not going to get paid, then why do it properly. We need some kind of credit to have people put in their best effort. If no one gets credit, then I am afraid that people will just overlook doing the critical reviews and peer assessments.*
>
> —Don

> *HOLD IT RIGHT THERE! [emphasis in the original] I'm putting in the time and effort, I want credit.*
>
> —Helen

In these two comments, the desire (demand) for immediate reward can be seen. Learning is not for the individual's improvement or development, but rather a task to be accomplished to get ahead.

This payment metaphor in schools is of particular interest because, although teachers are using a currency of grades, many students do not recognize or value that currency, as Don reflected in his comments:

> *It would be interesting to sit down and talk to your students about how assessment should be for "building and learning," but what does a teacher do with a student who does not want to be at school, period? Students like this don't really care about school in the first place and assessment would be the last thing that is on their minds.*
>
> —Don

Don's reflection reveals his own view that some students are not interested in the work of learning and that assessment is irrelevant to them.

When assessment is viewed as a value judgment, a very important issue for the student is for whoever is doing the assessment to be an expert or authority and be "fair" in his or her assessment.

> *I think that assigning grades at the peer level stops short of that [learning] process. It takes nothing into account about how that peer assessment was assimilated by the student. Also, it does not start everyone out as "even," since (for example) some people will tend to grade a paper "very good," where others may tend to grade "superb." That's (theoretically) not a problem if you have one teacher doing the grading. Peer grading introduces another level of uncertainty into an already somewhat arbitrary grade system. What if we don't agree with the grade we get? Who do we talk to? Or, what if we are afraid to give the grade we think the paper deserves because we don't want to make our peers angry?*

—Margaret

The learner's fear that others will get angry reflects a diplomat's level of thinking about the learning environment. Wanting to keep the relationships between peers friendly and smooth, the learner anticipates honest assessments as a threat to the learning environment. This student reflected that she would be more willing to approach an authority than her peers in demanding fairness. This tendency to value correctness based on authority reveals a thinker who is operating at a diplomat level of development. The learners rationalize why the change in roles for grading makes them inherently more uncertain. This notion, based in assessment as a value judgment rather than a way to improve, limits the usefulness of assessment. This issue of fairness, when taken to a level of liability, becomes a critical issue in making value judgments.

> I am coming from the position of a high school teacher in a public school, and I personally do not allow my students to grade each other's work. Parents would not be happy if they found out that students were assigning grades to other students, and when it came to report card time, they want to know how that student did according to the teacher, not his or her peers. If I allowed students to do my grading, parents would wonder what I was doing! This issue recently came up with a LD student, who is the child of one of my friends. My friend has reported the child's teacher to the school board for allowing other students to grade his work. Our policy is that each student has a right to privacy, and does not have to share his or her grades with any member of the class. We do not call out grades, we do not allow other students to assign grades, we hand papers directly to each student...Grades are a private issue and I wish to keep it that way, even in graduate school.
>
> —Mona

This learner also reflects a diplomat level of development because she brought up conforming to external protocols and rules as a rationale for not changing how assessment is traditionally done. The privacy issue reflects the learner's interpretation of assessment as a judgment process and keeping the grade private is important, particularly if one's own self-esteem is attached to that grade. Mona described herself as "an A student," thus using this external measure as a personal defining factor.

When grades become defining factors for individuals, fairness becomes particularly important when considering assessment.

> I think that any student that works hard should get what s/he deserves and I think that disadvantaged students, be they African American, ESL [English as a second language], poor or whatever, get tired of being made to feel that they get grades just because of their disadvantage and not because they have worked their butt off. Why can't grades be assigned based on effort?
>
> —Tonya

From the perspective of fairness and objectivity, establishment of clear criteria by which quality can be judged becomes paramount. When credit or payment is the metaphor through which grading is interpreted, the issue introduces an additional problem of differing individuals having to exert more effort to get the grades, thus being "paid" at differing rates. The potential for discrimination because of subjectivity is a real possibility in the minds of the individuals being assessed. The duality established between the learner and the teacher mediates against the establishment of a learning community.

Developmentally, Tonya's comments can be considered to be from an individualist level, wherein questioning the rules of authority occurs more frequently than at the diplomat level. A primary contribution from this level is the consideration of other's perspectives and equality issues. This questioning extends to the roles of assessment in learning, as Tonya did when she sought alternative ways to think about grading.

As the learners discussed the process of peer assessment, they applied the ideas to other classes in which they were currently enrolled. Physics for Teachers, a class in which many were concurrently enrolled, required them to make conceptual sense of physics content. In physics class, the students worked in groups, doing experiments. In their assignments, they explained what was happening, as they would to a middle-school student. The professor scored them not only on correct answers, but also on the clarity and understanding revealed by their writing. In this context, several of the students reflected a diplomatic level of development in their reluctance to rate peers, based on a perceived lack of expertise.

Nancy asked me an interesting question the other day... if Dr. C gave us the option to peer assess each other in Physics, would I choose to do it? I think I would say no. I don't feel my physics knowledge is at a level to do this. I feel that Dr. C's class demands the "right" answer, which I don't always have. What would you do?

—Susie

But what would you do about someone like me who has learned helplessness when it comes to my physics ability. I just don't see how I could do any type of assessment in a Dr. C's course because my own content knowledge was very limited.

—Don

Although the physics professor had sense-making as a goal, the students doubted their own ability to make sense of content in which they felt they lacked experience. The notion of "learned helplessness" caused them to be passive participants in the class and to act against the goals of the course. This notion of expertise is common in higher education classes and is counterproductive when attempting to establish a learning community based on sharing and continuous improvement. Using external measures against which they were compared influenced their ability to develop critical stances in the class. This is one of the unintended consequences of the standards movement prevalent in education today. These students were unable to see themselves as viable contributors in the physics community of which they were not a part.

The members of the learning community spent several weeks trying to establish what each of the criteria meant and tried to make their scoring process as objective as possible. About four weeks into the semester, most of the students expressed considerable frustration at trying to agree upon objective criteria for grading and realized that was getting in the way of accomplishing the course goals of establishing a learning community:

> Please correct me if I am wrong and I know some of you will—but I see what is being suggested by Susie [objective criteria] as going against the idea of building a learning community. It seems that somewhere along the way we have lost sight of the community and are thinking every woman/man for her/himself.
>
> —Tonya

Tonya, who recognized the competitive metaphor that underlay assessment as value judgment, was able to objectify the process and see how competition mitigated against the intents of establishing a learning community. As students competed for grades as limited resources or as comparisons of one against the other, the notion of building a learning community was compromised. Even in this context, in which the students were not grading one another, the issue continued to surface. This is an indication of how strongly the framework of value judgment is held by learners within the system.

When the establishment of a learning community is the goal for education, then grading tends to act against continuous improvement. Grading as value judgment and accountability establishes the instructor as an authority in the classroom. Reliance on external values undermines the individual's ability to look at assessment as continuous improvement.

Assessment as Continuous Improvement

My goal in the course was to use another intent for assessment: to reflect the learning process. Learning involves development, and to assess the learning process would be to provide feedback for the learner to continuously improve his or her own thinking in the content of the course. When continuous improvement is the goal, then learning becomes the focus. The learners in the course reflected on the importance of receiving information, or feedback, on their writing and thinking:

> I agree with those who feel that they want/need feedback in order to proceed. Would you say that we become stagnant without feedback?
>
> —Cally

This ability to welcome feedback represents the level of thinking of the achiever.

Quality is still an issue, but it takes on a different tone, valuing the subjectivity. As Peggy described:

> *An issue we are struggling with is the important criteria of quality. This is how I am trying to make sense of QUALITY as it relates to critical reviews. We have all sampled a particular dish at different functions, say, steamed fish, and liked it all the time. Then this day we taste steamed fish again and it is like we have never tasted before. It is of a high QUALITY. We cannot really describe it but it is above and beyond. To me, that is superb. There is a good blend of the spices and the herbs, just right. So, what are the spices and the herbs in writing a review?*
>
> —Peggy

Understanding the nuances of quality and being able to describe that in words enhanced the learning within the community as members developed a more sophisticated understanding of the process. Others in the community were able to see the power in developing communication about the ideas even as these ideas applied to the physics class:

> *Maybe it would be easier getting through Dr. C's course if there were some amount of peer assessment. Yes, it would mean more work than we already have, but, I think that as you read someone's explanation you would be forced to challenge your own content knowledge which I think does help in the sense-making process. Once there is a discrepancy or difference in your peer's work, you would be forced to sort this out, which in turn helps you. Don't you think? The problem I see would be giving the explanation in the way, form, or wording that Dr. C wants or requires. If the goal is learning, then peer assessment should not be a problem. I am reminded of von Glasersfeld's response to assessment, as long as assessment is based on performance, where performance means the ability to reproduce answers that were part of the instructional process we are not assessing what would be important learning from a constructivist point of view.*
>
> —Peggy

Peggy was beginning to look at assessment in a more complex manner, as a way to learn rather than merely a value judgment. The shared experience of the physics class provided the students with a place from which to look at their own learning and to think about the conflicting notions of assessment, as they developed their own sophistication in understanding the purposes of assessment within the learning community. This place from which to view the process allowed the learners to stretch themselves and encouraged the formation of multiple perspectives.

> *Although I am not in Dr. C's class, I see a connection to why some of students in our class opted not to assess others' work. Think back to the beginning of this class and your first attempt at writing a critical review. Now think about the critical reviews you write now. Have you seen any improvement? If so has some of that improve-*

ment been sparked by the comments you received from your peers. If the critical reviews don't do it for you, think about how much your peers have contributed to your overall learning since entering this class. I guess the point I am trying to make is that maybe you should look at peer assessment as a means of enhancing your learning.

—Tonya

Tonya's development as a learner is clearly highlighted in this quote because she considers assessment part of the learning process. As the learners continued to struggle with the process, they reexamined their notions of assessment and its purpose within the learning community:

What exactly is assessment? What is its purpose? I am seeing different answers in the recent conversation. Tonya presents a vision of assessment as skill development based on input from others. Allen presents a vision of assessment as an objective endeavor measuring individual learning. Don presents a vision of an activity that changes from setting to setting. My dictionary says to assess is "to fix the rate or amount of." It says that to evaluate is to "appraise, value." With definitions like these, it is difficult to separate assessment from value judgment. I am beginning to think we need a different vocabulary to better describe the activities/outcomes we want.

At the same time, is the-concept-formerly-known-as-assessment a stopping point or a continual process? As it is currently used, I say stopping point. Don raises a good question about the-concept-formerly-known-as-assessment in other settings. I think the-concept-formerly-known-as-assessment should fit the goals of the learning environment. But throughout the process the learners still confused the continuous improvement goal with grades.

—Helene

Helene identified the continuing struggle members of the class had because the multiple definitions of assessment created conflicts within the learners. Her comments reveal that she was developing a more complex level of understanding, including the notion of creating new words to describe the processes. Continuing to wrestle with the issue, Susie began to see a learning purpose even in the scientific context:

But wouldn't it be interesting if we tried to assess in his class? Maybe it would have to be assessed by both the peers and Dr. C. Maybe Dr. C could assess the "correctness" of the physics, and we could assess the clarity of the writing. We would be able to help each other with communication skills, presentation of concepts, etc. I think it could be possible.

—Susie

Although earlier in the course Susie could not consider assessing physics knowledge, her experiences in the teaching and learning course broadened her thinking about assessment. However, not all students were as creative as Susie, and these conflicting purposes of assessment continued to create dissonance within the class.

Assessment is a completely difficult issue. I thought I had it under control, but obviously, I am nowhere near. Nancy always poses the most difficult questions and I have to think about them a long time and I can't always give an answer. I am going to take the constructivist's way out and say that I am still constructing my understanding of assessment. I guess that is a good sign. I thought after 24 years of teaching and testing, I might have the definitive answer, but again I find myself at a bifurcation point full of perturbations. I am constructing! Change requires reflection on practice as ideas are applied.

—Patty

Patty's comments reflect the focus discussed in this chapter. Although the class was established with a goal of creating a community of learners, and assessment was defined as continuous improvement, the ways the learners viewed assessment were based on their levels of development and their previous experiences in schools. The competing notions of value judgment and continuous improvement worked against each other. Through the process of reflecting on assessment throughout the semester, the learners became more aware of the potential of reframing the intentions of assessment as a learning tool. It was a slow process, as students tried out the new framework and applied it to their experiences. Not all students progressed to the level of accepting assessment as a tool for change. They continued to wrestle with notions of assessment, and several of the students focused their graduate research on the processes of assessment. The point is that learning to think about assessment as continuous improvement is a developmental process and needs to be brought to the forefront of the conversations so students can learn from their own reflections. Individuals who attempt to integrate peer- and self-assessment into their own practices need to be aware that the learners may or may not be able to make the leap. As an instructor, being able to develop trust within the community is paramount in setting the stage. Establishing trust takes time and considerable effort, and an intentional awareness.

Creating an Integral Assessment

Throughout this chapter, I have drawn upon Cook-Greuter's (2002) action logics and the framework of the quadrants to inform me about the use of peer assessment to achieve my goals as a teacher.

Using the Four Quadrants to Inform Assessment

As I came to understand the varying purposes for assessment, using the four quadrants as a guide, I was better able to determine how I wanted to use assessment in the classroom. I was able to better articulate to others, in particular future classes, what my intentions were in using the forms of assessment I used. As we discussed, creating integral assessment has four aspects:

What interior learning do I want the students to gain? What opportunities do students have to reflect on what they are learning? What are the opportunities for self-assessment?	What measures of knowledge do I want the students to demonstrate? What products will they produce, and what are the standards against which they may be judged? What rubrics can be created to determine and communicate their gains?
How can a community of learning be established? What are the opportunities for the learners to negotiate and contribute to the learning process? How can the learners gain a voice in the grading proces? What are the opportunities for peer assessment?	What are the structures that contribute to the learning environment? How can the learners demonstrate the quality of their learning to those outside the context? What rubrics can be used to compare and contrast the products of learning?

Table 17. 3 Planning Tool Using 4-Quadrants

1. Assessment of the interior of the self (learning) through self-assessment;
2. Assessment of self, measured against established criteria;
3. Assessment of the population and the location of the individual within the population; and
4. Assessment of the quality within group norms—peer assessment or peer review.

I find the quadrants to be a useful tool when reflecting on my own intentions in teaching and assessing. I attempt to include all four quadrants in my planning, as well as in my assessment products. One might use the matrix in Table 17.3 to assist in planning:

Assessment from Developmental Levels

Although this research was limited to a few students, patterns began to emerge Utilizing Cook-Greuter's developmental levels to understand the students' reactions and comments regarding peer assessment provided me with clearer understanding of what I need to do to assist students in the assessment process. Because peer and self-assessment are not the norm in our educational system, being aware of students' fears and concerns can help us to provide structures to assist students' growth. One might ask the following questions to help understand students' developmental levels in relation to assessment practices:

- How complex is the language students are using?
- What perspectives are the students expressing?
- What fears are being expressed by the students?
- What type of reasoning is used?

These questions pose a preliminary frame for considering how learners are conceptualizing the assessment process. With further research, a framework for assessment might be developed.

Conclusions

Education is a complex endeavor (Davis, 2004), with many perspectives that can be used to understand what happens in learning environments and educational systems. Education is also a practice of cultural reproduction (Pinar et al., 1995). When this cultural reproduction, integral theory is viewed as a method of hope and as a way of achieving a more sophisticated development of culture, and provides a framework for action. Acknowledging and valuing the multiple purposes of assessment, while understanding that our students bring varying perspectives of assessment to the learning environment, we, as educators, can develop skillful means that can help us align our intentions with our practices, as we consider how the learners are interpreting what we do. We can act with compassion as we use the wisdom we gain from looking at our own practices and our students' conceptions of those practices through integral lenses. This chapter tells the story of my own ongoing journey of understanding of assessment as a tool, a skillful means to be used to enhance development, and I invite you, dear reader, to join with me.

18

Integral Program/Curriculum Design in a Technical World

Terri O'Fallon

Overture

Pam signed into her online class, Social Systems, to check her students' offerings for the day. They were in the process of putting together a "teach-in," an online approach to working with a literature review, but in this class, each of three groups were delving into one critical aspect of the material related to the class, and it was their assignment to prepare a "class" for the next week where they would teach the material they had researched to the other two groups. At the culmination of the teach-in, there was to be a downloadable paper with all the information they had researched, all in the appropriate formatting. By collecting all these "chapters" each student would have their own textbook for the course, one they had written themselves, with material they themselves had taught others or learned from others.

Pam checked into the online forum space for the first group of three. They had posted the minutes to their planning phone call and a reflection on their process for the week, with suggestions of how to improve their online work together along with a plan for the next week. There were also the various iterations of the work they had planned to teach. It was exciting for Pam to see that, in their teach-in, they began with a small reading assignment, followed by a short at-home research project that would make the material come alive in the other participants' bones.

After checking all three groups Pam signed into the coaching corner where she found several questions by students asking for suggestions, mentoring or references. Then she moved on to the journals to check in on the progress on the individual projects each student was completing over the quarter. The quarter was about to end and it looked to be a very successful one; this course was one of a number of specific courses, each one intertwined with the other to produce a program that was "whole-cloth" and completely integrated. Teachers from different classes were collaborating together on single projects that meet some of the requirements of all their classes.

Students seldom see the collaboration that the faculty does in the program planning or their cooperation, which guides projects and an integration of the material. In this combination of online and face-to-face learning, things move along so smoothly few people know about the integral planning process that brings it about.

The previous description is a snapshot of a day in the life of a University instructor who is teaching a course in an integrated Masters Degree program on Integral Transformative Learning. The platform that is used could be any one of a myriad of platforms in use at this level of education, and in this case the class is part of an integrated online and face-to-face program, which gives the students an opportunity to learn through multiple learning options. The rest of this paper will describe an integral step-by-step process that can be used to develop an entire program, or a course. The summary at the end will share more ideas related to creative options for online learning.

Introduction

The online medium has exploded as a means of conveying education and information to participants all over the world. There are numerous platforms and a multitude of approaches that have been used and are being invented, many of which attempt to replicate face-to-face experiences in the online environment. New platforms such as Web 2.0, and other integrated technologies, bring a new world of engagement to learning and teaching. These processes, including some of the interactive approaches, can be quite advanced, and still they do not capitalize on the capacities of the online possibility. It is important to take advantage of the hidden benefits of the online classroom in designing curricula. Infusing integral programs with an online focus can add benefits to learning that go well beyond face-to-face experiences. It is critical to engage the world of technology, as it is indeed the new generation's primary platform for learning.

Combining Technology-Based and Face-to-face Learning

The benefits of face-to-face learning are well known. There is a presence with others in the moment. One can experience live, human exchanges in the classroom through all of the senses, and multiple ways of knowing are relatively easy to use.

Face-to-Face (FTF) teaching and learning can be presented in many ways. Lecture format can be combined with engaging exercises, group work, fieldwork, research projects, art work and a number of other engaging ways of learning. FTF experiences are dependant upon the composure of the participant population, the maturity of present learning, participant ages, learning styles, levels, lines, states, and types.

Most of these pedagogical approaches may be supported in an online teaching environment as well. However, online pedagogy offers some benefits that FTF can't offer; it can bring together people from far-flung areas to form networks that would have never occurred otherwise. Information, class work and online spontaneous dialogues and conversations can be made permanent through archives so that the participants can review their work over a number of months or years. As a result, participants may track their personal changes, reflect on the differences between now and then as well as the trajectory of their translations and transformations. These archives may also be used to conduct research.

Since assignments can be put online for all to see, everyone learns from all of the assignments of all of the students. This advantage is in contrast to most FTF modes where individual students present their paper or project to instructors for private feedback. In the online arena, participants can provide feedback and reflections on their peer's work and receive feedback on their own work from many people with ease. An introverted student may reflect for a day or two and revise and reformulate her response until she feels confident before offering it. In an FTF class, she may never respond or participate to this extent.

It is far easier to invite a live guest speaker-expert from afar to present interactively on a topic. The online capacities make it possible for experts to engage with students without ever boarding an airplane. In addition, conference calling and video conferencing provide aspects of learning that FTF classes don't incorporate. Video/conference calling allows participants to ask questions in real time and engage in a timely dialogue together while still providing a connection with people all over the world. In this paper, several levels of technology-based, integral education will be described. The first level provides an example of setting up of an integrally informed online delivery system that incorporates a complete curriculum capable of delivering an integral degree or non-degree program of two or more years. The second level examines the design process of one integral course within such a program. The third area describes a technologically informed integral program carried out in real time. Woven throughout these three levels is the interaction among other media, such as video/conference calls and face-to face learning.

Designing a Long-term Integral Program through Infusing Technological Approaches

When designing a program that offers a degree or certificate or that is long-term (lasting a year or more), the Integral lens provides a remarkable platform upon which to situate the planning. For the purposes of this paper, "Integral" is defined in terms of the four-quadrant model developed by Ken Wilber (2006).

The chart below depicts the developmental nature of Wilber's four quadrants model; the Upper Left (UL) which depicts individual subjective, the Upper Right (UR) which depicts the individual objective, the Lower Left (LL) which depicts the collective subjective and the Lower Right (LR) which depicts the group inter-objective.

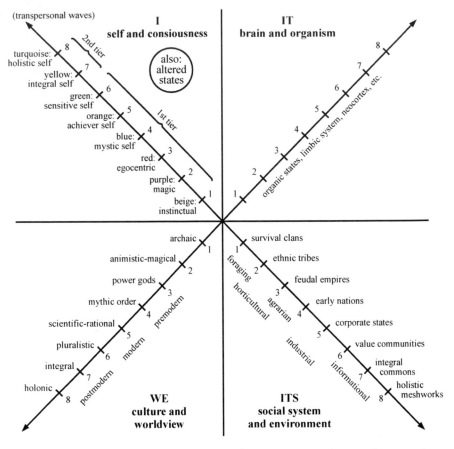

Figure 18.1: Ken Wilber's Great Chain of Being, Sex, Ecology and Spirituality

Program Vision

A program usually begins with one or more people who have a vision or insight for a long-term program offering. In this case, it would be the responsibility for the program founders (of the course, degree program, an entire school or learning organization program), to crystallize the vision, and this can be assisted by Wilber's Integral frame (2006). This process requires viewing the original vision through the Integral framework, crafting the vision statement (which works best when it honors multiple perspectives) and selecting an integral team in order to design the program, based on the vision.

Selecting the Curriculum Design Team

Selecting appropriate members of a team to plan the integral program, involving online and other technological media, calls for an array of integrally informed members who may be at various levels of development (Cook Greuter, 2002) and several members who reside primarily at the integral level (Strategist or later). Honoring all these voices in the curriculum serves to attract individuals from a variety of levels to the program. One might consider involving team members who are situated in different geographical areas, so that portions of their work would be designed together online. When the design team reaches the experience level of being immersed in the technological milieu that they wish to incorporate, they will be far more likely to include the experiences that they themselves find valuable and avoid the aspects that are less appropriate in the design they are creating. It is also important that they have the opportunity to work together FTF for part of the time.

Upper left (UL), upper right (UR) lower left (LL) and lower right (LR) quadrant planning involves intentional selection of individual planners who have skills and capacities in one or more quadrant perspectives.

Curriculum Planning Team Criterion for Selection

UL Individual Subjective	UR Individual Objective
Second tier or integral members Lines of Development • Intellectual • Moral • Values • Interpersonal • Intrapersonal Balance of types Male and Female	Skills to work with content in the Integral frame • Planning • Writing • Delivering specific topic content and curriculum artifacts in such a way that the program wilal be realized
LL Individual Subjective	**LR Interobjective Systems**
Willing to participate in a • Learning community approach • While designing the curriculum • As the team itself is engaged with their own learning and communi ty development through the pro cess of designing the curriculum	Design the curriculum in a system utilizing face-to-face, online and video=conference calling Credit, grading and evaluation systems for the program and the participants Reporting systems Payment, funding/accounting systems Case Management Application procedures Recuitment of participants System of standards of the integrally informed faculty

Figure18.2: Four Quadrant Curriculum Planning

Designing and Planning the Integral Program

The integral team is now ready to begin the Integral design, which 1) invites the development of purpose principles and their intended effect and 2) plans appropriate time segments for content that will form the basis of the program trajectory. Continually viewing the curriculum through the lens of each quadrant supports systematically taking a variety of perspectives on the design, as it is being developed.

This planning design team begins by meeting face-to-face to set up an online platform design for their use in-between conference calls and FTF intensives and to develop the principle purposes and intended effects of the integral curriculum.

What do they expect the principal purposes and effects represent (based on the perspectives of each quadrant, expressing all levels, accommodating a variety of lines, types and states for the outcome of the program)? Creating these principles from an integral standpoint sets the stage for an integrally informed curriculum.

The second step involves breaking the purposes and intended effects (springing from the vision) into time intervals in which blocks of information and experience can be delivered. This may involve a typical semester or quarter system or a series of two or more ecological intervals in which blocks of learning are completed. No matter how these segments are divided, it is important to place the classes so that there is a seamless flow of one knowledge segment or course to the next. A new set of integral purposes and intended results emerging out of the program principles is then created for each of these courses.

The third step involves seeing how these integral principles and intended effects may actually be delivered in an Integral format of learning that might appropriately involve online, face-to-face, and conference call formats.

Developing a Four Quadrant Plan with an Array of Integral Delivery Approaches

While developing the program design it is useful to look through as many perspectives as possible and plan three levels of learning. The first level includes curriculum prescribed by the program design itself (it), the second level focuses on curriculum which is designed by the faculty as needs arise (we), and the third level involves areas that are individually designed by the participant and/or faculty member for their own benefit and interest (I).

Planning for the development of a learning community (LL), including specific systems to support these experiences (e.g., written documents, processes, and platforms) that are available for everyone to refer to on a regular basis (LR), is important. Examples of specific program designs in three formats for each of the quadrants follow below.

AQAL Program Delivery Approaches

Planning Curriculum Delivery from a Team Perspective

Actual segments of learning, translated into courses or their equivalent, are developed with designated values (i.e. credits) and can be determined once awareness of various ways curriculum delivery is noted and opened.

UL Individual Subjective	**UR Individual Objective**
Faculty and participant delivery approaches evoking inner processes	*Faculty and participant delivery approaches evoking behaviors*
Online	**Online**
Online reflective interactive journals	Written or A/V lectures
Individual reflection papers	Individual criterion for assessment
Links to online typologies (e.g., Enneagram and Keirsey)	Individual participant presentation of written papers and other artifacts (e.g., self assessment integral research)
Intellectual inventories	Assigned postings journals
Online meditations	Assigned self-evaluations
Autobiographical writing—reading texts and other hard copy print materials while being aware of certain inner processes (e.g., marking the text they are attracted to (+) and that which they are repelled from (-) noting where they feel those states in their bodies	Faculty individual evaluations and individual assessments
	Coaching/mentoing delivered through online and email formats
Face to Face (FTF)	**Face to Face (FTF)**
Awareness of listening filers, reactions, states, etc. when in FTF intensives	Lectures
	Demonstrations
	Individual presentations and research
Video Conference Call	Art projects
Individual coaching	Story tellinn on life line
Mentoring	**Video Conference Call**
Question and Answer sesions	Individual conferences to support project development, and/or dissertation or project defense
Augmenting online inner processes	

Figure 18.3a: Upper Quadrants Delivery Approaches

LL Intersubjective	LR Interobjective
Faculty and participant deliery approaches for community learning	*Faculty approaches for support-ive systems*
Online	**Online technological platforms**
Online meditation	Websites
Learning community	Online grading and reporting
Paradoxes of group life	Online application
Integrative seminars	Pipeline procedures
Group norming	Scheduling of classes
Collaborating and making new knowledge together	Accounting systems
Self-organizing	Online communication
Evaluating a group project that engages material	Decision-making systems
Online "teach-ins" and drama	Strategic Plan
	Online AQAL program evalua-tion
Face to Face (FTF)	
Insight dialogue	**Face to Face (FTF)**
Learning Community ap-proaches	Applicant recruitment
Group norming	Interview and selection systems
Collaborating	FTF communication and decision-making systems
Making new knowledge together	Faculty recruitment, interview-ing and selection systems
Self-organizing a group project	AQAL evaluation systems
Improvisation and drama	**Video Conference Call**
Art projects	Recuitment and interviewing systems
Video Conference Call	
Group conference calls in which the participants sup-plment their group learning through plan ning and revlective feed back, feed-forward	

Figure 18.3b:Lower Quadrants Delivery Approaches

The team reviews all of the program's courses through FTF intensives, online inter-sessions and conference calls (alternated based on the specific needs of the program delivery). This alternative iterative process greatly benefits repetition in the learning.

Next, the online, FTF and conference call aspects of the curriculum design are planned, assuring the actual integration of all of the content and processes. An example of this planning would be the implementation of two ongoing courses through an entire 1-2 year (or more) program, reflecting all three delivery systems. 1) Learning community, (LL perspectives learned) could be used to enhance perspectives from the other three quadrants, and 2) an integrative seminar (which all faculty and students from the different courses attend), could provide an ongoing integration of all the content from the various courses and quadrant processes as they occur. In addition, individual, participant journals could enhance UL processes.

Learning Communities

Combining FTF activities with online learning brings together the best of both worlds, particularly when formulating a learning community. Bringing together a group of people in a FTF venue for several days can support the formation of community. There are specific FTF approaches one can use to support the development of a learning community that can be continued online to enhance community development. The online feature of this approach can inform learning through non-local communities, which seems worthwhile and inevitable in today's global arena.

Research may be conducted on the forming of community norms by reflecting on past postings. Hints of a birthing autopoietic process may be detected as communities form. This approach makes these typically unconscious norming processes conscious. The stages of community may also be apprehended with reflective processes on postings in the various online items, but especially in a learning community item, which may be ongoing for several years.

Alternating FTF and online work, the community can support each member to stand in their individual sovereignty while being completely dedicated to the group in a co-arising of self with other. The combination of FTF and online supports this co-arising. FTF interaction is generally very quick, but things slow down in the online forum. People have a chance to become aware of their reactions before they respond. They can activate the witness after an internal response, and their online posting may be a portrait of a second response coming out of a reflection of their initial conditioned response. Over a period of time, collective individualism can be taught with a combination of a FTF group that meets online in-between retreats, intensives or sessions.

When a group arrives at the point of working in a collective/individualistic approach, there is a palpable experience that cannot be mistaken. An experience of unity with the community and individuals within the community (coupled with a sense of being more of oneself) arises. There is no "group mind," because individuals have the capacity to stand in their own personhood and not be swayed by the group to support something with which they are not aligned. They may experience being honored for their stand, and then the group arises out of this capacity of individuals to stand without fear in their bare self and open to learning as self co-arises with the group and their work. This is different from a typical group-mind where people comply because they are afraid they will be rejected, judged, or will hurt someone's feelings (scape-goating those who don't comply with their way of thinking). Thinking, feeling and being can be fiercely independent and yet totally and palpably united. An experience begins to happen wherein individuals become sensitive to the group awareness and speak this knowledge into the group, recognizing that these words are not necessarily their own, and the ownership of words and multiple meanings of conceptions come into question.

At first, groups have this as a peak experience and then more frequently as the state becomes a stage. People who come to the online classroom with this experience may begin to experience this online, especially if there is group online meditation practice done in an asynchronous format in synchronous time, using the refresh button to access the latest in-time posting. This approach slows the conversation down so it isn't at all like a chat but more like slow meditative speech writing. The palpable connection begins to arise in this online meditative approach, and people begin to experience the expansion of self beyond their skin…many, many miles beyond their skin.

Integrative Seminar

An integrative seminar can serve as a means to assure that the AQAL vision; principles and intended results of the program are attended to on an ongoing basis. This seminar can run throughout the entire program integrating the experiences, learning, processes and content of all of the courses within the entire program. The integrative seminar incorporates all four-quadrant learning at once, providing ongoing insights and learning from both the faculty and students whom are all participants in the program.

Journals

An individual journal or internal blog for each participant to record his or her own internal learning, processes, and application of the course content into the world is a helpful online application. Assignments can be specifically made for these journals. Collaborative decisions about what can occur there may be created with the faculty, and individual choices, based on what they want to work with can be posted. These journals can be interactive; that is, everyone in the learning community may see the content of everyone's journal, but the owner of the journal may decide if they want comments or feedback from others in their journal. After a while, most often, participants appreciate these outside views and ask for the interaction within their journal. This approach supports their increasing sophistication of receiving and giving feedback.

Designing the Content Delivery System: Courses, Content Threads, Thematic Content

Content experts begin to create different courses or segments of learning. Individual courses might be stand-alone courses that have specific content, which is needed to complete the appropriate learning for the program. Other kinds of content might involve a series of courses, one building on another through the entire program, comprising specific content threads. However, thematic processes over time may still be important, such as an ongoing examination of norms or paradoxes of group life.

Use a collaborative inquiry approach to the planning process is a valuable Integral approach to designing the content of the program curriculum. Each content expert may work separately on the syllabi for their course, starting with an outline and an intention to make the course Integral (UR). Then, course developers come together and share what they have with each other, noting how the principles and intended effects of the time segment and the entire program (LL) are satisfied. The curriculum group working on this together can make suggestions for how these courses might mesh together, supporting each others' planning the online integrative seminar, integrating the material for the entire course, the FTF intensives (LL), identifying the compatibility of the grading system with each course and across courses (LR), including technology, grading and evaluation, recruiting, and funding needed to implement the delivery system for these courses (LR).

Each person, having learned from everyone else, may again work individually on their course document (UR), reflecting on what they had learned from the group interactions (UL) and cycling again to the group process (LL and LR). These cycles of individual reflection and action, and group reflection and action, may continue until the curriculum syllabi documents for the entire year or two-year plan are complete. Various classes may be offered within the context of FTF retreats and online intersessions, through the container of a learning community and integrative seminar.

A Sample Online Class

Online classes are most potent when they use multiple methods and processes in order to convey the information and the experience of applying the information. These classes are even more powerful if the participants are a part of a learning community because they already know each other in ways that a stand-alone class cannot provide. This approach offers a rich resource from which the material in an individual online class may arise.

For example, if an adult class is taught on worldview, belief systems, cultures, ways of knowing, certain English topics, history, and so on, one can begin by assigning groups of students to readings, including a typical online discussion in order to ground the basic knowledge of the class. Then, they could participate in a collabora-tive literature review on various parts of the content. For instance, a worldview, Eng-lish Literature/History class could research indigenous, egoic, traditional, modern, post modern and integral levels of the content area using the text books provided (augmented by using the library, World Wide Web, and other resources.) Highlight-ing development in a literature course, a history course, and even a mathematics course could serve to place any content area within a context of levels or belief sys-tems, which may support participants of most ages to learn about their own UL be-liefs and LL experiences in community.

After participants have been involved in their literature research deeply enough to have an idea about the content represented through the systems of worldviews, an expert in one of the content worldviews could be invited to engage with the class in a guest online forum. The students in the entire class can ask questions of the expert about the content within the worldview and everyone can read the responses. A new expert may be invited to join each week or every other week until each group has had visiting experts contributing to the knowledge base.

This knowledge could be supplemented by having the participants do FTF inter-views with people in one of those viewpoints (which can be compared to their litera-ture review and the guest speaker material may be incorporated into their reports). In addition, they could listen to audios, watch certain movies or read novels or stories where these particular areas within content are featured, identifying the worldviews or levels of the characters and perhaps the author.

Each group report can constitute a "chapter," which everyone downloads and reads, compiling their own textbook.

Also, each group could design a "teach-in" in order to teach the rest of the class the content within the area they have researched, including an "exercise" (often an activity the participants would do offline and report back on) that would support an experience of the content. The sponsoring group could host an interactive discus-sion. This may include participants reflecting, providing feedback and feed-forward regarding the presentation. The instructor may reinforce the worldview learning by providing a sample evaluation of each group from the perspective of the levels or content they represented; a recitation of facts for the traditional, competitive curve-based tests for the modern, a narrative for the post modern and an integral evaluation for each of the integral levels.

The culminating event could invite each person to step into a level or a belief sys-tem different from their own by developing a character based on the content within their selected level. They could begin with an online posting introducing themselves and describing their character. This activity may include a "photo" or drawing featur-ing a self-portrait, family work, and so on, which give the rest of the class a visual experience of their character. In each posting, the participant could use this portrait as a visual means of self-identification.

The instructor may then pose a question that the country or world is grappling with presently, related to the content area on which they are focusing. All of the par-ticipants step into the characters they developed. They begin a dialogue around the question posed, standing in the shoes of their character. Since the question is often a dilemma that may have multiple opinions around it, participants are challenged to stand in the shoes of this different level or worldview and have conversations depicting the character's view or level, even though their own opinions may personally be different.

Upon the culmination of the online improvisational drama, students could do a reflection assignment, describing what they learned as a result of being simultaneously engaged in dialoguing with one viewpoint and watching themselves with another. Ongoing reflections of the learning may be recorded in online journals, which every one in the class can see. The participant may decide if they want their journals to be interactive (that is, others in the class may respond to their reflections, asking questions, probing, making comments, and so on, which helps them expose shadow.) These journal entries may be used in a final paper, reflecting on what was learned in the class.

Each student could be evaluated based on completion of the work, contribution to the group, depth of questioning of the guest speaker, engagement in the teach-in, written skills, and the authenticity of their character during the improvisation. If grades are required, possibly use a point system for each area and decide which level would be used to evaluate the student, making it explicit to them. Overall grading and evaluation could be based on the criterion jointly decided by the curriculum team.

Planning for the Class

The example above might portray an ambitious plan for a one quarter or semester class, but perhaps it illustrates the creation of a class that works from all of the quadrants, several levels, lines and states and multiple ways of knowing (illustrating some of the combinations that might be considered when you are constructing the syllabi.)

First, it is important to know if participants of the class are naive about the subject. If it is an entry-level class, beginning with some traditional teaching may be helpful by assigning text pages that summarize the basic content of the class as an overview so they may begin to see what the material is all about. This would be important for both FTF and online approaches (UR, UL quadrants; level, traditional.) Traditional teaching approaches (show and tell) are very worthwhile for initiating participants into new worlds of material through direct instructional approaches.

The group works together to get the facts about content in the literature review and together write a paper with everyone owning the product. They also learn from an "expert/elder." This activity also has the flavor of indigenous and traditional teaching (LL quadrant, indigenous and traditional levels.) Each student, however, has the opportunity to ask the expert individual questions to satisfy their own curiosity and independently interview other people about their topic (UR, UL quadrant; level, Modern.) They have an opportunity to decide how they are going to compete for a grade in the class (UR quadrant; levels, Modernist.)

The group self-organizes (post-modern/integral) and constructs a "teach-in" for the other members of the class giving participants at least one experiential exercise to help the rest of the class embody the experience of the content they are presenting. This is a post-modern approach whereby students and teachers are all on the same level, working collaboratively in groups (levels, postmodernism in the LL quadrant.) The exercises often evoke different states.

Students are given the opportunity to construct their own drama character based on a worldview and to dialogue with others in different content areas, on an improvisational basis. They are standing in the witnessing (states) position as they engage, reflecting while in action (UL quadrant and integral lines.)

The journals reinforce UL quadrant learning and may be designed by each participant to support their own type (e.g., introvert vs. extrovert,) Other skills reinforced include: asking good questions, interviewing skills, collaborating and co-creating, learning literature review research, writing according to standards (i.e. APA, MLA, etc.,) witnessing one's reactions, and so on.

Thus far, this paper has described one design of an integral program curriculum and the design of a particular integral class within the program. Next, the implementation of this particular integral design is addressed.

Implementing a Technologically Informed Integral Program in Real Time

The integral faculty themselves comprise a learning community and design team. They have access to all classes, and they all participate in the integral seminar and learning community strands. They meet via FTF, conference call, or bimonthly chats for continuous evaluation and tweaking of the course work and participants' integral experiences.

Each faculty member teaches the individual classes for which they are responsible. They are involved in the learning community strand for the participants and also in the faculty learning community (one cannot easily teach "learning community" unless it has been personally experienced.) The learning community strand is specifically taught by one faculty member who supports the noticing of emerging group norms, calls attention to the paradoxes of group life, and works with decision making processes of the group. All of the faculty members are present in this strand. All faculty members have regular involvement in the integrative seminar strand, engaging with the students and other faculty in integrating and relating the material in the program in a way that everything is contextualized relative to the program vision, objectives, strategies and actions.

Each faculty member is involved in personal learning, group learning situations, and learning about systems in their own integral learning community of practice. This occurs as they plan together, learn together, and raise the bar on their program, which is evolutionary and ever-changing. They share their single, double and triple loop insights with one another and engage in the pursuit of collective individualism as they continue to evolve liberating ecologies for their student's experiences.

Conclusion

All of these approaches can be used with very simple online platforms, some of which are free of cost, providing equal access to global participants and those who are economically challenged. Though there is a lot to learn about applying some of these ideas into some complex platforms, very exciting things are possible with the simplest technology. Technological media, though it is sacred in its own right, is empty. It's what we put into its form and what we condition into its system that brings the experience to the participants. The key is often not so much the bells and whistles of the media but how one plans activities that are one-to-many, many-to-many, many-to-one, engaging perspectives from all quadrants, and incorporating as much as possible multiple levels, lines, states and types. Most important, after an integral design, appropriate technology and positive FTF and online delivery system are created, it is still the integral teacher (with heart and knowledge in content and processes involving the good the beautiful and the true) that makes the difference.

19

Mutuality, Engagement and Transformation: A Case Study in Coaching

Shayla Wright

In times of change, the learners will inhabit the earth, while the knowers will find themselves beautifully equipped to deal with a world that no longer exists.

—Fred Kofman

Introduction: Themes and Inquiries

What is the source of long-term commitment and engagement in our students, and how do we draw forth this capacity? How do we evoke their innate courage and intelligence, and support them in nourishing these fundamental aspects of their being? This is one of the themes that I want to explore in this chapter. As someone who has spent her life teaching and coaching, I have grown more and more curious about this, because it has revealed itself as a key factor, one that makes an enormous difference, especially in the face of the profound obstacles and challenges that arise in both our outer and inner lives.

The great Zen teacher, Suzuki Roshi, (Chadwick, 1999) had been working with his students for quite a while when he was first diagnosed with cancer. He would pray to the Buddha, and ask him, "Please, just give me ten more years, that's all I need, just ten more years." Quite clearly he had a deep sense of a long-term engagement with his students, and the kind of fruit that it could bear. The Buddha did not give him those ten years.

I'd also like to inquire into the relationship between teacher and student, or coach and coachee, and how the nature of this relationship impacts this whole process of transformative learning. How can I learn to support students or clients as they struggle to bring what they receive in sessions or groups with us into their everyday lives? How can I find ways to close the gap between something we think and talk about in class, and something we can contact directly when we really need it?

I'd like to explore these questions using inquiry in quite a specific way, which is the way I offer it in all of my courses and workshops. This approach to inquiry is a spiritual practice, not an academic exercise. This kind of inquiry is integral—we bring our whole being into our engagement with these questions: heart, body, mind and spirit. We have the opportunity to actually live with these questions, to bring them into the centre of our work and our lives, without expecting a fixed answer or conclusion. Instead, as I inquire, I find that I am not so certain of what I think I know—the limited viewpoints through which I am perceiving myself and the world are expanded. This can include even the fixed sense of who I take myself to be. In this process of inquiry, my own identity can reveal itself to be open, fluid, and quite mysterious.

Case Study: Sean Williams

I'm not sure now how Sean heard about me, or how he knew that he wanted to commit himself so thoroughly to the work we did together. Maybe he didn't know at the beginning-- perhaps he was just riding on a hunch, and his commitment grew as he allowed himself to become more and more engaged. The first thing Sean did with me was an eight-week Gift of Presence course. The Gift of Presence is what I call an integral approach to awakening unconditioned awareness, based on the work I have done in Advaita, (Müller, 1962) Yoga, (Feuerstein, Trans. 1989) and in the non-dual traditions of Buddhism: Zen, (Merzel, Dennis, Genpo, 2005) Dzogchen and Mahamudra (Fenner, 2007). I have also been strongly influenced by the Shambhala teachings, developed by the Tibetan Buddhist teacher Chogyam Trungpa Rinpoche (Kneen, 2002). Also, many of the ways in which I am reflecting on this case study have been inspired by the Radiant Mind work I do with Peter Fenner (Fenner, 2007).

In *The Gift of Presence* students learn to access and then to gradually embody the non-dual ground of being, the state of timeless, effortless presence. There are many ways in which this work is based on an Integral model. One of the most basic is that an embodied non-dual awareness is one that has no preference for the transcendent or the relative level of life. An organic kind of integration starts to happen when we are not fixated on either the formless transcendent dimension, or the human side of our experience. Sometimes we call this "standing with one foot in each world."

The Four Core Modules

The Gift of Presence works with the four core Integral modules of body, mind, emotion and awareness or spirit. All of the work that happens in the course is strongly grounded in the body and the breath, and in the subtle intelligence that begins to reveal itself naturally, through this kind of mindfulness. In Integral terms this aspect of practice is one that focuses on the "subtle body." The subtle body is a whole way of experiencing or feeling, through the living energetic field of the body. This is not abstract, but an actual phenomenological reality that presents itself to our immediate awareness as we practice. Becoming aware of this subtle body expands the whole sense of identity, which is often fixated on the physical or gross body only.

This approach also works on the level of intellect, through cognitive deconstruction, on both the personal and impersonal levels of being. There is an inquiry into fundamental values, similar to what is referred to in the Integral approach as discovering your "ultimate concern."

Ultimate Concern

In the work I have done over the years, I have found, over and over, that people are disconnected from their ultimate concern, from what they really care about, from what matters most. In fact, in our society, we have very few practices and opportunities for people to discover for themselves what the most important thing is. Not for someone else, but for them. This begins very early on in the post-modern world. Somehow people are expected to magically know what their area of ultimate concern is, just by going through our school system.

In many of the indigenous societies, the young people go through a powerful initiation, and are then sent away to wander, far from village, family and tribe, so that they can find out, without being influenced by anyone else, what really matters to them. In one sense, part of the work we do in my courses is this wandering, looking for signs and clues that will make this "ultimate concern" more visible.

The work that focuses on relationship and the emotional body happens in small groups and in dyads (partner work). Quite often this turns out to be shadow work, because it is the disowned aspects of our own being that create most of the suffering that happens in relationship.

Beginning to Work

When Sean showed up for our first session, I experienced him as one of the most disconnected and contracted people I had ever met. I could not understand how he had ended up there, in this room where we were all gathering, ready to participate in the course. He did not seem to have any of the natural capacities that support people in this kind of practice. He was very shy and withdrawn, profoundly cut off from both his body and his feelings. I felt a sense of numbness in the field of his energy, and under that, a great deal of pain, helplessness and despair. He spoke openly about having very little joy, connection or motivation in his life.

I'm someone who responds well to challenges, but that first evening with Sean was not easy. I found myself really questioning what I could offer him in the context of this group. At the same time, I noticed something else: Sean evoked a natural and spontaneous respect in me as well as fondness, tenderness in the heart. Whenever he spoke, I felt his intelligence and integrity very strongly. He seemed almost incapable of being dishonest, and quite keenly aware of the state of his body and mind, without a lot of excuses or denial.

Trapped in the Cocoon

By the end of that first eight-week course, there had been a few moments for Sean—moments of aliveness, connection with others, moments of laughter and softness. I was happy for those moments, and at the same time, I felt sad that what I perceived as his fundamental state of "stuckness" was pretty much untouched. I experienced Sean as trapped inside a cocoon of his own creation, a small world of fixed conditioning that was smothering the life and vitality in him. In an effort to protect and care for himself, he had withdrawn into a state of isolation and separation that was deeply familiar and very difficult to release.

In Integral terms, I perceived a strong element in Sean of the "sick boy." This means that many of the qualities connected to the healthy masculine principle had been distorted and were functioning in a destructive way. Strength had become rigidity, independence and autonomy had become isolation and an inability to reach out or communicate. The healthy feminine principle that expresses itself as flow, play, compassion and connection seemed to have been buried long ago.

I spoke to the group on our last night together, about how it can seem sometimes like not much has happened for us, until we look a little deeper and see that invisible seeds have been planted—seeds that will flourish and flower in their own time.

Embodiment through Communication—The Lower Left Quadrant

A few weeks later Sean registered for my Heart of Communication course. I was shocked. The work in both of these courses rests on the foundation of unconditioned awareness. In The Heart of Communication we are exploring this awareness through the vehicle of communication, intimacy and self-expression, opening to and cultivating a vulnerability, an honesty, and a willingness to allow ourselves to be deeply touched and transformed by others. The emphasis is on allowing the fixed and solid sense of our identity to open and expand to include the collective and universal levels of experience. In Integral Language, I can say that The Gift of Presence begins in the top left quadrant, with the subjective experience of "I," and The Heart of Communication begins in the bottom left, with the subjective experience of "we."

One of the metaphors we work with is from the Indian tradition: Indra's net (Cook, 1977). Indra, one of the Hindu gods, has a net that stretches across the universe—that is the universe itself. The vertical threads in this net are time, the horizontal threads are space, and in each place where they intersect is a living being, sparkling like a jewel. With Indra's net, our familiar frames of reference begin to dissolve: each jewel or living being in this vast net reflects every other jewel inside itself.

In the "we space" I am aware of myself as a space that embraces and includes much more than just my individual being. The field of my awareness opens and I am able to receive the experiences, the feelings and thoughts of others, into my own being.

As we explore this developing awareness, we find that our "body" —far from being restricted to "me" —is actually, in some strange way, inclusive of the other embodied ones, the other people in the world.

—Ray 2008

Silent Conversations

One thing that happens in this <we space> is that I begin to hear the silent conversations that go on all the time, underneath the explicit ones. There are many different kinds of silence, and different kinds of conversations that happen in these silences.

When Sean registered for the second course with me, I could feel a silent conversation begin. As we began to work together again, the same silent conversation continued: it expanded, deepened and became an essential part of what was unfolding.

It began something like this:

Shayla: Wow, Sean, you're going to do it all over again. I'm surprised. The last course was really hard for you. And you're willing to go through it all again.
Sean: Yes I am.
Shayla: What is it that's bringing you back?
Sean: Something changed, something opened—just a tiny bit. In the middle of all my hopelessness I feel something, yet I don't know what to call it. And I trust you...even though I still feel very hopeless.
Shayla: I am honored by your trust Sean. I care about you a lot. I respect you. But your conditioning is very strong. I can't promise you anything. There are no guarantees in this kind of work.
Sean: I understand. And I think what allows me to be here is that I don't hear you asking me to be different than the way I am.
Shayla: That's true. I am not asking you to try and change in that way. You've already tried that. Now we are trying something different. We're just going to see what happens when we shine the light of our non-judging awareness on each moment of our experience, when we allow ourselves to be truly intimate with what is.

The Heart of Communication course was even more challenging for Sean than The Gift of Presence. He was facing what seemed like insurmountable obstacles in his marriage at the time, and I told him quite frankly that I had a lot of compassion for his wife. I realized that he was doing this work in part because of the immense struggles he faced every day, just trying to communicate with the people around him.

A Real Life Practice

My deepest interest in this transformation of consciousness hinges on the difference between two levels of practice. The first is a more formal or traditional practice, in which we do whatever we are doing for a certain length of time each day, or maybe a few times a week. Whatever our practice is, it is something that happens within a particular time and space, with a clearly defined beginning and end.

The second level of practice is one is which we are simply willing to work with ourselves, just as we are, moment to moment, day after day, right in the middle of everything that is going on. Most of the "homework" I offer people in my courses— the exercises, contemplations and inquiries, can be done right in the middle of life. They actually need to be done that way, not cross-legged in a silent forest grove. If we cannot work with what actually arises in our lives—the real, messy, chaotic situations we are faced with, life becomes very difficult.

I was in a health food store a while ago when a young mother and her three or four year old daughter came in. The little girl started getting upset about something, and this escalated into a full blown tantrum, with the child on the floor of the store, kicking and screaming and pulling things off the shelves. All of the adults in the store were frozen, and the mother was trying to control her child with very little success. I called to her across the store, because I wanted the others to hear.

"It's so hard, isn't it," I said, "being a parent in a situation like this? I remember how helpless I sometimes felt as a mother, and how ashamed. We feel helpless too, because we can't do anything, and for the moment, neither can you. For me, it just helps to remember that it's nobody's fault."

The mother turned and replied to me briefly, while the rest of the people in the store relaxed and started talking again. I left, and a few minutes later, the mother came running up behind me on the street and thanked me. "What a difference that made," she said, "just to hear you acknowledge it like that took all the shame I was feeling away."

This is what happens as we learn to access our deeper resources. We no longer get entangled in the kind of thinking that creates loops of suffering: "This should not be happening," or "There's something wrong with me because I can't control what is going on." We are finally willing to work with life as it is.

Sean had two small children and a full time job, so he had very little formal time for practice. However, he did engage in the work whenever he could find the time, to the best of his ability. He would return to each session with questions, and often clear and succinct reports on his failures. The more I worked with him, the more I could sense his pain, his isolation and his despair—and the strength of his motivation. I became aware of an immense power in him that had been distorted, turned against himself. Many times it would have made sense for him to say, "I can't do this anymore—I give up." But he did not.

Accessing Natural Resources: Shadow Work

One of my jobs as a teacher or coach is to help my students access their deepest and most natural resources. Our work together strengthens the connection to, and the recognition of, these deep capacities and qualities. How do I nourish these aspects, these dimensions of being? How do I help my students to recognize and call them forth? And how can I support them in seeing the other side of each quality, in opening to an awareness that does not exclude any part of themselves?

Our gifts and our challenges are intricately connected. Our greatest strength is our greatest weakness, and our greatest weakness is our greatest strength. In the non-dual understanding, polarities are inseparable—we can't have one side without the other. So I need to support my students in opening to their own wholeness, the totality of who they are. This involves a willingness to inquire into the other side, that which is hidden—either the positive or negative energy which has been disowned.

Here we find ourselves working with the shadow. For me, this begins with becoming familiar with an awareness that does not exclude any part of ourselves. Our conditioned mind can only function in terms of good/bad and right/wrong, which is why it is always excluding what it considers the negative parts of our being and of our experience. As our core sense of identity opens and expands, we are able to access unconditioned presence, the open ground of being. From this place we can experience intense feelings without being thrown around by them, and by our negative judgments about what they mean.

As I worked with Sean, I engaged with him on all these levels. I encouraged him, in many different ways, to consider letting go, just for a few minutes, of the heavy judgments he carried about himself and his way of being in the world—to open, even briefly, to a willingness to be with himself as he was. I invited him to see what happened when he allowed himself to simply feel whatever he was feeling, and to open to that experience in the body. Together we engaged in a process of inquiry regarding his core thoughts and beliefs. I was looking for ways to mirror back to him the innate gifts he was carrying, the qualities that were intrinsic to his natural way of being.

The main gift that Sean offered me was his persistence, his stubborn refusal to give up on himself. I felt as if the depth and ferocity of his ability to persevere was actually working on me. In the Shambhala tradition (Trungpa, 1984) they describe this energy or capacity as "windhorse," something that enlivens us, lifts us up, and cuts through obstacles. I recognized it as a positive dimension of the healthy masculine principle. It was a palpable, mysterious, implacable force that had awakened in him, and now in me. I felt awed by it, intrigued, perplexed. I would ask him about it, try to understand what was driving him, what brought him back, again and again to this room where he had to face so much pain, struggle and unease.

As time passed, I experienced our relationship more and more as a sacred contract, an unspoken agreement, which kept deepening as we worked together. I could feel it in my heart: as long as Sean was willing to continue working with what life was bringing to him, I would be there too, allowing the way that I showed up with him to change, evolve and transform as we went along together.

Cognitive Work

The module of mind was one I used a lot in my work with Sean. I found it quite easy to work with his innate intelligence—it was so strong and alive in him. I encouraged him to question everything, especially the things I was saying. He responded very well to this kind of suggestion. I began to work with his cynicism, which is often the other side of an intelligence like his. Slowly, he began to see for himself how his cynicism was actually blunting his intelligence—locking him into a rigidity and a certainty that was blocking the free flow of his inquiry. I could feel a new perspective opening up in him—a way of looking at his own cynicism and realizing that it was just another fixed position. Underneath the cynicism and despair was something else. Often it felt to me like a tiny stream in winter, flowing beneath layers of snow and ice. Little flashes of sweetness, tenderness and vulnerability would sparkle through the grim surface of Sean's experience, announcing the presence of something the conditioned mind knows nothing about.

Trust, Respect and Mutuality

At a certain point I realized that a great part of his ability to persist was connected with me—and his simple trust in me as a teacher. This is the last theme I explore here, and perhaps the most central for me. It's certainly not a new one in the field of education. The subject of trust has been addressed in a myriad of ways.

What I have discovered about trust is something that emerged during this period of working with Sean, and it has been growing and unfolding for me ever since. This kind of trust emerges from a relationship based on mutuality, and a willingness to be vulnerable and transparent. In essence they are the same thing.

For me, mutuality is an understanding that has to be there in my cells and in my bones, on the deepest level of my being: we are absolutely equal, and ultimately non-separate. In each moment of communication, your being and my being interpenetrate. We influence each other, and are ultimately participating in a vast, universal web of infinite spheres of influence. As a human being, you may have capacities, skills, gifts or experiences that are far superior to mine in many areas. But as beings, as expressions of the same life, the same presence, the same awareness, we are equal, and we influence and impact each other, mutually and without end. When I know this to be true, this knowing is part of what I am transmitting to you in every moment.

Then it becomes very difficult to hold myself above you, to pose as someone who holds some kind of superior position. I am keenly aware that real wisdom is not a commodity—it is a living thing that does not belong to anyone. On one day, or in one moment, that wisdom may come alive in me, in the next moment it could be expressing itself through you. A genuine willingness to learn from our students—this is the ground of true education.

I experienced this mutuality in a very natural way with Sean. I experienced him as shutdown, cut off, and full of suffering, and at the same time, I felt this ongoing spontaneous respect. It was a deep respect for his being that just kept on growing. It was not something I could have manufactured—it was just there. He knew it and I knew it. Sometimes, once in a long while, I would express some of this to him, but not very often. I sensed it would be difficult for him to receive that much kindness. So most of the time, it remained part of our silent conversation.

The other aspect of this mutuality is my willingness to be vulnerable—to reveal myself, just as I am, again and again, even when parts of my identity have no interest in doing that. The more I teach, the more this willingness in me grows. With Sean, it just became clearer and clearer that it wasn't possible to be any other way.

Transformative Insight

One evening we were working in dyads. I was encouraging an inquiry that was grounded in the body, a willingness to ask and question without grasping for any sort of answer from the mind. Something happened for Sean at one point. "Oh, I see." he said. "I think that I really want to reach out and connect, but what I actually do is retreat. I go into this cave inside myself, and hide, because it feels safe there, even though it's incredibly lonely. I've been doing this since I was a child."

I encouraged him to stay right where he was and to keep opening to whatever was happening for him. "Now I'm aware that I really don't want to go there anymore," he said. "That's kind of scary. It feels like stepping out, into the world, naked and unprotected."

"Which one is stronger," I asked him, "the impulse to protect yourself, or to reach out and connect"?

"Right now," he said, "the impulse to open and connect is much stronger. I don't even have to think about it. I'm just going to see if I can actually remember this, the simplicity of this, when I am trying to speak to someone outside this room."

Sean spent the next few weeks exploring this key insight. In the family constellation work of Bert Hellinger, (Hellinger, 2001) what had begun to awaken in Sean could be called the simple reaching-out movement of the human heart. This movement is often crippled in our childhood, especially in men living in cultures like ours that emphasize the value of strength and independence over connection and co-operation. What Sean reported to me was a slowly growing capacity to open to other people, and remain present, even when he wanted to retreat back into the solitary confinement of his cave.

About halfway through The Heart of Communication, Sean's mother had a stroke. She was in the hospital in a city five hours away, where Sean and the whole family were going to visit her. Sean called me before they left, to tell me that he might be gone for a while. "We have no money right now, so it will all have to go on the credit cards—a cheap hotel and the kids all day long, and the hospital. I don't think it's going to be very much fun," he said.

They were gone for several weeks, returning in time for our final session. Sean arrived that evening, very present and alive. I could tell he was happy to be back. He told us a story about something that happened on one of their last days in the city.

"We were driving home from the hospital one afternoon. It had been a long, exhausting day for all of us. The kids were really tired and grumpy, and we were all desperate to get back to the motel, have dinner and crash into bed. We were downtown, right in the middle of rush hour, and the truck broke down. I couldn't believe it. Horns were honking at us, the kids started screaming, and I couldn't get the ignition to start. "I felt this huge wave of indignation and self-pity arise in me. I just wanted to have a temper tantrum and tell the universe what I thought of the way it was treating us. But something happened. I was watching the connection between my thoughts, my feelings and my body, and I heard myself asking, 'Do I really want to believe this thought? What happens to me when I believe this thought? Who am I?'

"I wasn't looking for answers," he said, "but immediately everything shifted. I wasn't angry, bitter and at the end of my rope any more. I dealt with the situation, and we went back and slept."

Good work and Great Work

This was the moment, the revelation, not just for me, but for everyone in the room. We had all been carried into that experience in the truck with Sean, knowing the kind of frustration such a scene would evoke in us. Nobody spoke. There was just silence in the room, all of us looking at Sean in wonder.

"How did you do that?" I finally asked. "Where did you find the power to stop and inquire, in a moment like that one?"

"I don't know," he replied. "I really don't know. It just felt like something else was called for."

These are the moments we are waiting for. They arrive unexpected and unheralded, like the moment when Rosa Parks (Parks, 1992) was asked to go and sit at the back of the bus, and she said "No," because something else was called for.

I found myself that evening, standing right in the centre of a moment of genuine transformation. The nature of this kind of change is right at the heart of my own work and the Integral vision as well. My experience with Sean was profoundly open-ended. The challenge of working with him evoked something in me: an ongoing investigation, genuineness and a spontaneity that impacted all of us together. He called me into new territory, where the consequences of my actions were not predictable. I didn't know where we were going. I was not able to control the environment, so I was right inside the change that was occurring. I was being carried along by the same river in which we were all swimming. My only choice was to be open, transparent and courageous, without clinging to any ideal, or any idea of outcome. In this "we space," I am totally responsible for the wake I am leaving, and so my choices reflect that, even though I have a deep sense of no agenda and no control. I have referred to this way of being with students as "mutuality." We can also look at it as the essence of collaboration or partnership.

In working with children and adolescents, a lot depends on our capacity to enter into the kind of dynamic and spontaneous interchange with our students. The "identity systems" of young people are much more fluid and undefined. This leaves a natural ground from which to work that is full of possibility, vitality and magic. Core beliefs and fixations in young people can be revealed and allowed to dissolve; new ways of perceiving themselves and the world can unfold quite naturally, when the field of learning is opened up in this way.

Michael Bungay Stanier, the Canadian coach, describes this as the place of "great work." We do good work when we are confident, competent and full of knowing. Good work is something wonderful and necessary, but it needs to leave room for the emergence of great work. Great work happens somewhere else, and it is an opportunity, full of grace, to benefit others, to help this world, from a place that is tender, raw and full of mystery.

I'd like to finish this article by including an email I received from Sean a few weeks ago, almost five years after we finished working together.

Hi Shayla,

This was a moment of speaking from the heart:

Last month my brother in law and his twin brother had celebrated their 50th birthdays. The conspiracy to celebrate their birthdays reserved a big part of a brew-pub restaurant, and I knew that decorum demanded that I give a speech. I picked a couple of funny moments that I thought illuminated deeper parts of their characters and wrote a little speech around that. But I didn't bother to memorize it. Rather I familiarized myself with the essence of how I felt about these moments and about them. Getting ready to go out, I stuffed my printed sheet into a pocket somewhere, but it never made it to the restaurant. And I knew that it wasn't important. When the time came to speak I was so at home with the material and my feeling for these two wonderful men that I was able to speak through the speech directly to the 40 or so people there. People came up to me for the rest of the night and said that I made the best speech of the night. You were with me then in some way.

Sean

20

Integral Practices: The Personal in the Professional

Patricia Gordon, Ph.D.

I and mine do not convince by arguments, similes, rhymes, / We convince by our presence.

~ Walt Whitman

As Whitman indicates, our presence, our being, is the most powerful teacher. Integral educators realize that their teaching is an outflow of who they are, so they keep further evolving their being in order to be a powerful, positive presence in their students' lives. Henry David Thoreau remarked,

> *Men say, practically, Begin [sic] where you are and such as you are, without aiming mainly to become of more worth, and with kindness afore-thought go about doing good. If I were to preach at all in this strain, I should say rather, Set [sic] about being good. As if the sun should stop when he had kindled his fires up to the splendor of a moon or a star of the sixth magnitude, and go about like a Robin Goodfellow, peeping in at every cottage window, inspiring lunatics, and tainting meats, and making darkness visible, instead of steadily increasing his genial heat and beneficence till he is of such brightness that no mortal can look him in the face, and then, and in the mean while [sic] too, going about the world in his own orbit, doing it good, or rather, as a truer philosophy has discovered, the world going about him getting good. (160)*

Integral teachers aspire to an increasingly sun-like presence in the classroom, opening their students to greater truth, goodness, and beauty in the ongoing creative process of the Kosmos. Since a healthy and evolving being is the path to attaining this enlightening presence, integral educators engage in a personal integral practice, and consider their teaching as part of this practice, a radiant outflow of integral service to students, society, planet, and Kosmos. Here I explore the interfused being and do-ing of integral teachers in-process, sharing integral perspectives and practices, giving some examples of my college classroom applications of these in my literature courses. These examples are preliminary and incomplete, and may you, *camerado*, as Whit-man says, add your own teaching activities to the framework offered here.

Jelaluddin Rumi, the Persian mystic and poet says, "Angels only began shining when they achieved discipline." (n.p.) Spring-boarding from philosopher Ken Wil-ber's use of Plato's the Good, True, and Beautiful in his discussion of quadrants (e.g., *Integral Spirituality* 19) and from physicist Brian Swimme's suggestion "to create as a spiritual discipline" (*Earth's Imagination*, video, part 7), I propose that the basic integral discipline, both personal and professional, may be expressed as increasing our own and our students' flourishing and evolution through practices of the true, the good, the beautiful, and, as is appropriate and exciting in our time of evolutionary awareness, the creative.

Truth Practices

Perspective Taking

A major truth practice of integral teachers is increasing their awareness of per-spective- taking possibilities, which are summarized in Ken Wilber's *Integral Spiritu-ality*. For example, when I first started applying the integral approach in my personal life, I realized that, to my disadvantage, I had been neglecting to take into account all four quadrants when analyzing and solving problems (20-23). I now include this as part of my life and my students' activities. (See Appendices A and B.) In teach-ing, when I first started applying an integral approach to my classroom and reflected upon specific lines (7-9, 23-24), I realized that I had not been including activities to encourage a higher level of my students' moral line, so I began including empathy ac-tivities in my teaching. (See Appendices C and D.) This led to my extending empathy to such things as spiders in my personal life. Also, I began to use such perspectives as quadrants and the moral levels of egocentric, sociocentric, and worldcentric (6-7) in my own and my students' analyses of fictional worlds and characters. In this way I practice truth-fullness by taking into account more completely aspects of reality (in the above cases, quadrants, the moral line, and its levels.) These aspects of reality are always in play whether I acknowledge them explicitly and intertwine them in my life and teaching or not. In addition to quadrants and the moral line, other integral perspective-taking possibilities with implications for personal life and the classroom are the inside and outside perspectives of quadrants (zones), other lines, levels, types, and states (33-40, 23-24, 4-7, 11-15, 3-4). (See Appendices E through J.)

Another way I practice perspective taking is during class discussions when I point out the partial truths and limitations of student contributions and then weave them into a more complete, complex view. In this way, I model for students the practice of dis-identifying with partial truths and excluding their limitations by transcending them with a more complex view that embraces what is valuable from each partial truth. Also ongoing feedback originating from my own self-reflective awareness, and from others, is another valuable perspective-taking practice. I engage students in this practice in a variety of ways, some of which are mentioned in this chapter and some in the appendices.

Helpful for me in all these perspective-taking practices is keeping in mind Reverend Michael Beckwith's inquiry into our truth-fullness: "How much of Yourself are you willing to let touch you?" (audio, part 3).

Open Presence

Resting in Open Presence helps dis-identification with partial truths. It is also a truth-fullness practice in that practicing awareness in the moment, resting in Presence, is dwelling in my true identity. (See Appendices G and H.) I offer my students this practice under the name of one of its effects: stress reduction. I ask them to move to the place inside themselves that is "home," that is "you, you just being you, you in your you-ness." I find this leads students into a meditative state very naturally and successfully, one they can easily return to on their own.

Goodness Practices

Playing Attunement

A major goodness practice of integral teachers is attunement, the creation of an understanding, empathy, or "we" in both personal life and in the classroom. (There are different types of "we," such as the "we" of mutual understanding and the "we" of a more developed person resonating with a less developed person, such as teacher with student.) Many new approaches are needed for the practice of creating "we," *camerado*, and sharing your own discoveries with other integral teachers would be welcomed. As regards my own attunement practices, I have found the following helpful in the classroom and, except for the last practice, also in personal life: facilitation of a shared group vision and understanding about how we all will interact to create that vision; periodically asking for feedback on "the state of the we;" and reading of student educational autobiographies so that I can get a better feel for, and empathize with, student attitudes toward education.

Dis-identification with partial truths supports my ongoing aim to play the perspectives, to consistently attune and flow freely, with awareness and appropriateness, among my and others' partial perspectives of states, lines, levels, types, quadrants, zones, and the polarities that arise within all of these. In my classroom I especially play the levels, the types, and "the eight" (zones) (Gordon, 2008a; 2008c, 16). Most especially, I shift among and shape communication and activities attuned to the self-identity levels, moral levels, Myers Briggs personality types, and visual, auditory, and kinesthetic learning types.

Some of these perspectives I make very explicit to the students so that they may begin to flexibly dis-identify from their own types and moral level, for example, and become more constructive in their classroom and world presence. I also ask students to attune to the particular "mind" they happen to be in at the moment, for example, Thinking Mind, Distracted Mind, Curious Mind, Bored Mind, Tired Mind, Creative Mind, Closed Mind, Open Mind, Lizard Mind, Mammal Mind (social mind) and Aware Mind. I then ask how these minds affect how they experience their courses and life and how they affect their classmates and other people.

Increasing awareness, dis-identification, and flexible flow is a lifetime project for our integral development of the play of creation's perspectives, the One playing Many. Songwriter David Wilcox in *"Party of One"* beautifully expresses this play:

> *Party of one*
> *This way, your place is waiting*
> *We've been expecting you*
> *Party of wonder, full*
> *Right on time*
> *Just begun*
> *Party of one*
> *Sailing free*
> *Untangled*
> *Through the Bermuda Triangle of joy…*
> *Party of one*
> *Party of wonder*
> *You've been invited to a party of one.*

Highest Purpose Centering

Partying, playing attunement, is a powerful means to achieving students' and others' benefit. However, maintaining Open Presence as relaxed body, loving heart, and receptive awareness with an intention for the highest good for all is perhaps the foundational goodness practice in both personal life and teaching. My particular conception of the highest good, as I hold my students, others, and the Kosmos in positive intentionality, has been that we all fully become the creation that we are (healing our unhealthy aspects and flourishing in our healthy aspects); offer our unique extrinsic contributions that enrich and evolve the universe; evolve into greater intrinsic value (higher levels of awareness, perspectives, intentions, caring, emotions, actions, and qualities); and enjoy pleasures in doing all of this. I introduce my students to an abbreviated version of this intention in the classroom empathy practice mentioned earlier. May all this goodness be ours and our students,' *camerado*.

Transforming Projection

Centering in this intentionality when I feel inappropriately negative about a student or someone else is one way of transforming destructive emotions, another key goodness practice. (In some situations negative emotions, such as anger, are of course very appropriate.) Other ways of transforming "the dark" in a classroom or personal situation that I have found helpful are Brother Steindl-Rast's in-the-moment practice of gratitude for the opportunity to engage a virtue or take constructive action. Following exercising gratitude for opportunity, I take the other's perspective and, when appropriate, also do an abbreviated version of 3-2-1 shadow work (Wilber 2006, 136-137; 2008, 49-51)), a practice that I have found very helpful. Abbreviated shadow work involves in-the-moment inner acknowledgement of the existence of the undesirable trait in question in myself, however faint or in the past it may (or may not!) be. Shadow practices can also be done later, after the situation. Maintaining Open Presence is necessary to be aware of projections. As the poet Rumi says in "No Wall," "The clear bead at the center changes everything. / There are no edges to my loving now." (n.p.)

Beauty Practices

Three-Level Physical Radiance

In our classroom performance as teachers, we are radiating the beauty of three kinds of physical energy: our still, causal energy of Open Presence; our loving, inspiring subtle emotional energy; and our human form's vital life energy (Wilber 2006, 16-17). Author and workshop presenter David Deida comments on these three physical energies, "As a performer, what you do is you feel where someone's at and where you want to bring them. And you feel that difference. And you orchestrate that difference through the gross, the subtle, and the causal." He speaks of the performer's causal centeredness in the Ground and of their eye contact calling the audience deeper. He explains that performers also bring their audience to deeper or higher states through a vitally energetic but strongly grounded physical presence. This is where teachers' practices of health and fitness can serve well. On the subtle level, Deida tells performers to "breathe in the [mental or emotional] closure" of their audience, empathize with them, synchronize with them, become them, and then "...offer beyond there." Performers can imagine their emotional state is the emotional state of the audience and infuse the audience with it. They give their deepest gross, subtle, and causal self (audio, part 3).

I have already spoken of Open Presence earlier, and I will discuss performance and subtle level emotional health and inspiration in the next section. Here I would like to focus on teachers' and students' vital life energy. Integral teaching considers the body as sacred, as expressed so eloquently by the ancient poet Symeon the New Theologian:

> *... all our body, all over,*
> *every most hidden part of it,*
> *is realized in joy as Him ...*

we awaken as the Beloved
in every last part of our body. (38-39)

Given this perspective of sacredness, an important beauty practice, which is neglected in most college teaching unless it is in a physical education class, is to attend to the physical harmony, energy suffusion, and further development of our and our students' physical form. I usually bring to my classroom the physical presence and energy of someone who generally gets enough sleep, eats a healthy diet, and exercises. I take care to provide opportunities for them to reflect on their body and brain's well being and plan next steps on how to increase their health and fitness, presenting this activity as a necessary base for successful learning. I also make sure to offer the opportunity for students to take brief stretching breaks in the classroom whenever needed.

Performance

An additional beauty practice is the performance not only of the in-the-moment kind of radiant causal, subtle, and physical connections described by David Deida above, but also the performance of the course itself considered as an artwork and the performance of various arts within the course. If we teachers can also be considered as artists creating and performing the artwork of the course, then artist Alex Grey's remark, "Art is the transmission of states of being," is illuminating (79). Grey speaks of artists visualizing themselves joined with and transmitting the highest forces of love and wisdom while they are working (217). The teacher's entire course, created to be a work of art, can transmit inspiring states, as the students experience the good, the true, the beautiful, and the creative.

My courses, called the Good Life series, offer one way of doing this, which is to focus on positive, inspiring visions (in literature) of humans' relations with their inner selves, each other, nature, and the universe. They also include inspiring performances of music, art, and film. One of the beauty practices of my own life is to permeate myself with positive literature and other art so that my courses are an outflow of the positive creativity that I have taken in.

In addition, a beauty practice that I use in the classroom and that may be adaptable to other teaching contexts is what I call "participatory reading." As I perform or read aloud to the students, they perform, as intensely and completely as possible, the literary scene or passage in their imagination, seeing the sights, hearing the sounds, tasting the tastes, smelling the smells, touching the textures, and feeling the associated emotions. Students are also encouraged to use this approach when they read silently to themselves at home, and they also sometimes physically enact scenes from literary works in group performances in the classroom. A similar performance of beauty may be used for voyaging through the elegance of a molecule's structure, the nobility of an historical moment, or any number of phenomena taught in a classroom. An inspiring experience is more likely if the object has been placed in a Kosmic context of creative emergence or a positive human role on the planet.

This beauty practice is perhaps the most difficult in the context of the ugly boxes of most contemporary college classrooms, boxes which change teachers every class period. One simple but powerful approach that I have successfully used in this context is to put the desks in a U shape, which not only allows students to see each other, but also opens up space and creates a graceful form and atmosphere.

Creation Practices

Study and Praise of the Evolving Kosmos

Nanao Sakaki's poem *"A Love Letter,"* takes the reader out into the physical aspects of the Kosmos in widening celebratory circles:

Within a circle ten thousand kilometers large
Walking somewhere on the earth.
Within a circle one hundred thousand kilometers large
Swimming in the sea of shooting stars.
Within a circle a million kilometers large
Upon the spaced-out yellow mustard blossoms
The moon in the east, the sun west.
Within a circle ten billion kilometers large
Pop far out of the solar system mandala.
Within a circle ten thousand light years large
The Galaxy full blooming in spring.
Within a circle one billion light years large
Andromeda is melting away into snowing cherry flowers. (477)

In another celebration of the physical universe, Brian Swimme in an interview by Susan Bridle highlights the mystery of the evolution of the universe in his one-sentence history: "You take hydrogen gas, and you leave it alone, and it turns into rosebushes, giraffes, and humans" (40).

One of my most joyful personal practices is the creation practice of celebrating and studying the evolving Kosmos, including individual interiors and collective (cultural) interiors, in addition to the beauty and creativity of the universe's matter and energy celebrated by Sakaki and Swimme above. Professionally, in one of my courses I invite students to read literature about the universe, re-enact in imagination or in group performance the evolutionary story of the physical aspects of the Kosmos in all its grandeur, and open to wonder, awe, and delight.

Evolutionary Productions for the Kosmos

In my course, students contemplate what it means to be a contemporary human being in this large Kosmic context; some of the positive contributions humans can give to the Kosmos; and how they as individuals can participate in these contributions. By including in our courses, our professional creations, the collective dimension of human evolution, we teachers can kindle in our students a positive vision of potential human greatness in carrying forward the Kosmos' creativity.

My students participate in future visioning, papers, and action projects that utilize unique self-expression, course content, and course skills to contribute, in however small a way, to snatching Earth away from becoming one of the Kosmos' evolutionary duds. These constructive opportunities trigger powerful positive states, as I have witnessed during my students' production of collaborative papers focused on imagining in detail (from the perspectives of all four quadrants) an ideal, worldcentric city or college. Students need to be explicitly included in the vital work of this evolutionary moment, ideally working side by side with adults when possible, contributing their ideas and creations in a state of high morale, feeling that they are needed and that their lives matter.

Especially honored by integral educators is the deep, base capacity of creating, of bringing something into existence. I believe that student's nature, nurture, intentionality, and base creativity as Ground Arising are always at work together and the complexity of their interactions means that any particular student's potential in evolution and creation, both in college and beyond, is always unknown (Gordon, 2005, 29). As the Kosmos is the manifestation of Mystery's creativity, all acts of creativity, including those in teaching and learning, participate in and are literally inspired by the Ground's outflow, from the bubbling up of novel self-expressions, to original gifts streaming into one's group or discipline, to the rippling out of unique contributions to the world, to the ultimate act of creativity: surging forward on a new wave of evolution.

Conclusion

This chapter has shown that inhabiting an integral worldspace in teaching involves embodying the truth practices of perspective taking and Open Presence; the goodness practices of playing attunement, highest purpose centering, and transforming projection; the beauty practices of three-level physical radiance, performance, and pleasure in place; and the creation practices of study, praise, and evolutionary productions for the Kosmos. Personal and professional practices are entwined, a seamless way of embodying integral in our lives, of lighting up the many facets of Being.

These practices in their ensemble are an ideal: all integral teachers are integral teachers in-process, on the move, opening to the infinite horizon of Light before them. I invite you, *camerado*, to journey here with me on the open road. In wonder, exploring, experimenting, may you create further, better practices than those presented here and share them with the rest of us, your *camerados* here on the airy, brightening path, expanding into greater presence as we go.

21

Future Horizons

Miriam Mason Martineau and Stephan Martineau

Taking some time to sit with the many insights, questions and experiences shared throughout this book, and imagining you're perhaps doing similarly, a question arises in us, "What's next? What next step will we take to keep evolving education as a whole and in its many facets?"

In concluding this book we invite you to become quiet, to sink within and listen to the future, to what it calls into being inside of you. What do we mean by that? Rather than primarily looking at where you have come from and being informed by the past as to where you must go, we invite you to become still and present with an inner orientation to listening for what lies ahead. Allow yourself a moment to sense the unknown quality of this inquiry, with curiosity and alert receptivity. As you head to your classroom tomorrow, or wherever you are engaged as an educator, can you suspend for a while what you already know, and take the risk of being equipped for your next teaching moment with just the bare willingness to be as present as possible and to listen as deeply as you can? In doing so, what might you notice—within yourself, in the classroom, your town, the state, the country, our world and the universe that we all inhabit? What do we need to prepare our students for? Here is an opportunity to hold multiple perspectives simultaneously. From where we currently stand as a human family, certain trends and tendencies are noticeable. At the same time, we have a choice as to how we shape the future. So we can both "be informed by what is and draw a likely line ahead from here forward," as well as, "listen to what a preferred future could be and see if in our work as educators we might contribute to that preferred future coming about." There's also a third perspective that weaves the other two together in its conclusions: Given we don't ultimately know what lies ahead, what skills and qualities do we need and want to impart to our students so that they can be well-equipped, whatever the future may bring? We would like to briefly review these three perspectives.

The first one: looking forward from where we stand now, what are some likely scenarios? Rather than laying out a specific prediction of education and a future reality we need to prepare our selves and our students for, and which could so easily miss the mark, we would like to note some likely trends and tendencies that may unfold, given our current trajectory. For one, looking at the rate of change we have seen over the last few decades, it seems safe to say that change will continue to be part of the picture, and likely even an ever-greater rate of change in many arenas, from technology, to climate change and other environmental conditions, as well as the geopolitical state of affairs. Indeed, change may be the one constant factor we can depend on! In addition, it looks very likely that some of these changes will bring with them significant challenges, partly because of the rate of change itself, as well as their magnitude. We have never, in human history, faced so many challenges of global scope and consequence as we do today. At the same time we are seeing an increase in our capacities to meet these challenges. Integral consciousness, which is emerging in individuals around the world, enables us to embody a greater level of presence and integrity, and to perceive, interpret, make meaning and synergize in ways that pay attention to the wholeness and interconnectedness of things, while also going right to the core of issues. In August 2008, we at Next Step Integral held a five-day seminar especially for 20-35 year olds and were struck, deeply moved, and heartened to witness a degree of intelligence combined with heart and presence that enables these emerging leaders to grasp increasingly complex issues and tend to the subtleties of an issue, as well as the overall picture and timeframes that go well beyond their generation. With global crises at hand we are also seeing unmatched creativity, brilliance and innovation, fuelled by a sense of urgency.

Second, as educators—and this might sound rather grand, but it is true—we are actually co-creators of the future. We have one of the most important jobs on earth—that of providing orientation, skills and perspectives that will serve and equip those we teach as they head out into the world to contribute, as they head out into the world to flourish their potential, create, contribute, and flourish their potential. Indeed, we are blessed and burdened with the opportunity and responsibility to co-create a new world culture, to help re-invent the world we live in. Education is one of the most powerful tools we have to transform as a human family, which in turn will greatly effect what kind of future will one day be our present reality. When we see education and ourselves as educators in this way, the context we operate within broadens and deepens dramatically. Bringing an integral perspective to education enables us to think beyond the personal sphere, expanding our awareness and care to the whole planet and universe, and to consider much longer timeframes. What kind of a future do we wish to co-create? As we contemplate this question, we can allow the emerging responses to inspire and inform how we presently show up as educators. In addition, there are so many wonderful tools, books, and other resources available to us. It is a matter of putting them into action, of taking seriously the call to offer our wholehearted contributions to each teaching and learning moment.

Third, at this time in history, when our very survival as a human family rests on our ability to navigate with determination, grace, and intelligence of heart and mind, what skills and qualities shall we impart to our students so that they are well-equipped, whatever the future may bring? We don't know exactly what lies ahead. However, by taking note of likely trends, such as the many paradoxes presenting themselves, the experience of many-a-time not knowing, technological tools and advances, and a fast-changing environment, we know that the qualities of adaptability, the fearless ability to navigate the unknown, and the capacities to innovate, imagine and collaborate will be essential. By letting ourselves be informed by our preferred future, we can teach toward authenticity, integrity, contemplation, responsibility, emotional and spiritual intelligence, a high level of interpersonal and intrapersonal skills, and the capacity to understand a multi-tiered and systems-wide approach to design, story, symphony, empathy, play and meaning (from A Whole New Mind, by Daniel Pink.) As these young adults will be relying on a whole-brained approach to working, being and thriving in a high concept, high touch professional culture, such capabilities will be the future baseline of cultural literacy.

This kind of education begins right at birth (and before!) when we enable, through attentive, attuned and loving parenting, a child's sense of self and will to develop with congruence and integration. In addition to conveying these qualities to our students through our teaching, we can greatly enhance our efforts with a personal commitment to transformation, willing to be at our own growing edge, however uncomfortable that may be, to share what we know, and to inquire together with our students into what is still unknown. Integral education in this sense is not so much about "getting it" with our minds, but about embodying an ever-growing degree of presence, integrity, and love of life.

Given the larger context we place ourselves in as we become more integral in our perception of education, we may feel both daunted and inspired by the task—the task of transforming ourselves, as well as of accompanying and guiding our students in their growth and learning within a universe unfolding into increasing consciousness and complexity. When facing questions, such as how to work to develop current capacities, and to create the conditions for the emergence of more complex perspectives in the future, we encourage each of you to find or co-create learning communities—collectives wherein you can be held, supported and connected. As you develop a supportive and transformative culture for yourself, your colleagues and your students, you stand a much greater chance of proceeding sustainably, joyfully and purposefully.

To end we would like to suggest that we continue asking questions, such as the ones that have been asked and begun to be answered in this book. While this may not leave you with a very definitive conclusion, We do so for two reasons—one because we think they are calling out for ever-fuller answers and the more of us who ask, the more complete the emerging response will be! Secondly, becausewe would like to encourage inquiry as a posture and catalyst for forward movement that will continue to open up and guide us in our next steps as educators.

Here some examples of questions a variety of educators have touched on in this book that we can continue to seek answers to collectively in order for integral education to flourish:

- What classroom settings and teacher qualities facilitate transformation in students?
- What hinders change? Why are we often immune to change?
- How do we hold a space that generates inspiring, orienting and guiding state experiences in our students to serve their evolution?
- How/where/with whom might we create communities of practice and support?
- What opportunities can we include in our educational system that facilitate students to discover themselves, their gifts, and how they can participate in a meaningful way in our rapidly changing world.
- As Duane Elgin says, "Now is not the time for half-hearted contributions —the world needs our greatest talents." What are your truest, greatest gifts to offer and be in service of humanity's future?
- How might we tend to that most precious of qualities in our students, the one that sustains and engages their evolutionary spirit: their curiosity?

Please add your own questions and allow them to guide you and others onward and upward! Above all, may integral education be a joyous, meaningful life experience where learning, evolving, relating, and transforming become deeply exciting and satisfying for yourself as an educator, as well as for your students and the universe at large.

Blessings,
Miriam and Stephan

Appendices

Appendix A
Learning Reflections

[Below is a handout for students.]

In typed and paragraph form, but informally and spontaneously (you don't have to revise) please write at least one paragraph on EACH number below, detailing

(1) what **helps** you to learn and
(2) what are **obstacles** to your learning.

What you write should be about **you** personally and refer to your **own** learning.

A. Inner Self:

1. What are your strongest capacities and talents? How do your weakest capacities and talents affect your learning? Examples of types of capacities and talents: linguistic (writing, reading, speaking), naturalist (ability to categorize), logical, mathematical, perspective-taking (ability to take different perspectives), interpersonal, moral, intrapersonal (self-awareness, self-reflection, self-management), attentional (ability to focus attention), spatial, musical, aesthetic (appreciation of beauty), creative, imaginal (ability to form images), kinesthetic (sports, dance).

2. Which of your beliefs, feelings, or attitudes about yourself as a learner, about college in general, and about English classes in particular help your motivation to learn in school? Which of your beliefs, feelings, and attitudes hinder it?

3. Does the presence or absence of long-term goals and related short-term goals personally affect your learning? Explain.

4. (*Please label this as an Action Paragraph*) Considering the inner factors above, what are the most important specific actions that you personally can take to strengthen the factors that help you to learn and overcome the obstacles that prevent you from learning?

B. Physical Factors and Behavior:

5. Do any of the following factors especially affect your learning either positively or negatively: sleep, nutrition, drugs, alcohol, exercise, overall health, eyesight, energy level, response to stress, ability to concentrate, and ability to process information? Please explain the effects of the most positive and negative factors for you.

6. Does your ability to speak more than one language, your frequency of reading and writing in English in the past and present, or the frequency of your learning new words in the past and present affect your learning? Please explain.

7. Do any of the following factors affect your learning: time management, energy management, procrastination, utilization or not of the best approaches to learning each subject, and classroom behavior (talking, listening, note taking, attendance, punctuality, and participation)? Please explain.

8. (*Please label this as an Action Paragraph*) Considering the physical factors and behavior above, what are the most important specific actions that you personally can take to strengthen the factors that help you to learn and overcome the obstacles that prevent you from learning?

C. Culture:

9. Do any of the following factors affect your learning either positively or negatively: the attitudes and values of your family toward school and learning and the attitudes and values of your friends toward school and learning? Please explain.

10. (**Please label this as an Action Paragraph**) Considering the cultural factors above that affect you, what are the most important specific actions that you personally can take to strengthen the factors that help you to learn and overcome the obstacles that prevent you from learning?

D. Environmental and Social Factors:

11. Do any of the following factors affect your learning either positively or negatively: your study environment; your living situation or life circumstances; your commitments outside of school—job, sports, family responsibilities, and social life; and your course load and choice of academic program? Please explain.

12. (*Please label this as an Action Paragraph*) Considering the environmental and social factors above, what are the most important specific actions that you personally can take to strengthen the factors that help you to learn and overcome the obstacles that prevent you from learning?

Thanks to Penny Ross, who inspired the creation of this text.

Appendix B
Integral Approach to Achieving Goals

[The integral approach to achieving goals below, which you may find useful in adapting to various assignments in your courses, has been excerpted and adapted from a course assignment in my Nature course.]

(A) (**Inner support**) In this inner support section please write down the three layers of motivation that can support your goal:

(1) **An egocentric layer:** How will achieving your goal benefit you personally (for example, having less stress)?

(2) **A sociocentric layer:** How will achieving your goal benefit *you* socially (for example, meeting new people) or benefit your *social group(s)* (for example, making life happier and healthier for them now or in the future)?

(3) **A worldcentric layer:** How will achieving your goal benefit Earth's community of life (plants, animals, and humans) and its continuing evolution?

The beauty of having the three layers of motivation is that the alignment of all these layers in support of your goal will create a powerful, robust motivation that can last through obstacles and difficulties much better than one layer alone.

(B) (**Steps**) How will you regularly touch base with your three layers of motivation? What other concrete steps will you take to enable you to achieve your goal?

(C) (**Cultural Support**) what values of your family, friends, or others can support you in achieving your goal? How will you take advantage of these supportive cultural values?

(D) (**Environmental and social support**) how can you arrange your environment to enable you to achieve your goal? What kind of actions can others take to help you achieve your goal? How will you enable them to do this?

The four kinds of supporting actions and three layers of motivation above make success much more likely.

Appendix C
Expanding Compassion and Awareness

[This practice especially cultivates empathy and also awareness. In addition, it serves as a pressure for eventually moving up a moral or cognitive stage. Students in my "Nature" course, after reading various natural history essays where the narrators relate in a positive way to the "dark" side of nature (e.g., predators, spiders), complete an assignment where they choose a being in nature they feel negatively about and then through becoming informed and exercising empathy, try to cultivate a more compassionate attitude. Another variation of the activity, included below, broadens the scope of that assignment to humans and transforms it so that students, if they wish, can continue to practice increasing their compassion and awareness after the course is finished.]

Expanding Compassion

A. (1) Make a list of individual humans, groups of humans, kinds of plants, or kinds of animals that you dislike, fear, or even wish harm.

(2) Choose one and imagine yourself in their place (exercise empathy). What are their sufferings, fears, and joys? Learn as much as you can about their lives. For humans, you might even imagine them as an infant and then imagine them growing up with their genetic, family, and cultural influences taking effect. If you had been born them, you might feel and act in a similar way.

(3) Next, for humans, you might wish for them that their unhealthy, harmful aspects become healthy; or that their positive aspects increase; or that they evolve to greater awareness and compassion. For both humans and nonhumans you might wish for them, for example, that their lives be happy and benefit others.

(4) Once you have succeeded doing this for one being or category of being, move on to the next in your list. The overall ideal is to eventually increase caring for your family, friends, and various social groups in larger and larger circles (everyone in your neighborhood, city, province, nation) (**cosmocentric** level) and expand your circles of compassion to other countries, human cultures, animals, plants, and the whole Earth Community (**worldcentric** level).

Caution: Don't slide into idiot compassion. Harmful actions must be stopped or prevented. Authors Roger Fisher, William Ury, and Bruce Patton in *Getting to Yes* suggest, speaking of humans, **Be soft on the people, hard on the problem** (13). You can deliberately choose to exercise compassion for someone or some group, but you don't have to actually be their friend, accept their behavior, or let the behavior continue.

B. Become involved with the branch of your religious tradition that encourages and offers specific practices for expanding compassion to the worldcentric level.

Expanding Awareness

C. Practice increasing the expanse of your awareness through actively seeking understanding of ever larger sociocentric and worldcentric circles.

D. Widen the expanse of your awareness by practicing continually taking others—perspectives (human, plant, and animal) when you are in their presence and also by imagining periodically during the day what is happening in different places on the planet or the universe.

E. Strengthen your capacity for awareness: keep bringing back your focus and awareness to the present time and place for sustained attention. Another way to do this is by becoming involved in the contemplative or meditative branch of your religious tradition.

In another approach using moral levels, my "Nature" course helps students enact the worldcentric moral level for their own reasons by appealing to the motivations of their own level, be it egocentric, sociocentric, or even worldcentric itself. When we discuss how the main character in Kim Stanley Robinson's novel *Pacific Edge* is acting from egocentric motives, sociocentric motives, and worldcentric motives simultaneously, I ask them to brainstorm how they can feed their personal passions and their joys with family, friends, and romantic relationships while at the same time aligning them with worldcentric actions. One student, for example, planned to combine her passion for being on the beach and her love of her friends by participating with her social group in actions helping an international organization that saves beaches at risk. A mature student decided to combine her love of plants and love of her daughter by teaching her daughter to care for domestic plants and also for plants and forests around the world.

In general, educators make students feel the limitations of their moral (and cognitive) level in three main ways: by alluring students into inspiring experiences of the higher perspectives through the students' use of imagination or through their being in the presence of role models; by posing a problem that students have to move to a more complex point of view to solve; and by arranging for students to enact, for their own stage's reasons and motives, the behavior or attitudes of a higher level.

Appendix D

[Below is an adapted version of a handout concerning moral development given to my students.]

Expanding Circles of Awareness and Caring

Levels of Compassion

Levels are determined by someone's degree of awareness and/or degree of compassion. Please start reading from the bottom (number 1) up. Definitions of terms are at the bottom of the page.

3. WORLDCENTRIC (WORLD-CENTERED) LEVEL:

Most inclusive level: this level includes all the levels below, plus all plant and animal species, or in other words, it includes the whole Earth community (plant species, animal species, the human species.) All plants, animals, and humans have varying degrees of intrinsic and extrinsic value, and all of them also have ground value. (This is the only level to include ground value.)

2. SOCIOCENTRIC (SOCIAL GROUP-CENTERED) LEVEL:

Even more inclusive level (anthropocentric): this level includes all the levels below, plus the whole human family (all humans around the world). All humans have intrinsic value; plants and animals have extrinsic value.

More inclusive level (anthropocentric): this level includes all the levels below, plus an increasing number of friend groups and groups such as religious, cultural, interest, professional, geographical groups. Your group(s) has intrinsic value; everyone else has extrinsic value.

Less inclusive level (anthropocentric): this level includes the level below, plus family. Your family has intrinsic value; everyone else has extrinsic value.

1. EGOCENTRIC (SELF-CENTERED) LEVEL:

The most limited level (anthropocentric): this level includes just yourself. You have intrinsic value; everyone else has extrinsic value.

239

Anthropocentric: human-centered; caring is limited to humans.

Extrinsic value: value based on usefulness.

Intrinsic value: (a) something's value in and of itself. (b) Philosopher Ken Wilber bases (a) on the degree of consciousness and complexity a being has.

Ground value: equality of foundational or fundamental value.

[Ground value is explained more fully in the handout for the students below.]

Worldcentric Ways of Relating to Nature

Why do all individuals and species have equal ground value, in addition to possessing varying degrees of extrinsic value and intrinsic value? Different worldcentrists base this ground value on different things, as shown below.

Philosophers: Some worldcentrists point out that living beings engage in autopoiesis or self-making (self-reproducing and self-repairing) activities. This autopoiesis makes all beings, as ends-in-themselves, of equal ground value, aside from whatever greater or lesser extrinsic and intrinsic value they also possess. In this way, the Philosophers ground worldcentrism on life's survival activities.

Earth Tribe Members: Some worldcentrists, while honoring the Philosophers' survival focus, also think in terms of an Earth Tribe. Even if those of us on Earth eventually encounter beings from other planets, they won't be genetically related to us and a member of our Earth Tribe. We must bond deeply to our wild kin, our only companions in the vastness of space, and stick together as one Earth Family. We must be proud of each other's creativity and accomplishments, our Earth's unique contributions to the Universe, and embrace every member as precious.

Heroes: Some worldcentrists add on a Hero's view. To help the Family survive, they believe the strong and advantaged should rescue the innocent and helpless (both powerless humans and other species, who are unable to protect themselves from human expansion.) These Heroes see their role as the dynamic protector of Earth and its species, with innocence and powerlessness entitling all species to this protection. These men and women are willing to undergo intense challenges to achieve this goal and are often on the cutting edge with unique, creative, and daring solutions. Wealth, fame, and glory may be lavished on these heroes by a grateful community, or they may be ignored or disparaged during their lifetime, but become an admired legend after their death.

The Noble: A noble tradition keeps many Heroes inspired and guided in their battles for the Earth. Some honor the worldcentric aspects of the truth, stories, and images of the world and the Universe upheld by their cultural group. Rooted in their tradition's vision of human purpose and goodness, they strive to live an honorable, noble life and fulfill the worldcentric Laws, Way, Will, or Mission, either secular or divine.

Vast Minds: Some worldcentrists not only honor their specific cultural group's worldcentric aspects, but also see how their tradition enriches and finds a place in a more universal context of rationally-based rights. Some have realized that *human* rights, particularly in the West, have been expanding outward for centuries: first only powerful warlords, kings, and aristocracy had rights (might makes right,) then white males, all males, women, tribal peoples, gays, physically challenged, and onward. These worldcentrists, with their Vast Minds, propose a sweeping vision of expanding rights to *all* beings who live, enjoy, and suffer on this planet.

Celebrators: Some Vast Minds are also Universe-centered. They have immersed themselves in understanding and being inspired by the whole evolutionary history of the Universe and Earth, from the first cosmic fire, or Big Bang, to the present moment.

Their knowledge of the dazzling transformations of matter, energy, life forms, and ideas throughout the grand story of evolution leads them to feel awe for the creative potential of the Universe and its ever dynamic parts. Celebrators are aware that bacteria invented photosynthesis; worms began the development of what would eventually be the backbone; fish created the beginning of the symmetrical four-limbed form and air-breathing lungs; and Palaeolithic humans brought forth symbol systems. We never know what marvelous future feats will emerge from seemingly humble species. For the Celebrators, since all beings on Earth or beyond are parts of the ever-transforming matter and cosmic fire of the Universe, they contain vast creative potential and are worthy of profound respect.

Vast Hearts: Ever greater reaches of awareness make possible an ever-widening embrace of compassion. Over the centuries many people's caring has expanded from their own families and cultural groups to their nations, and then expanded further to people in other cultural groups and nations. Some worldcentrists, with their Vast Hearts, propose an immense embrace of unconditional love for all beings, human and nonhuman, who are trying to live their lives in our Earth Community. Some would go further and envelope also all those in the Universe Community.

Integrators: There are those worldcentrists who enfold most or all of the above approaches to ground value, calling them forth from the various dimensions and aspects of themselves and letting them shine out when time, place, and desire call them forth. They honor the Philosopher's focus on survival concerns, the Earth Tribe's embrace of family relations, the protective Hero's assertion of uniqueness and creativity, the Noble's fulfilling of human purpose, the Vast Mind's awareness of the universal and the Universe, and the Vast Heart's love of the whole. They may go even further and also experience the sacred oneness of The Radiant.

The Radiant: Some worldcentists' awareness and love expand until they feel a mystical oneness with the Earth and Universe, experiencing them as being Divine. Others not only experience the Earth and Universe as Divine, but also experience a mystical oneness with a transcendent Divine, considering the Earth and Universe as part of this transcendent Divine in manifest form. Both of these kinds of worldcentrists experience everything as sacred. The Radiant are on fire with the light of the Spirit and act from a place of beauty in themselves to cherish all.

And who knows what other kinds of worldcentrists are arising now or may arise in the future?

Appendix E

The Eight Zone Perspectives as Applied to Teaching

Zone perspectives are the inside and outside view of each quadrant. A brief, rough idea of each view is presented below. For a discussion of related theoretical issues and a more complete and nuanced discussion of the zone perspectives and applications to college pedagogy, see Gordon, 2008.

Upper Left Quadrant

Zone 1 (the inside view): Using this perspective, teachers try to empathize with a student, feeling "where the student is coming from." They attempt to attune to, intuit, or empathically perceive a student's inner self, including such things as attitudes, intentions, thoughts, and emotions.

Zone 2 (the outside view): Here teachers try to look at the student's Zone 1 objectively and form an understanding or idea about it, for example categorizing the student's motivation as worldcentric or the student's cognition as being at the formal operations level.

Lower Left Quadrant

Zone 3 (the inside view): Taking this view, educators attempt to attune to, intuit, or empathetically perceive such things as the shared values, understandings, and feelings of one or more student groups.

Zone 4 (the outside view): Enacting this perspective, teachers try to look at a student group's Zone 3 objectively and form an understanding or idea about it, for example categorizing a group's motivations as sociocentric or their worldview level as modern.

Upper Right Quadrant (This account is nonstandard. For a discussion of the theoretical issues involved, see Gordon, 2008.)

Zone 5 (the inside view): Teachers can take this view only if they use equipment connected to a student to actually register, measure, image, or track educationally relevant bodily phenomena inside the skin, such as the presence or absence of impediments to neuronal processes in cognition; integrity of immune system feedback processes; and level of nutrients, for example. However, teachers can hold Zone 5 phenomena generally in their awareness when teaching and, in ways possible in their teaching context, try to support student health.

Zone 6 (the outside view): Taking this perspective, educators register, measure, or track such things as an individual student's classroom behaviour, learning performance, and (in the case of physical fitness, sports, music, and dance programs,) physical form and performance.

Lower Right Quadrant (This account is nonstandard. For a discussion of the theoretical issues involved, see Gordon, 2008.)

Zone 7 (the inside view): Using this view, teachers observe or track such things as students' classroom interactions and collective behavioral states, for example noticing a group's exclusion of a non-native speaker; class members' interactions being slower than usual; or students leaning forward in their seats.

Zone 8 (the outside view): Taking this perspective, educators observe or track the larger, embodied context of their classroom, for example the ways institutional policy affects the classroom physical environment and interactions or the ways that the infrastructure of the educational system affects the ecological system.

Appendix F
Lines of Development Adapted for Educators

Ken Wilber in *Integral Spirituality* lists cognitive, self, values, moral, interpersonal, spiritual (ultimate concern), needs, kinesthetic, emotional, and aesthetic lines (60). A longer list (which includes creativity, for example) may be found in his *The Eye of Spirit* (637-638). For educators' purposes, Wilber's subtle and causal cognitive lines, discussed in his *Integral Psychology* (556-557; 685, n. 16; 686, n.17) could be called imagination and attention lines respectively.

Howard Gardner in *Intelligence Reframed* describes linguistic, logical-mathematical, musical, bodily-kinesthetic, spatial, interpersonal, intrapersonal, and naturalist (based on the ability to categorize) lines (he uses the word "intelligences") (41-43, 52).

I have selected and organized those developmental lines presented either by Howard Gardner or Ken Wilber, or both, that are especially relevant for educators. In order to facilitate professional self-inquiry and educational planning, I have taken Wilber's two major line categories, self-related lines and capacity-related lines (2004), and added two other categories: base cognitive lines and base capacity line.

1. Base Cognitive Lines: perspective-taking; imagination; attention.

2. Self-Related Lines: intrapersonal; self-identity; self-needs; moral; spiritual (ultimate concern); values.

3. Capacity Lines

Base Capacity: creation/creativity.
Intellectual: linguistic; logico-mathematical; spatial; naturalist (the latter is based on the ability to categorize).
Social: interpersonal.
Physical: bodily-kinesthetic.
Musical: musical.
    Artistic: aesthetic appreciation. (As for creating art, Gardner in *Intelligence Reframed* points out that many developmental lines can be used for artistic ends as well as nonartistic ends (108-109). Also, creating art involves the entwining of various lines.

Appendix G
Development of State-Stages

Terri O'Fallon, in her "Leadership and the Interpenetration of Structure and State Stages: A Subjective Expose" gives a succinct overview of state-stages:

Gross state-stages: "[In the first stage] people experience the sensation [a touch, taste, sight, smell, or sound] without awareness; next they become *aware* after the fact that they have had a sensory experience [such as when someone is eating something without really being present to the experience], and finally they are *aware* in the moment that they are experiencing sensory experience."

The same three stages apply to **subtle** (for example, thinking, emotions, imagining, or dreaming) and **causal** (vast openness, emptiness, formlessness) state-stages: (1) unaware; (2) aware after the fact; (3) aware during the experience, such as in (subtle) lucid dreaming or (causal) deep dreamless sleep.

One also develops from intermittent-self-recognized witnessing to constant-self-recognized witnessing of all states (witness state-stage), and from intermittent-self-recognized to constant-self-recognized resting in the witness-as-one-with-everything-it-witnesses (nondual state-stage.)

Appendix H
Development of Perspective-Taking

Drawing upon Robert Kegan's and Susann Cook-Greuter's work, I have adapted Wilber's list of levels of perspective-taking, or cognition of "what is," from Wilber's *Integral Spirituality* and included this adapted version below, aiming for a continuity in terms and description that can aid teachers in their work.

1. The Preconventional Levels are **Sensorimotor (Instinctual Mind)**, which consists of perceptions and reflexes; **Preoperational (Impulsive Mind)**, which subsumes reflexes under impulses; and **Preoperational (Opportunist Mind)**, which treats impulses as objects to manipulate and reflect on, making it possible to create categories embedded in its own needs and point of view.

2. The Conventional Level is **Concrete Operational (Conventional Mind)**, which treats categories and needs as objects to manipulate and reflect on, making it possible to internalize society's rules and roles.

3. Added to Wilber's list here is the Transition Between Conventional and Postconventional Levels, which is Cook-Greuter's **Abstract Operational** level (**Expert Mind or Technician Mind**), which subsumes social norms under craft logic.

4. The Postconventional Levels include **Formal Operational (System Mind)**, which subsumes craft logic under system effectiveness and, like the Expert, treats society's rules and values as objects to reflect upon, making it possible to create its own ideology and identity; **Early Vision-Logic (Pluralistic Mind)**, which treats its own ideology and identity as an object to reflect upon, making it possible to respect diversity, with radical relativism subsuming the single system view; **Middle Vision-Logic (System-of-Systems Mind)**, which treats pluralities and contradictions, both inner and outer, as objects to reflect upon, making it possible to use global commonalities or principles to organize plural systems; and **Late Vision-Logic (Nth-Degree Systems Mind)**, which reflects upon systems of systems as objects, making it possible to correlate and organize them into metaframeworks.

5. The Transpersonal Levels consist of the **Illumined Mind,** which regards the individual rational mind, its systems, and its thinking as an object, from the perspective of mystical oneness with material aspects of the Kosmos, such as nature and other people; the **Intuitive Mind,** which regards the material Kosmos as an object, from the perspective of oneness with the Divine; the **Overmind,** which regards all manifestation as an object, from the perspective of oneness with the Empty Witness; and **Supermind,** (Ground Arising), the all-inclusive, nondual recognition of Emptiness and all the ever-emerging Forms above.

The college educator may challenge students with Conventional Minds to become self-authoring by presenting them with different points of view on a problem or social issue and requiring them to formulate a reasoned defence of their own position, while taking the views of others into account. Students who have moved out of Conventional Mind and who erroneously hold that all opinions are equal can be helped to learn how evidence and logic may have different degrees of validity. Students with Expert Minds can be asked to research the larger context of a problem or to question their proposed solution from various system-wide angles. Stretching students with System Minds may require proposing that they culturally or techno-economically contextualize their choice of a solution to a problem. Those few undergraduate learners with Pluralistic Minds might be challenged to discover commonalities among a global range of value systems or to apply systems principles.

Appendix I
Types Relevant for Educators

Integral educator Sean Esbjörn-Hargens has categorized educationally-relevant types according to quadrants (83). He gives the examples of Myers Briggs personality types (usually referred to as MBTI—Myers Briggs Type Indicator—types) and Enneagram personality types (Upper Left); neurolinguistic programming sensory types (Upper Right); masculine and feminine gender types (Lower Left); and preferred narrative styles of writing (Lower Right). To Esbjörn-Hargens' examples, I would like to add the learning style types of David Kolb (Upper Left); kinds of learning disabilities and physical disabilities (Upper always linked to masculine and feminine genders (Lower Left); and John Holland's vocational/environmental types (Lower Right).

[A handout for students' self-reflection concerning types can found on the following page.]

[I have found an awareness of the Myers-Briggs types to be especially helpful in teaching. Below is a Myers-Briggs-related handout given to students in all of my courses. During class, I periodically relate these preferences to what we are doing so that students are more self-and other-aware and more tolerant of activities outside of their preferences. This handout also helps me to relate to students more effectively in one-on-one sessions. I don't reveal the meaning of the capital letters until later in order to avoid prejudicing their responses. (I=Introvert; E=Extravert; S=Sensory; N=Intuitive; T=Thinking; F=Feeling; J=Judgment; P=Perception]

What are your preferences?

Please circle what is usually more energizing, easy, or enjoyable for you to do. All things being equal, what are your usual preferences?

1. Choose one preference below:

E: being sociable; doing mental work by talking to people, focusing on people, objects, actions, and events in the surrounding environment; taking action

I: being quiet; doing mental work privately before talking or acting; focusing on inner thoughts, ideas, feelings

2. Choose one preference below:

S: paying attention to concrete, real-life items; practicalities; being patient with details; avoiding complications; having prior experience in solving any problems present; using skills already learned

N: paying attention to meanings of facts and how they fit together in patterns or a "big picture;" using imagination to come up with new possibilities; not minding complicated situations; avoiding details; using imagination to come up with new ways of doing things; solving new problems; learning new skills as opposed to using skills already learned.

3. Choose one preference below:

T: logic; ideas; fairness; improving things; competence
F: empathy; feelings; social harmony; intimacy

4. Choose one preference below:

J: being systematic; planning; being decisive
P: being casual; spontaneity; keeping things open

Appendix J
A States Overview for Educators

Below I have applied Ken Wilber's general categories for different states to the educational context, adding some material and subcategories that seem helpful to educators. Wilber remarks, "states occur in all quadrants (from weather states to states of consciousness)," and I also take this fact into account, giving an all-quadrant overview.

Upper Left

The Five Natural States: The foundation here is the Always Already Nondual state, "which is not so much a state as the ever-present ground of all states..." (Wilber, 2006, 74) with integral educators holding the recognition of their students as Always Already in their minds and hearts. Witnessing or attentional states are especially important to educators in the Waking states since student states of attention, focused or unfocused, are key for learning. Also important for educators in the waking states category are states of intention, consciously or unconsciously holding an intention for oneself or others, and emotional states, for example, inspired, anxious, or bored. (The exceptions, one hopes, to natural states relevant to the educational context are the REM Dream and Formless deep dreamless sleep states.)

Altered States: Of special interest to integral educators are imaginal states, for example, creative flow states (Csikszentmihalyi; Murphy, 140-141) and directed imagination or visualization and Meditative, Attentional or Witnessing states, for example, reflection or contemplation on one inner or outer object, witnessing whatever is arising, and witnessing awareness itself (Wilber, 2006, 74). These may (or may not) lead to Unitary states, for example, experiences of oneness with others, nature, the Divine, or Emptiness; or experiences of oneness with all of these in temporary nondual awareness (Wilber, 2006, 93). Concerning Psi states (for example, inner sensing or knowing; telepathy; precognition (Radin, 13-247), in the future as integral teachers move into working more extensively with meditational, unitary, and collective intelligence states (Hamilton) in educational contexts, they and their students may increasingly experience psi states and desire to know more about them.

Upper Right

Natural States: These states, for example, healthy, clear-headed, optimally energized on all levels (gross, subtle, causal) (Wilber, 2006, 74), tired, and ill, obviously have an enormous effect on learning and teaching and need to be taken into account.

Altered States: Of special relevance here for educators is extraordinary individual athletic performance (Murphy, 443-444).

Lower Left

Natural States: Examples of these collective states are a group of students feeling inspired during a classroom presentation or anxious because of world events.

Altered States: Here, a number of students can simultaneously experience individual states, such as during group meditation and group visualization. Also, states of collective intelligence (Hamilton) are being explored in the context of adult learning and problem solving (Scharmer; also, Senge, Scharmer, Jaworski, & Flowers) and have exciting potential for the college and university context.

Lower Right

Natural States: Examples would be a group of students behaving in a distracted or cooperative way. On a larger scale, institutional states significantly affect the classroom. Examples of institutional states are universities being in the midst of implementing education-enhancing policies or, conversely, being in the midst of cutting funding to educational programs because of lack of money.

Altered States: These include such things as extraordinary functioning of sports teams (Hamilton, 67, 69; Murphy, 282; 139-140), embodiment of collective intelligence experiences, and classroom synchronicities (Bach, 189-196; Senge, Scharmer, Jaworski, & Flowers, 164-166).

References

Argyris, C. (1985). *Action science, concepts, methods, and skills for research and intervention*. San Francisco: Jossey-Bass.

Aurobindo. (n.d.). *The Life Divine and The Synthesis of Yoga*. XVIII-XXI. Pondichcherry: Centenary Library.

Awbrey, S. M, Dana, D., Miller, V. W., Robinson, P., Ryan, M. M. & Scott, D. K. (Eds.) (2006). *Integrative learning and action: A call to wholeness* (studies in education and spirituality). New York: Peter Lang.

Bach, C. M. (2000). "Teaching in the Sacred Mind." *Dark Night, Early Dawn*. Albany: SUNY Press, 183-212.

Balder, S. (n.d.). "TSK and the Public Self," Gaia Community blog. Retrieved December 17, 2008, from http://pods.gaia.com/tsk/discussions/view/148428.

Banathy, B. H. (1992). *Comprehensive systems design in education: Building a design culture in education*. Educational Technology, 22(3), 33-35.

Bayne, R. (2005). *Ideas and Evidence: Critical Reflections on MBTI Theory and Practice*. Gainesville, Florida: Center for Applications of Psychological Type (CAPT).

Bassesches, M. (1984). *Dialectical thinking and adult development*. New Jersey: Ablex Publishing.

Beck, D. E. & Cowan, C. C. (1996). *Spiral dynamics*. Malden, MA: Blackwell Publishers.

Bogdan, R. & Biklen, S. K. (1982). *Qualitative research for educators: An introduction to theory and methods*. Boston: Allyn and Bacon.

Bohm, D.. (1996). *On Dialogue*. London: Routledge.

Bohm, D. (1992). *Thought as a System*. London: Routledge.

Bohm, D. (1980). *Wholeness and the Implicate Order*. London: Routledge.

Brown, J.S., Collins, A., & Duguid, P. (1989). *Situated cognition and the culture of learning*. Educational Researcher, 18(1), 32-42.

Bruffee, K. (1999). *Collaborative Learning: Higher Education, Independence and the Authority of Knowledge*. 2nd ed. Baltimore, MD: John Hopkins University Press.

Bruner, J. (1966). *Toward a theory of instruction*. Cambridge, MA: Harvard University Press.

Chadwick, D. (1999). *Crooked Cucumber: The Life and Zen Teaching of Shunryu Suzuki*. Broadway.

Collins, A., Brown, J. S., & Newman, S. E. (1989). Cognitive apprenticeship: Teaching the craft of reading, writing, and mathematics. In L. B. Resnick (Ed.), *Knowing, learning, and instruction: Essays in honor of Robert Glaser* (pp. 453-494). Hillsdale, NJ: Lawrence Erlbaum Associates.

Commons, M. L., Richards, F. A., & Armon, C. (Eds.) (1984). *Beyond Formal Operations: Late Adolescent and Adult Cognitive Development. New York: Praeger.*

Cook, F. H. (1977). *Hua-Yen Buddhism: The Jewel Net of Indra*. University Park, PA: Penn State Press.

Cook-Greuter, S. (n.d.). Two Ways of Conceptualizing the Spectrum of Development. Adapted from Paul Landraitis. Integral Development Associates. Retrieved July 30, 2007 from http://www.cook-greuter.com.

Cook-Greuter, S. R. (2000). Mature ego development: A gateway to ego transcendence. *Journal of Adult Development, 7*(4), 227-240.

Cook-Greuter, S. (2002). *A Detailed Description of the Development of Nine Action Logics: Adapted from Ego Development Theory for the Leadership Developmental Framework*. Retrieved from http://www.cook-greuter.com.

Cook-Greuter, S.R. (2005). Ego development: Nine levels of increasing embrace. Available at www.cook-greuter.com.

Csikszentmihalyi, M. (1997, July/August). Finding Flow. Retrieved 9 2009, from *Psychology Today*: http://www.psychologytoday.com/articles/pto-1999701-000042.html.

Csikszentmihalyi, M. (1997). *Creativity: Flow and the Psychology of Discovery and Invention*. New York: Harper.

Davis, B. (2004). *Inventions of Teaching: A Genealogy*. Mahwah, NJ: Lawrence Erlbaum Associates.

Davis, N. T. & Blanchard, M. (2005). Collaborative Teams in a University Statistics Course: A Case Study of How Differing Value Structures Inhibit Change. *School Science and Mathematics*, 104(6).

Davis, N. T., Kumpete, E., & Aydeniz, M. (2007). Fostering Continuous Improvement and Learning through Peer Assessment: Part of an Integral Model of Assessment. *Educational Assessment*, 12(2), 1-23.

DeBono, E. (1970). *Lateral thinking: A textbook to creativity*. London: Ward Lock Educational.

Deida, D. (n.d.). "The Three Ways of Love: Excerpted from Intimate Communion: Awakening Your Sexual Essence" Retrieved 5/14/10 from http://www.enotalone.com/article/4205.html.

Dewey, J. (1926). *Democracy and education*. Plain Label Books. http://www.cafepress.com/7391.

Dyer, A. (2003). The Knowledge of Good and Evil. Retrieved 5/14/10 from http://faculty.etsu.edu/dyer/lectures/Knowledge_of_Good_and_Evil/knowledge_of_good_and_evil.htm.

Elbow, P. (2008). The Believing Game or Methodological Believing. Conference Presentation available at http://works.bepress.com/peter_elbow.

Esbjörn-Hargens, S. (2007). "Integral Teacher, Integral Students, Integral Classroom: Applying Integral Theory to Education." *AQAL: Journal of Integral Theory and Practice* 2(2), pp 72-103.

Esbjörn-Hargens, S. (2008, 4). An All-Inclusive Framework for the 21st Century: An Overview of Integral Theory. Retrieved 12 12, 2009 from Integral LIfe: http://integrallife.com/node/37539.

Esbjörn-Hargens, S. (in press). Integral theory in service of integral education: Illustrations from on online graduate program. In S. Esbjörn-Hargens, J. Reams, & O. Gunnlaugson (Eds.) *Integral education: Exploring multiple perspectives in the classroom*. Esbjörn-Hargens, S. Reams, J. & Gunnlaugson, O. (Eds.) (in press). *Integral education: Exploring multiple perspectives in the classroom*.

Evans, N.J., Forney, D.S., & Guido-DiBrito, F. (1998). *Student Development in College: Theory, Research, and Practice*. San Francisco, California: Jossey-Bass.

Ewert, G. D. (1991). Habermas and education: A comprehensive overview of the influence of Habermas in educational literature. *Review of Educational Research*, 61(3), 345-378.

Feldman, L. (2008). The transformative and adaptive potential of integral pedagogy on the secondary educational level. Paper presented at Biannual Integral Theory Conference, John F. Kennedy University. Pleasant Hill, CA.

Feldman, A. & Minstrell, J. (2000). Action research as a research methodology for the study of teaching and learning of science. In A. Kelley & R. Lesh (Eds), *Handbook of research design in mathematics and science education*, pp. 429-455, Erlbaum: Hillsdale, NJ.

Fenner, P. (2007). *Radiant Mind, Awakening Unconditioned Awareness*. Sounds True.

Feuerstein, G. (1987). *Structures of consciousness: The genius of Jean Gebser*. Santa Rosa, CA: Integral Publishing.

Feuerstein, G. (2001). *The Yoga Tradition*, paperback edition, Hohm Press.

Fisher, R., Ury, W., & Patton, B. (1981). *Getting to Yes: Negotiating Agreement Without Giving In*. (2nd ed.). New York: Houghton Mifflin.

Fischer, K. W. & Farrar, M. J. (1987). Generalizations about generalizations: How a theory of skill development explains both generality and specificity. *International Journal of Psychology*, 2, 643-677.

Fosnot, C. T. (Ed.) (1996). *Constructivism. theory, perspectives, and practice*. NY: Teachers College Press.

Freire, P. (1996). *Pedagogy of the Oppressed* (2nd revised edition ed.). New York: Penguin.

Fuhs, C. (2008). An Integral Map of Perspective-Taking. Paper. Integral Theory Conference. John F. Kennedy University. August 8. cfuhs@integralinstitute.org.

Gardner, H. (1999). *Intelligence Reframed: Multiple Intelligences for the 21st Century*. New York: Basic Books.

Glasersfeld, E. von (1995). *Radical constructivism: A way of knowing and learning*. London: Falmer Press.

Goleman, G. (2006). Social Intelligence. New York: Bantam Books.

Gordon, P. (2005). "Integral Practice in University and College Teaching." Unpublished paper. pgordon@johnabbott.qc.ca.

Gordon, P. (2008). Going Beyond Current Understanding of The Eight Native Perspectives: Applications to Pedagogy, Integral Theory Conference, August 10, 2008, San Francisco.

Gunnlaugson, O. (2007). "Revisioning Possibilities for How Groups Learn Together: Venturing an Integrally-Informed Model of Generative Dialogue". *Integral Review*, http://www.integral-review.com.

Gunnlaugson, O. (2006). "Exploring Generative Dialogue as a Transformative Learning Practice within Adult & Higher Education Settings." *Journal of Adult and Continuing Education*. Scotland.

Gunnlaugson, O. (in press). Reexamining and Integral Approach to Education. In S. Esbjörn-Hargens, J. Reams, & O. Gunnlaugson (Eds.) *Integral education: Exploring multiple perspectives in the classroom*.

Habermas, J. (1998). *Between Facts and Norms* (W. Rehg, Trans.). Cambridge, MA: MIT Press.

Habermas, J. (1999). *Moral Consciousness and Communicative Action*. Cambridge, MA: MIT Press.

Hamilton, C. (May-July, 2004). "Come Together: The Mystery of Collective Intelligence." *What Is Enlightenment?* (25), 57-79.

Hampson, G. (in press). Western-Islamic and Native American genealogies of integral education. In S. Esbjörn-Hargens, J. Reams, & O. Gunnlaugson (Eds.) *Integral education: Exploring multiple perspectives in the classroom*.

Harris, C. (2002). The experience of support for transformative learning. Harvard Graduate School of Education Dissertation.

Hartman, D., & Zimberoff, D. (2008, September 22). Higher Stages of Human Development. Retrieved June 2009, from *Journal of Heart Centered Therapies*: www. thefreelibrary.com.

Hooks, B. (1994). *Teaching to transgress: Education as the practice of freedom*. NY: Routledge.

Illich, I. (1975). *Tools for conviviality*. London: Fontana.

Isaacs, W. (1999). *Dialogue and the Art of Thinking Together. A Pioneering Approach to Communicating in Business and in Life*. New York: Bantam Doubleday Dell Publishing Group.

Johnson, B. (1996). *Polarity management: Identifying and managing unsolvable problems*. Amherst, MA: HRD Press.

Kegan, R. (1994). *In Over Our Heads: The Mental Demands of Modern Life*. Cambridge, Massachusetts: Harvard.

Kegan, R. (2002). "Epistemology, Fourth Order Consciousness, and the Subject-Object Relationship, or How the Self Evolves." *What is Enlightenment?* (Fall/Winter 2002), 143-154.

Kegan, R. & Lahey, L.L (2009). *Immunity to Change: How to Overcome It and Unlock the Potential in Yourself and Your Organization*. Cambridge, MA: Harvard Business School Publishing.

Kneen C. (2002). *Awake Mind, Open Heart*. Marlowe & Company.

Koestler, A. (1967). *The Ghost in the Machine*. New York: Macmillan.

Kögler, H. H. (1992). *The power of dialog: Critical hermeneutics after Gadamer and Foucault*. Cambridge, MA: MIT Press.

Lakoff, G. & Johnson, M. (1999). *Philosophy in the flesh: The embodied mind and its challenge to Western thought*. New York, NY: Basic Books/Perseus Books Group.

Lave, J. & Wenger, E. (1991). *Situated learning: Legitimate peripheral participation*. Cambridge, MA: Cambridge University Press.

Lawrence, G. (1993). *People Types & Tiger Stripes*. (3rd ed.). Gainesville, Florida: Center for Applications of Psychological Type (CAPT).

Marshall, H. H. (1990). Beyond the Workplace Metaphor: The Classroom as a Learning Setting. *Theory into Practice* 29:94-101.

Mayer, R. (1998). Cognitive, metacognitive, and motivational aspects of problems solving. *Instructional Science*, 26, p. 49-63.

McNab, P. (2005). *Towards an Integral Vision: Using NLP and Ken Wilber's AQAL Model to Enhance Communication*. Victoria, BC: Trafford. Phone: (250) 383-6864.

Mendaglio, S. (2008). *Dabrowski's Theory of Positive Disintegration*. Great Potential Press.

Mendizza, M. (2003). *Magical Parent Magical Child: The Art of Joyful Parenting*. Berkeley, California: North Atlantic Books.

Mervis, B. & Rosch, E. (1981). Categories of natural objects. *Annual Review of Psychology*, 32. p. 89-115.

Merzel, D.B. (2005). *The Path of the Human Being, Zen Teachings On The Boddhisattva Way*. Shambhala.

Mezirow, J. (1991). *Transformative dimensions of adult learning*. San Francisco: Jossey-Bass, Inc.

Mezirow, J. (2000). *Learning as Transformation: Critical Perspectives on a Theory in Progress*. Jossey-Bass, San Francisco.

Moltz, M (in press). Contemporary integral education research: A transnational and transparadigmatic overview. In S. Esbjörn-Hargens, J. Reams, & O. Gunnlaugson (Eds.) *Integral education: Exploring multiple perspectives in the classroom*.

Montessori, M. (1965). *Dr. Montessori's own handbook*. New York: Schocken Books.

Moseley, A. (n.d.). Philosophy of Love. Retrieved 5/14/10 from http://www.iep.utm.edu/love/.

Muller, M.F. (2004). trans. *The Sacred Books of the East: The Vedanta Sutras*, 1962, New edition, Kessinger Publishing.

Murphy, M. (1992). *The Future of the Body: Explorations into the Further Evolution of Human Nature*. Los Angeles: Jeremy P. Tarcher.

Murray, T. (2006). Collaborative knowledge building and integral theory: On perspectives, uncertainty, and mutual regard. *Integral Review*, 2,. 210-268.

Murray, T. (2008). Exploring Epistemic wisdom: Ethical and practical implications of integral theory and methodological pluralism for collaboration and knowledge-building. Paper presented at Biannual Integral Theory Conference, John F. Kennedy University. Pleasant Hill, CA.

Murray, T., & Arroyo, I. (2002). Toward measuring and maintaining the zone of proximal development in adaptive instructional systems. Cerri, Gouarderes & Paraguacu (Eds.) *Intelligent tutoring systems: 6th International Conference*, ITS 2000 (pp. 749-758). Berlin: Springer Verlag.

Myers, I. B. (1998). *Introduction to Type.* (6th ed.). Mountain View, California: CPP.

Neufeld, Gordon & Mate, Gabor (2004). *Hold on to Your Kids: Why Parents Matter.* Toronto: Random House.

Norgaard, R.B. (1989, February). "The case for methodological pluralism." *Ecological Economics*, Elsevier, vol. 1(1), pp. 37-57.

O'Fallon, T. (in press). Grounding integral theory in the field of experience. In S. Esbjörn-Hargens, J. Reams, & O. Gunnlaugson (Eds.) *Integral education: Exploring multiple perspectives in the classroom.*

Palmer, P. (1993). *To Know as we are Known. Education as a Spiritual Journey.* San Francisco: HarperSanFrancisco.

Palmer, P. (1998). *The Courage to Teach: Exploring the Inner Landscape of a Teacher's Life.* San Francisco: Jossey Bass.

Parks R. with Haskins J. (1992). *Rosa Parks: My Story.* Scholastic Inc.

Patton, M. Q. (1980). *Qualitative evaluation methods.* Beverly Hills, CA: Sage Publications.

Pearce, Joseph Chilton (2002). *The Biology of Transcendence: A Blueprint of the Human Spirit.* Rochester, Vermont: Park Street Press.

Piaget, J. (1972). *The principles of genetic epistemology.* New York: Basic Books.

Piaget, J. (1977). *The Essential Piaget.* Eds. H. Gruber and J. Voneche. New York: Basic Books.

Pinar, W.. F., Reynolds, W.M. Slattery, P. & Taubman, P. M. (1995). *Understanding Curriculum.* New York: Peter Lang.

Pinker, S. (1997). *How the mind works.* New York: Norton.

Polya, G. (1973). How to solve it. Princeton, NJ: Princeton University Press.

Polanyi, M. (1962). *Personal Knowledge Towards a Post-Critical Philosophy.* Chicago: University of Chicago Press.

Pringle, R. M. (2000). *When Grades Get in the Way of Learning: An Interpretative Study of Developing Assessment as Continuous Improvement in Science Teacher Education.* Ph.D. diss., Florida State University.

Radin, D. (1997). *The Conscious Universe.* New York: HarperCollins.

Ray, R.A.(2008). *Touching Enlightenment.* Sounds True.

Reigeluth, C.M. (2008). Chaos theory and the sciences of complexity: Foundations for transforming education. In B. Despres (Ed.), *Systems Thinkers in Action: A Field Guide for Effective Change Leadership in Education.* New York: Rowman & Littlefield.

Riso, D. R. & Hudson, R. (1999). *The Wisdom of the Enneagram: The Complete Guide to Psychological and Spiritual Growth for the Nine Personality Types.* New York: Bantam.

Robinson, K. (2001). *Out of our minds: Learning to be creative.* Oxford: Capstone.

Rosenberg, M. (1999). *Non-violent communication: A language of compassion.* Encinitas, CA: Puddledancer Press.

Ross, G. (1998). Pleasantville. Retrieved 5/14/10 from http://www.imsdb.com/scripts/Pleasantville.html.

Ross, S. (2005). Toward An integral process theory of human dynamics: Dancing the universal tango. *Integral Review,* 1(1) 64-84.

Rotten Tomatoes (2010). "Pleasantville" Synopsis. Retrieved 5/14/10 from http://www.rottentomatoes.com/m/pleasantville/#synopsis.

Scharmer, O. (2007). *Theory U: Leading from the Future as it Emerges.* Sol Publishers.

Schoenfeld, A. H. (1985). Metacognitive and epistemological issues in mathematical understanding. In E. Silver (Ed.), *Teaching and learning mathematical problem solving* (pp. 361-380). Hillsdale, NJ: Lawrence Erlbaum Assoc.

Senge, P. M., Scharmer, C. O., Jaworski, J. & Flowers, B.S. (2004). *Presence: Human Purpose and the Field of the Future.* Cambridge, MA: Society for Organizational Learning.

Smith, M. K. (2008). Infed: The Encyclopedia of Informal Education. Retrieved November 26, 2009 from Howard Gardener, Multiple Intelligences and Education: http//www.infed.org/thinkers/gardner.htm.

Stack, S. J. (2007). Integrating science and soul: The lived experience of a science educator bringing holistic and integral perspectives to the transformation of science teaching. Retrieved March 13th 2008, www.stack.bigpondhosting.com/thesis.

Steckler, E. & Torbert, W. (in press). A "developmental action inquiry" approach to teaching first-, second-, and third-person action research methods. In S. Esbjörn-Hargens, J. Reams, & O. Gunnlaugson (Eds.) *Integral education: Exploring multiple perspectives in the classroom*.

Stein, Z. (2008). Intuitions of altitude: Researching the conditions for the possibility of developmental assessment. Paper presented at Biannual Integral Theory Conference, John F. Kennedy University. Pleasant Hill, CA.

Steiner, R. (1965). *The education of the child in light of anthroposophy*. London: Rudolf Steiner Press. Strickland, B. (2002, February). Bill Strickland Makes Change with a Slide Show. Retrieved December 7, 2009 from Ted Talks: http://www.ted.com.

Thurman, R., trans. (1976). *Vimalakirti Nirdesa Sutra*. The Pennsylvania State University. Retrieved from http://buddhasutra.com.

Tolstoy, L. (1907). "The Three Questions.," *Twenty-Three Tales*. New York: Funk & Wagnalls Company.

Tomlinson, C. A (1995). *How to Differentiate Instruction in Mixed-Ability Classrooms*. Alexandra, VA: Association for Supervision and Curriculum Development.

Torbert, W. R. (2004). *Action Inquiry: The Secret of Timely and Transforming Leadership*. New York: Berrett- Koehler Publishers.

Varela, F. & Scharmer, O. (2000). The Three Gestures of Becoming Aware: Interview with Francisco Varela. Retrieved February 10, 2008, from http://www.dialogonleadership.org/interviewVarela.html.

Vaughn, F. (1995). *Shadows of the Sacred*. Wheaton, IL: Theosophical Publishing House.

Vygotsky, L. S. (1978). *Mind in society: The development of higher psychological processes*. M. Cole, V. John-Steiner, S. Scribner, & E. Souberman, (Eds.). Cambridge, MA: Harvard University Press.

Walsh, R. (1995). The Spirit of Evolution: An Overview of Ken Wilber's Book Sex, Ecology, Spirituality: The Spirit of Evolution (Shambhala, 1995). Retrieved 5/14/10 from http://cogweb.ucla.edu/CogSci/Walsh_on_Wilber_95.html.

Wertenbaker, C. (2006). The Home of the Self. *Parabola: Tradition, Myth and the Search for Meaning*. Society for the Study of Myth and Tradition.

Wilber, K. (1999-2000). *The Collected Works of Ken Wilber*. Boston: Shambhala.

Wilber, K. (1999-2000). *The Collected Works of Ken Wilber*. v. 4 Integral Psychology and v. 7, The Eye of Spirit. Boston: Shambhala.
Wilber, K. (2000). *Integral Psychology*. Boston: Shambhala Publications.

Wilber, K. (2000). *Sex, ecology, spirituality* (in collected works of Ken Wilber, Vol. 6). Boston: Shambhala Press.

Wilber, K.. (2001). *A Brief History of Everything*. Boston: Shambhala Publications.

Wilber, K. (2004). Integral Education: Introducing the AQAL Approach. (Audio). Retrieved December 27, 2004 from http://www.integralnaked.org.

Wilber, K. (2004a). Excerpt C. In Excerpts from volume 2 of the Kosmos trilogy. Retrieved January 15, 2004 from http://wilber.shambhala.com.

Wilber, K. (2004b). Excerpt D. In Excerpts from volume 2 of the Kosmos Trilogy. Retrieved January 15, 2004 from http://wilber.shambhala.com.

Wilber, K. (2005). "Introducing the AQAL Framework: A Guide to Integral Theory and Practice." in *Integral Life Practice Starter Kit*. Version 1.0. Boulder, Colorado: Integral Institute.

Wilber, Ken (2006). *Integral Spirituality: A Startling New Role for Religion in the Modern and Postmodern World*. Integral Books: Shambhala.

Wilber, K. (2008). States Stages and Skillful Means. Retrieved December 6, 2009 from Integral Life: http://integrallife.com/node/53521

Wilber, K. (2009). Integral Spirituality, Chapter 4 States and Stages. Retrieved December 3, 2009 from Integral Life: http://integrallife.com/editorial/chapter-4-states-and-stages.

Wilber, K. & Kegan, R. (2004). The Evolving Self. Part I. Why the Hierarchy Within Can Heal the Hierarchy Without. (Audio). Retrieved December 20, 2004 from http://www.integralnaked.org.

Wilber, K., Patten, T., Leonard, A., Morelli, M. (2008). *Integral life practice: A 21st-century blueprint for physical health, emotional balance, mental clarity, and spiritual awakening*. Boston, MA: Shambhala Press.

Winne, P. H. (2001). Self-regulated learning viewed from models of information processing. In B. J. Zimmerman and D. H. Schunk (Eds.), *Self-regulated learning and academic achievement: Theoretical perspectives,* (pp. 153-189). Mahwah, NJ: Lawrence Erlbaum.

Wittgenstein, L. (1953). *Philosophical investigations* (3rd ed.). (Anscombe, Trans.). New York: Macmillan.

Index

G

L

M

P

Contributors

Nancy Davis, Ph.D., is a professor of science education at Florida State University. She uses integral theory to inform her interaction with prospective and practicing teachers. She is actively involved with schools and practicing teachers as they adapt to the changing climate of education. Her primary focus is the development of professional teachers, fostering a more sophisticated understanding of teaching and learning science. This focus involves assisting teachers to understand themselves and to align their values with enacted practice. In addition to this individual focus, professional empowerment is enhanced through understanding of cultural and political influences in teaching. Her research focuses on assessment practices and integration of developing technologies into classrooms. She has published articles in School Science and Mathematics, Educational Assessment, International Journal of Science Education, Research in Science Education, and numerous other journals. In her personal life she puts much energy into interacting with 10 grandchildren, gardening, raising chickens and reading.

Willow Dea, M.S. OTR (Editor), is deeply inspired by the impact of transformational practices in emerging educational systems. Her thirst for working with systems began with the human body. After a combined bachelor's and master's degree program in occupational therapy, the science of human performance, she was certified in five additional modalities of human integration, which facilitate sustained peak performance and conscious embodiment. Willow has used an integral approach with her clients in private practice and in educational settings for 15 years, providing leading edge services for people of all ages. Willow serves on the board of trustees for The Khabele School in Austin, Texas, where she lives with her husband, the grackles, and cacti. www.teachingwholeness.com.

Lynne D. Feldman, M.A., J.D., is an attorney and educator who has been active in creating and sharing integral applications to education, parenting, law, mediation, transformational change, leadership, and spirituality. She worked closely with Ken Wilber and Integral Institute. She is on the editorial board of the Journal of Integral Theory and Practice, and is an Integral Scholar. Her writings have been published in the AQAL Journal, Kosmos Journal, and bar association magazines. She created the

Center for Integral Education; Integral Education Consultants; and New York Integral, which presents workshops and services in the New York metropolitan area. She presents workshops on integral spirituality, leadership, life practice, and the AQAL map at the One Spirit Learning Alliance as well as Rutgers University, Maezumi Institute, Eagleton Institute, the Integral Theory Conference, and integral education seminars. Her work with adolescents has won her praise and honors from the White House, Dateline on NBC, Peter Jennings, Teen People magazine, Eagleton Institute, New Jersey state legislature, and her local board of education. The Governor of New Jersey named her to the Character Education Commission, and she headed the action team of the NJ Character Education Network. She belongs to many associations that relate to mindfulness, cognition, education reform, attachment parenting, and alternative dispute resolution. She lives in New Jersey.

Kyle Good, Ph.D., has a doctorate in integral studies with a concentration in learning and change in human systems. He is currently the principal of an elementary school that has implemented integral education concepts through transformational learning communities that have become the fabric of the school. Kyle also applied integral education perspectives as a district-level administrator. After 23 years of service in public education, Kyle launched his own integral education counseling, consulting, and professional coaching firm, (Opening Doors to Endless Opportunities), in which he is employing his skills and passion for helping others live an integral life and embracing unity in diversity. Kyle participated in the Creativity Workshop in Barcelona, Spain, where he began writing his new book on integral education, How Magic Happens in the Surprise (forthcoming, November 2009). www,drkylke.org.

Patricia Gordon, Ph.D., applies integral theory to the teaching of her literature courses at John Abbott College in Montreal, Canada. In the summer of 2008 she presented a theoretical extension of Ken Wilber's eight native perspectives in her paper "Going Beyond Current Understanding of the Eight Native Perspectives: Applications to Pedagogy in Higher Education" at the Integral Theory Conference, John F. Kennedy University. She also has written the paper "Integral Practice in University and College Teaching." She has participated in the Next Step Integral Education group and attended integral and integrally related seminars, such as Integral Institute's Integral Life Practice seminar, Susanne Cook-Greuter's Developmental Coaching Intensive seminar, and Don Beck's Spiral Dynamics 1 seminar. She graduated from Indiana University with high distinction and received a Clara J. Goodbody scholarship for her graduate studies in comparative literature, during which she taught in the honors division. She has served as chair of the board of directors of the Social Justice Committee of Montreal, is a member of the board of directors of The Epic of Evolution Society, is the education editor of their newsletter, and is the coordinator of John Abbott College's English Challenge Program.

John Gruber, M.S., holds an undergraduate degree in environmental studies and a graduate degree in medicinal chemistry and Pharmacognosy. As an undergraduate faculty scholar at Brown University, he worked to integrate studies in biology, geology, and environmental science, and received the C.F. Ma Research Fellowship for Natural Products research as a graduate student. In 2001, he was a Teacher Recognition awardee in the United States Presidential Scholars Program. As a science teacher and long-time student of evolutionary biology and natural history, he is particularly interested in ways to apply integral thinking to the secondary school classroom. Having taught a botany seminar for 12 years, John uses that particular class as an experimental ground, a place to explore the application of integral approaches to teaching with a group of willing and interested students. He emphasizes fieldwork, experimental observation, and direct perception, alongside conceptualization, in his science courses and continues to develop ways to build interior and exterior experiences into his science teaching. In addition to his work and research as an educator and administrator, he is involved in an active research program in insect ecology and systematic biology of moth species. John is one of the directors of Next Step Integral and currently also serves as chairman of the Upper School Science Department and director of the Summer Science Institute at Friends' Central School, an independent Quaker day school where he has taught for 16 years.

Olen Gunnlaugson, Ph.D. candidate, worked as program coordinator, lecturer, and integral coach at Holma College of Integral Studies (Sweden), playing a central role in helping the college make the transition from holistic to integral studies. His graduate research, which focuses on applying and building upon Scharmer's four fields of conversation within transformative, contemplative, and integral education contexts, has been fully funded by both master's degree and doctorate scholarships from the Social Sciences and Humanities Research Council of Canada. Olen is in the final stages of completing his Ph.D. at the University of British Columbia (Vancouver), where he is exploring presencing as a conversational practice for fostering second-person forms of contemplative learning in higher education classroom settings. Olen teaches courses in dialogue processes as part-time faculty at Langara College (Vancouver) and the University of Massachusetts's (Boston) Critical and Creative Thinking Masters program. His scholarship in integral theory, presencing, and dialogue education has been presented at numerous international conferences and appeared in peer-reviewed journals, such as Journal of Transformative Education, Journal of Adult and Continuing Education (Scotland), Journal of Further and Higher Education (UK), and Integral Review. He is presently co-editing a book on integral education (Suny Press) with Jonathan Reams and Sean-Esbjorn Hargens.

Miriam Mason Martineau, M.A. Miriam has a Masters Degree in Psychology from the University of Zurich, with a specialization in Youth and Child Psychology, and is also a certified teacher of Laban Modern Dance, as well as a singer and vocal instructor. From 1992-2002 Miriam lived in an integrally-informed intentional community and there honed the skills of group facilitation, conflict resolution and generative dialogue. Miriam works in private practice as an integral therapeutic counsellor for adults, couples, youth and children, and her interest in peak performance, vitality, integral business and leadership building have led her to work with Univera, an international health and nutritional products company leading the way in its field with world-wide resources, cutting-edge research, scientific development, and revolutionary products. Miriam is vice-president and faculty member of Next Step Integral, an international organization that applies integral consciousness to parenting, education, ecology, and community. For the last 15 years she has studied and researched how parenting can be pursued as a spiritual practice. This has led her to offering courses on the topic, working as a coach for parents, and writing a book (forthcoming) titled Integral Parenting. . www.nextstepintegral.org   www.integralhealth.myunivera.com/about

Stephan Martineau is the founder and President of Next Step Integral and an integral consultant for not-for-profit organizations. www.nextstepintegral.org

Tom Murray, Ed.D., has been consulting, researching, publishing, and leading workshops in areas including cognitive tools, online communities, adaptive educational software, and knowledge engineering since 1985. He is an associate editor at Integral Review Journal. Previously a visiting/adjunct faculty member at the University of Massachusetts and at Hampshire College, Tom currently is working as an independent scholar and as the "chief visionary and instigator" at Perspegrity Solutions. He is particularly interested in action research in second-tier communities and has published essays on the relationship between integral theory and topics such as education, ethics, learning communities, dialog and deliberation, and leadership. www.tommurray.us

Chris Nichol, a literacy program coordinator and artist at heart, has lived in the West Kootenays since graduating from Queen's University in 1992. Chris is married with two daughters, aged 14 and 11. She and her family spent six years living off the grid in a small cabin in the woods before buying raw land and beginning the long process of building a home and gardens in 2000. Part of her do-it-yourself approach to life has included homeschooling. She spent several years researching learning styles and pedagogy while observing her children growing and learning naturally. She infuses everything she does with an eye for beauty. Connecting with learners of all ages is what keeps her inspired in her work.

Terri O'Fallon, Ph.D., views learning and change in human systems as her life-long pursuit. She has taught, consulted, and led in this field for nearly 46 years. Her work includes the initiation, launching, and leading of a non-profit corporation; administration in three public schools; teaching at seven colleges and universities; and consulting in various inner city schools around the United States as a catalyst for school transformation. Terri has a bachelor's degree in education; a master's degree in special education; and a Ph.D. in integral studies, with a concentration in transformative learning and change in human systems. Terri's research specialized in building online and face-to-face learning communities, and teaching dialogic approaches to making new knowledge, as well as designing learning systems. She is also a certified spiritual director and has completed her certification as a scorer of the leadership development framework with Suzann Cook-Greuter.

Jonathan Reams, Ph. D., is currently an associate professor in the Department of Education at the Norwegian University of Science and Technology. He teaches a course on organizational counseling, coaching, and leadership, as well as some general counseling. His research interests are in the areas of leadership, integral theory, and the evolution of consciousness. Jonathan is editor in chief of Integral Review, A Transdisciplinary and Transcultural Journal for New Thought, Praxis and Research. He finds his work with Integral Review to be a highly rewarding venue for supporting and engaging in inquiry involving a wide range of perceptions on the human condition and how consciousness shapes it. A passion for understanding human nature has guided much of his experience and eventually led to a doctorate in leadership studies, with a dissertation on the consciousness of transpersonal leadership. His current work focuses on developing leadership capacities for students as well as a wide range of clients. This includes developing and delivering curriculum, consulting, coaching, facilitation, research, writing, and teaching. In addition to this work, Jonathan has presented at a number of international conferences on topics such as leadership, consciousness, transformative learning, spirituality, and science and religion dialogue. http://www.integral-review.org

Nancy Simko, M.A., received her undergraduate degree from the Pennsylvania State University, and a master's degree from the Bank Street School of Education. She is actively involved in the field of early education and has taught young children for the past 15 years in Hawaii and in Manhattan and Brooklyn, New York. Currently, she is teaching kindergarten at Blue School in New York City. Nancy resides in Brooklyn with her two children. www.blueschool.com

Sue Stack, Ph.D., is a Tasmanian educator who has worked at all levels of the education system (from primary to university) as a teacher, leader, and researcher. Sue is co-founder of the Holistic Education Network Tasmania. Her dissertation, Integrating Science and Soul in Education, brings integral and holistic lenses to the exploration and transformation of science education. She is interested in creative, experiential, and integrative learning opportunities that help to make flourish and transform the development of the whole person. She is currently teaching pre-service teachers in a bachelor of education program at the University of Tasmania. www.hent.org www.stack.bigpondhosting.com

Andrew Suttar is an artist, educator, scientist, and entrepreneur, of which all roles revolve around a profound relationship with soap bubbles, sparked by a high school science investigation in 1994. He set the Australasian record for the most popular science center show ever a year later, at age 17. Andrew has since developed a comprehensive range of education and entertainment services. A social enterprise, Bubble Media seeks to support whole community education and well being by "bringing bubbles to the people." Thanks to the simplicity and accessibility of soap bubbles, Bubble Media is able to easily introduce the concept of a holon, providing a set of cognitive tools to sharpen understanding of a person's experience of the physiosphere, biosphere, and noosphere. His life goal is to reorganize global mainstream curricula around a bubble model, one that grows holarchically outward from the self-bubble to the Kosmos.

Shayla Wright, Ph.D., has spent a lifetime studying and teaching inquiry, creativity, communication, and the transformation of consciousness. She worked with Mother Teresa in her children's homes and in her Home for the Dying in Calcutta. Shayla was a senior teacher and coach in her community in the Himalayas, the International Meditation Institute, where she lived for 23 years. She has a doctorate in non-dual philosophy and a teaching degree in Soma Yoga, and is a certified coach. She is known for her warmth and humor, and has a gift for making her subjects accessible, enjoyable, and alive. She is delighted by the fact that one of the most enthusiastic readers of her digital life-letter is a blackjack dealer from Las Vegas. She is now engaged as a non-dual coach with Peter Fenner and the Radiant Mind course full time, with people from all over North America. www.barefootjourney.net

Jamie Wheal, M.A. is a lifelong learner and career educator who taught a range from three-year-olds to corporate executives. He served as the dean of studies at the High Mountain Institute in Colorado, where he pioneered an integrated academic and leadership curriculum that spanned classroom and wilderness. Jamie was head of upper school for the Telluride Mountain School, where he introduced an integral global studies program, including the international baccalaureate. He also was head of school for Misty Mountain Montessori, an integral Montessori school, serving children aged two to twelve. Currently, he consults to integral schools; is on the faculty of the Esalen Institute; and leads integral leadership programs through Stagen, a consulting firm dedicated to conscious capitalism.

CPSIA information can be obtained at www.ICGtesting.com
Printed in the USA
BVOW020356070113

309945BV00009B/166/P